THE IMPERFECT STORM:
RACISM
AND A PANDEMIC COLLIDE IN AMERICA

*HOW IT IMPACTED PUBLIC EDUCATION
and HOW TO FIX IT*

———————————— ★ ————————————

JAMES A. TAYLOR, PHD & WANDY W. TAYLOR, EDD

ARCHWAY
PUBLISHING

Archway Publishing books may be ordered through booksellers or by contacting:

Archway Publishing
1663 Liberty Drive
Bloomington, IN 47403
www.archwaypublishing.com
844-669-3957

ISBN: 978-1-4808-9848-6 (sc)
ISBN: 978-1-4808-9847-9 (hc)
ISBN: 978-1-4808-9849-3 (e)

Library of Congress Control Number: 2020921369

Print information available on the last page.

Archway Publishing rev. date: 02/03/2021

CONTENTS

The collision between COVID-19 and racism was thunderous and created an "imperfect storm" that revealed major imperfections hidden in America's society. Virtually everyone became clear-eyed with 2020-vision and could see the imperfections in major institutions like health care, housing, banking, employment, criminal justice, and education. These institutions are part of an ongoing system of racism that continues to suppress the upward mobility of people of color. The authors provide common sense ideas and research-based solutions to begin the process of erasing racism in our society and it begins with our schools.

"Drs. James and Wandy Taylor are extremely insightful, committed educational leaders who remain unapologetically focused on helping adults to serve all children. *The Imperfect Storm* should remain on the essential bookshelf of educational leaders."

Dr. Calvin J. Watts, Superintendent,
Kent (WA) School District

"...while many people wring their hands over this issue [systemic racism in public education], the Taylors dig deep and lay out concrete strategies. This book could not be more timely."

Carolyn Bourdeaux, Ph.D.
US House of Representatives (GA 7th Congressional District)

"We should not be satisfied to 'get back to normal'...we should strive for something better. What could 'better' look like? This book provides a profound response to address that vision."

Jackie Beasley, Education Consultant

"This publication is very timely. It comes at a point when inequities and injustices are very prevalent. I am sure it will be a valuable resource and an informative aid to all who read it. Great work!"

Dr. Angela E. Burse, Regional Principal
Georgia Preparatory Academy

"A timely book for a time such as this! Having experienced examples in many of the areas described in *The Imperfect Storm*, I strongly encourage everyone to read it and internalize it. Many lessons to learn."

Norris Wallace, Jr.
Retired Educator,
Retired School Board Chairman
Retired Judge

"The Taylors' book is timely and provides a candid account of challenges related to implicit biases that infiltrate public education. It is a must-read for educational leaders who strive to serve all children under their charge, inclusive of every race, gender, religion, and socioeconomic status."

Everton Blair Jr., School Board Member
Gwinnett County (GA) Public Schools

ABOUT THE AUTHORS

Wandy W. Taylor, Ed.D., holds a doctorate in educational leadership and management from Capella University, an Ed.S. in educational administration from the University of West Georgia, an M.Ed. from South Carolina State University, and a BA from the University of South Carolina. She has worked in public education for twenty-three years, having served as a counselor, assistant principal, principal and director. She is a consultant with the Georgia Leadership Institute for School Improvement and CEO of Taylor & Taylor Education Consultants, LLC, a company she co-owns with her husband, James A. Taylor.

James A. Taylor, Ph.D., has worked in public education for more than forty years, having served as a teacher, high school principal, executive director, and associate superintendent. He earned a doctoral degree from the University of South Carolina in 1978 and completed additional post-graduate work at Auburn University and the University of North Carolina. He is also the author of *From Unequal to Unwanted: Reforms Needed to Improve K-12 Public and Higher Education*. He is a consultant with Taylor & Taylor Education Consultants, LLC., a company he co-owns with his wife, Wandy W. Taylor.

INTRODUCTION

The term "perfect storm" was first used on May 30, 1850, when a meteorologist described a "perfect storm of thunder and lightning" had engulfed most of England and created major damage. The term reached the shores of the United States on March 20, 1936, when a meteorologist assigned to the *Port Arthur (Texas) News* reported, "The weather bureau describes the disturbance as 'the perfect storm' of its type." This was in reference to an unusual chain of weather systems that collided and led to a massive flood.

Essentially, the term is used to describe a fierce storm that occurs when a rare combination of two opposing weather systems arise at the same time. In October 1991, three large weather systems collided in the North Atlantic Ocean off the coasts of New England, Nova Scotia, and Newfoundland, and the results were devastating. Although the center of the storm never reached shore, it created waves that reached nearly 100 feet; had wind gusts of 75 miles per hour; killed 12 people; and caused roughly $200 million in damage. The wrath of that storm inspired Sebastian Junger to write his best-selling novel in 1997 titled *The Perfect Storm*. This was followed by a movie in 2000 starring George Clooney.

Recently, two opposing forces or systems collided in America in 2020 to create another type of storm with catastrophic effects—it was an "imperfect" storm. While the colliding forces that created the so-called perfect storm were both weather-related, the colliding forces that created the imperfect storm were not. One force was a centuries-old, long-term system of racial injustice, and the other was the onset of a sudden pandemic that preyed on humanity. That collision created an "explosion" that exposed centuries of "imperfections" or serious flaws that crept inside the core of America's society. The impact of that imperfect storm created such an uproar that it caused people of all religions, races, ethnicities, and languages across the globe to shout in unison that "Black Lives Matter!"

To fully understand the dynamics of the imperfect storm, this book will take the reader on a journey through America's past, with a special focus on two areas—education and systemic racism. The first stop on that journey begins in the Jim Crow era of the late nineteenth century when America had two very distinct "separate and unequal societies." One society was black and disadvantaged; the other was white and privileged. That journey will extend into the summer of 2020.

During the Jim Crow era, a harsh system of racial segregation made it extremely difficult for black children to receive anything resembling a quality education. Even after public schools were finally desegregated in the mid-1970s, black students were the primary victims of implicit (covert) and explicit (overt) biases that were held by the mostly white, middle class, English-speaking teacher workforce across America. The consequences of biases in schools are both powerful and measurable. Invariably, teachers' biases lead to lower academic outcomes for the students they stereotype.

Moving into the twenty-first century, we make our second major stop on the journey. During this time, America's schools are becoming increasingly more racially and culturally diverse. This creates a culture gap between most teachers and the students in their classrooms. This culture gap inhibits teachers' ability to engage their diverse students into meaningful teaching and learning. Moreover, their biases perpetuate inequitable punishments for students of color. The federal government confirmed the inequities when it released statistical data in April 2018 indicating that racial disparities in school discipline were worsening. Black students are shown to have had far greater rates of school arrests and suspensions than their white counterparts.

Despite arguments from some pundits, we know that research findings consistently indicate that there are no distinct differences in the way black students behave in school when compared to students in other ethnic groups. The disparities are a manifestation of the way adults in the school buildings are responding to black students' behavior. This is the essence of implicit racial bias in our public education system.

The setting for the third major stop on the journey in this book is the onset of the year 2020. This is when a highly infectious coronavirus disease (COVID-19) created a path of destruction across the four corners of the globe. This worldwide pandemic raged like a wildfire and crippled daily activities throughout America. Entire school systems and countless businesses across the nation were shut down; unemployment soared; hospitals were overflowed with patients; and mass transit systems came to a screeching halt. Despite numerous efforts to contain and mitigate COVID-19, this silent-but-deadly virus caused death and destruction throughout the world. Between January 1, 2020, through December 31, 2020, its path of destruction claimed the lives of over 346,000 innocent people in the United States and over 1.8 million across the globe.

The federal government's Centers for Disease Control and Prevention (CDC) developed guidelines to mitigate the virus' path of destruction. Some of the most effective strategies included sheltering-in-place, "social distancing" (i.e., a public health practice that required people to stay at least six feet apart to reduce the chances of cross contamination), and wearing facemasks. Unfortunately, the CDC's guidelines were not totally effective simply because many people refused to follow them. The President of the United States was among the people who refused to follow the federal guidelines; subsequently—he contracted the virus!

During the same time COVID-19 was wreaking havoc, it was joined by another silent-but-deadly system or disease that was also carving out a path of destruction in America. Unlike COVID-19, however, this was not a new disease. This disease has lurked in America for centuries, and many white Americans had grown so accustomed to its presence that they tended to ignore it. The presence of this camouflaged "killer"—racism—was exposed when its path collided with COVID-19's path. That collision occurred on May 25, 2020, when four policemen murdered an unarmed black man in broad daylight in Minneapolis, Minnesota. That incident triggered an international outrage and a demand to eradicate systemic racism.

The collision between COVID-19 and racism was thunderous and created an "imperfect' storm that revealed major imperfections that were hidden in America's society. Virtually everyone became clear-eyed with 2020-vision and could see the imperfections in major institutions like health care, housing, banking, employment, criminal justice, and education. Those institutions were part of a system of ongoing racism that continued to suppress the upward mobility of people of color.

The last stop on the journey in this book deals with how to make systemic changes in America's major institutions, with a particular focus on education. A nine-step process is presented that state and local officials can use to address systemic racism in their schools. That process is both evidence-based and cost-effective.

Finally, a few terms will be used throughout this book that require some clarity. The terms "black" and "African American" will be used interchangeably; they bear the same meaning. Also, there is a difference between "equality" and "equity" in education systems. In an "equal" system, all students are treated equally and given the same resources. In an "equitable" system, resources are given to students based on their individual needs. Enjoy the book!

"Not everything that is faced can be changed,
but nothing can be changed until it is faced."
— James Baldwin
August 2, 1924 – December 1, 1987

★ ★ ★

CHAPTER 1

PUBLIC EDUCATION IN AMERICA: A HISTORY OF SYSTEMIC RACISM

---★---

ESSENTIAL QUESTION

*Does the stain of racism in America's educational-
past pose a problem for its educational-future?*

---★---

During his campaign for reelection, President Donald Trump scheduled a rally for June 19, 2020, in Tulsa, Oklahoma. The announcement of that rally sparked an uproar because of Tulsa's history as the site of one of the worst incidents of racial violence in the nation's history. In 1921, hundreds of blacks were attacked by white mobs that looted and burned many black-owned businesses in an area that was known as "Black Wall Street."

Holding a rally on that day in Tulsa was viewed as another afront by Trump, who frequently avoided having meaningful discussions about systemic racism unfolding in this country. Trump claimed that no one had ever heard of Juneteenth, the holiday that occurs on June 19 to commemorate the emancipation of black slaves in the United States. After yielding to pressure to reschedule the day for his rally, Trump proclaimed, "I did something good; I made Juneteenth very famous." This was a clear example of Trump's lack of cultural sensitivity and cultural awareness. We will have a more detailed discussion of Donald Trump and his legacy later in this book.

For now, suffice it to say that America must be mindful of her cultural past. This must occur before any substantive changes can be made to ensure that all people have equal access to the institutions in our system, especially in public education. The ugliness of our nation's past is captured in the infamous Jim Crow system or culture that operated primarily in southern and border states between the middle nineteenth and early twentieth centuries. The Jim Crow culture was steeped in the beliefs or rationalizations that whites were superior to blacks in all important ways, especially in the areas of intelligence, morality, and civilized behavior.

The story of Margaret Crittenden Douglass provides a backdrop for America's mindset regarding public education for black children during the Jim Crow era. Pursuant to an 1847 Virginia Criminal Code: "Any white person who shall assemble with free Negroes…for the purpose of instructing them to read or write…shall be punished by confinement in jail…and by fine…"

Mrs. Douglass, a former slaveholder in Virginia, was arrested under this code. She was subsequently jailed for one month in 1854 when authorities charged her with teaching "free colored children" of a local church to read and write. Upon her release from jail, she published her memoir of the event titled *Educational Laws of Virginia: The Personal Narrative of Mrs. Margaret Douglass, a Southern Woman, who was Imprisoned for One Month in the Common Jail of Norfolk, Under the Laws of Virginia, for the Crime of Teaching Free Colored Children to Read.*

Margaret Douglass' story is merely a snapshot of America's history of not providing black children with equal access to a quality free public education. For years, black children were treated as second-class citizens and separated in schools by law. If we were to compare the plight of black children to running a marathon, many of them would be lagging behind by miles. The next sections of this chapter will shed light on why disparities in outcomes in education between African American and white students existed in the past and persist today.

IDEOLOGY OF TWO BLACK SCHOLARS

During the Jim Crow era of institutional segregation and racism, two key black scholars offered divergent views regarding education. Booker T. Washington, who was the most influential black man in America during that era, expressed the most dominant educational ideology for blacks. He urged blacks to accept racial subordination as an unavoidable circumstance at that time, and he encouraged them to elevate themselves through hard work and economic gain. Washington insisted that an education in the *industrial arts* would enable black Americans to win the respect of whites and allow them to escape the bondage of sharecropping and debt.

W.E.B. Du Bois, the first black man to earn a doctoral degree at Harvard, argued against the principles that were espoused by Booker T. Washington. Du Bois argued that blacks should never entertain the idea of accepting the belief that whites were biologically superior to them and the notion that their best pathway to a meaningful education was through the industrial arts. Instead, he urged blacks to pursue an education in the *liberal arts* to broaden their intellectual acumen. Du Bois was also a vocal supporter of women's rights, and he co-founded the National Association for the Advancement of Colored People (NAACP) in 1909.

The ideological dispute between Du Bois and Washington polarized African American leaders at that time. This wasn't an especially bad thing, so to speak. The unintended consequence of the dispute was the fact that it caused people to take a closer look at the socio-political ideologies and institutions that existed at that time. The dispute produced two wings in the African American community; namely, the "conservative" supporters of Washington and his "radical" critics.

The Du Bois philosophy of agitation and protest for civil rights flowed directly into the civil rights movement, which began to develop in the 1950's and exploded in the 1960's. Today, Booker T. Washington is associated with the wing of the black community and its leaders that espouse the so-called colorblind politics of Clarence Thomas, the ultra-conservative Republican Supreme Court Justice.

Despite their philosophical differences, both Washington and Du Bois wanted the same thing for blacks—first-class citizenship. They agreed that *education* was the best way to earn respect and prosperity in a white-dominated society. Many African American scholars and historians consider Washington and Du Bois the pioneer civil rights leaders of the twentieth century.

SUBSTANDARD SCHOOLING

In a 2020 report by Dr. Bruce D. Baker titled *Money Matters*, the author provides data to indicate that the availability of resources in schools is positively correlated with high outcomes for students. He concluded that schools and districts with more money clearly have a greater ability to provide higher quality, broader, and deeper educational opportunities to the children they serve. If money does matter, then one can only imagine the substandard schooling that was available to black children in the early twentieth century. Most of the school facilities were dilapidated, the curriculum was woefully inadequate, and all of this impacted the self-esteem of black children.

SELF-ESTEEM AMONG BLACK CHILDREN

In 1896, the U. S. Supreme Court upheld a Louisiana law and ruled that if racially separate facilities were equal, they did not violate the Constitution. This ruling represented the legitimization of two school "societies" in America. One society was white-and-advantaged, the other was black-and-disadvantaged. The court said segregation was not discrimination. In reality, blacks never experienced anything "equal" during that era. On the contrary, society for black Americans was "separate-and-unequal."

Social psychologists Kenneth and Mamie Clark sought to challenge the court's prevailing opinion that "separate but equal" public schools were suitable and constitutional. They did this by conducting a research study to determine whether African-American children were psychologically and emotionally damaged by attending segregated schools. In their classic 1939 study, the Clarks showed 250 black children (ages two to seven) two sets of dolls that were identical except for their skin and hair color. The children were asked to select a doll according to each of the following specific verbal requests:

- Show me the doll that you would like to play with.
- Show me the doll that is a nice doll.
- Show me the doll that looks bad.
- Show me the doll that looks like a white child.
- Show me the doll that looks like a colored child.
- Show me the doll that looks like a Negro child.
- Show me the doll that looks like you.

The Clarks found that most of the children overwhelmingly selected the white doll as the "nice doll" and the one they wanted "to play with." Only 61 percent of the children selected the black doll (their own race) when asked to "give me the doll that looks like you." Some of the children refused to pick either doll or simply started crying and ran away. The study showed that in Jim Crow America the stereotyping of black people as "bad" and white people as "nice" began as early as age four.

Perhaps the most disturbing aspect of the Clarks' findings is that an entire generation of black children was plagued with episodes of low self-esteem. It is conceivable that the lack of self-esteem in black children related to a hostile segregated society extended well into the 1980s, especially in school settings. School psychologists agree that children with low self-esteem feel less confident in their abilities. These children typically may not feel motivated to try things that are hard for them, and they have a tough time dealing with mistakes.

Over the years, most black families have done a good job of

insulating their children from the stench of racism and discrimination. As a result, most black children today appear to have high levels of self-esteem and self-confidence. Research findings indicate that much of black children's low achievement in school is due to external factors (i.e., implicit racial bias of teachers and inadequate instructional materials), not internal factors (i.e., low-self-esteem and low intelligence).

The real impact of the Clarks' doll study occurred on May 17, 1954, when the U.S. Supreme Court issued its decision on the case of *Brown v. Board of Education.* "To separate [black children] from others of similar age and qualifications solely because of their race generates a feeling of inferiority as to their status in the community that may affect their hearts and minds in a way unlikely ever to be undone," wrote Chief Justice Earl Warren in the opinion. Kenneth and Mamie Clarks' work helped strike down segregation in the United States.

Facilities

Given the oppressive economic and social challenges that black communities faced entering the twentieth century, one can only imagine the condition of their schools. In a report compiled by the American Council on Education in the 1930s, we are given a glimpse of what those schools were like. Many of the school buildings for blacks had leaking roofs, sagging floors, and windows without glass. The dilapidated facilities ranged from being untidy to outright filthy and unsafe. In addition, the classrooms were crowded and typically all grades were taught in the same room by one teacher.

Remarkably, one of the greatest positive impacts on the reformation of school facilities for black children during that oppressive Jim Crow era was due to the philanthropy of a white man, Julius Rosenwald. This multimillionaire president of Sears, Roebuck & Company took a special interest in the plight of black children and the deplorable condition of the schools they attended. Consequently, he created a charity—the Rosenwald Foundation—that committed large sums of money in fifteen southern states for the construction of safe, comfortable schools affectionately called "Rosenwald Schools." Over the course of nearly two decades (1917–1932), the foundation contributed to the construction of over 5,000 school buildings, nearly 200 teachers' homes, and five industrial high schools for black students. Ultimately, hundreds of thousands of black children received a good education in the Rosenwald Schools.

Rosenwald also supported higher education for black students. He became a trustee of Tuskegee Institute and befriended Booker T. Washington. This humanitarian donated over two million dollars for facility improvements at Tuskegee, Howard, Fisk, and Dillard universities. Through his philanthropy, Julius Rosenwald played a huge role in providing opportunities for many black students to learn in a safe, healthy, and stimulating school environment.

As evidenced by the philanthropy of Rosenwald, improvements to school facilities require money. Throughout the first half of the "separate but unequal" twentieth century, blacks simply did not have access to the funding needed to build first-class schools. After the Supreme Court issued its *Brown v. Board of Education* decision in 1954, the expectation was that school facilities for blacks and whites would be equally funded by state and local authorities. Although that expectation was met with stiff resistance, local and state authorities reluctantly provided additional funding to black districts for school improvements.

In response to the *Brown* decision, many southern states adopted equalized school funding programs for black and white schools as a strategy to avoid integration. In South Carolina, for example, the state launched a multimillion-dollar campaign in the late 1960s to build schools for blacks under the guise of improving education for all children. However, the intent of the equalization programs throughout the South was to try to maintain segregation by improving schools in black communities.

The construction projects for improved school facilities were well-received in many black communities, especially in rural areas. Hundreds of schools were built throughout the South under state-funded equalization programs. Families and teachers were thrilled with their new buildings. For some, it was the first time their schools had indoor plumbing and centralized heating. Although the equalization programs did, indeed, improve school facilities in many black communities, significant problems in other areas emerged.

While the equalization-schools were attractive and appealing, many of them lacked gyms, football fields, and textbooks were outdated. Moreover, many of the southern states' equalization plans did not provide for the equalization of salaries for black and white teachers. This disparity led to several lawsuits involving equal pay and other programmatic disparities in the equalization plans of segregated school systems. Ultimately, those state-funded plans could not hold back the tide of integration. By 1975 (two decades after the *Brown v. Board* decision), all states in the South had abandoned their "separate-but-equalization" plans and complied with federal mandates to desegregate all public schools.

Historically, the federal government played a rather small role in school funding. After the failed attempts by many southern states to maintain school segregation through their equalization plans, the federal government became more involved with school funding. In 1960, state and local governments funded 96% of a public education and the federal government funded four percent. In 1980, state and local governments funded 90% of public education and the federal government funded ten percent. With this increase in funding, the federal government assumed greater oversight of spending in public education.

In theory, all public schools in America were supposedly "integrated and equal" by 1999. In reality, they were not. According to a report by the Harvard Civil Rights Project, our nation's schools became increasingly more segregated in the 1990s. This "re-segregation" was explained in terms of "white flight" to the suburbs. As schools in the suburbs became "whiter"— schools in the inner-city became "browner." This de facto segregation has resulted in a disparity in education finance. This is because school systems in the suburbs can generate more revenue through local property taxes from their more affluent residents. With more money available, school systems in the suburbs constructed better facilities. Thus, by 1999, many school facilities in rural and inner-city districts were unequal or inferior to those in affluent, suburban America.

According to education scholars at Penn State University, a growing body of research has found that school facilities can have a profound impact on outcomes for both teachers and students. For teachers, poor school facilities adversely influence morale, commitment, and effort. For students, inadequate school facilities have been linked with low achievement, poor engagement, and poor behavior. The researchers concluded that without adequate facilities and resources, it is extremely difficult to serve large numbers of children with compound needs.

Private donations from people like Julius Rosenwald helped to provide better school facilities for black children in the Deep South in the early to middle 1900s. Certainly, the upgraded facilities had a positive impact on outcomes for both black students and teachers. However, since public education is controlled by each state, and state governments in the United States did not consider the education of black children a priority at that time—black children continued to receive "separate and unequal" educational opportunities.

Curriculum

Educators have different perspectives regarding the definition, purpose, and types of curriculums. They do, however, tend to agree that a curriculum refers to the strategies and materials teachers use to interact with students to achieve desired educational outcomes. During the first six decades of the twentieth century, many segregated school systems with white student populations used two types of curriculums. First, there was the *written curriculum,* which comprised of the documents that were produced by the state and local boards specifying what was to be taught. Then there was the *taught curriculum,* which was the one that teachers actually delivered.

The curriculums for segregated school systems with black student populations during that same period were different. Their two curriculums can be described as what we call situational and adaptive. The *situational curriculum* was a quasi-written set of manual labor skills that were compiled to help the students adjust to the demands of their socio-economic environment. For example, the situational curriculum for poor black children that lived in a farming community would focus on rudimentary skills such as tallying, using proper techniques to grow produce, fixing farm tools, and recognizing the symptoms of diseased crops. The *adaptive curriculum* was largely unstructured; teachers typically used their personal experiences and imagination to deliver instruction.

The racially segregated school systems in America reinforced the presumption that was held by many whites at that time (and even today); that is, blacks were inherently incapable of learning at an advanced level. Segregating white children from black children was rationalized as a means of ensuring that the educational advancement of white children would not be hindered by the presence of "less-intelligent" black students. Consequently, black schools were woefully underfunded and, in many instances, states did not provide them access to meaningful curricular and instructional materials. Metaphorically speaking, while black children struggled along the path to an education in their bare feet with blinders, white children traveled the same path with the aid of a motorized vehicle and an adult navigator.

A great example of a *situational curriculum* occurred during the 1960s. The situation involved the Freedom Summer in Mississippi. In 1964, a campaign was launched in Mississippi to combat voter suppression by registering as many black voters as possible. This campaign received national support from congressmen, leaders of the civil rights movement, the NAACP, and organizations like the Student Nonviolent Coordinating Committee (SNCC).

During that summer, members of SNCC were appalled by what they described as the "sharecropper education" that blacks received in substandard schools. Therefore, they created freedom schools throughout Mississippi to provide six weeks of relevant, rigorous instruction. The curriculum they developed was designed to address the oppressed "situation" that blacks were facing at that time. A key element of instruction was to teach students how to become social change agents and how to participate in the ongoing civil rights movement. The education at the freedom schools was student-centered, leadership development was encouraged, and proficiency in traditional academic skills was expected.

Unlike what transpired in many black schools during the first half of the twentieth century, there was no unstructured delivery of instruction (i.e., *adaptive curriculum*) in the freedom schools. Many highly-qualified teachers were recruited to Mississippi to teach in the schools, and they used proven instructional strategies (e.g., open discussions and lesson plans) to engage students. The United Federation of Teachers in New York sent the largest contingent of teachers to teach in the schools. During that summer, nearly 40 freedom schools were established and served approximately 2,500 students, including parents.

At the end of the summer of 1964, many of the students remained in the freedom schools rather than return to their segregated schools. The students that did return to their segregated schools learned their curriculum well; they wanted reform. These students demanded improvements, and they insisted that white educators (i.e., the superintendent and local members of the school board) include African American history and literature in their curriculum. They resisted the goals of the infamous "sharecropper education" and insisted on having a curriculum that would prepare them for college.

The political awareness the freedom students gained during that summer had a profound and lasting impact on their perspective of human and civil rights. In January 1965, after over 200 students in two all-black high schools in two counties in Mississippi were suspended for wearing "One Man, One Vote" buttons—the entire student body in those schools walked out and shut down the schools. A court case ensued that was used as a precedent in the U.S. Supreme Court's landmark ruling in *Tinker v. Des Moines (1969)*, which protected students' right to free speech.

The legacy of the freedom schools was reborn under the leadership of Marian Wright Edelman, founder of the Children's Defense Fund (CDF). In 1995, sites for the first two CDF Freedom Schools were established in South Carolina and Missouri. The CDF Freedom School employed a transformative curriculum that continues even today to serve as a model for public education systems across America. Students are expected to use high-level reasoning skills to solve problems that are relevant to their local community and the nation within a world context. Teachers are trained to have high expectations for all students and to use culturally responsive pedagogy to engage students. These high-quality strategies were not embedded in the oppressive, now-defunct "sharecropper" curriculum.

At the beginning of the twentieth century, the basic curriculum in black primary schools reflected the limited jobs that were available to African Americans. During the early 1900s, most blacks lived in the Deep South and over half were employed as sharecroppers on white-owned farms. A white landowner typically saw little value in educating black children, because they believed education would have no positive impact on their ability to pick cotton or wash laundry. Besides, in the minds of many white landowners, an education would only serve to encourage black children to seek higher wages and employment elsewhere. Therefore, it was socially and economically advantageous for most white landowners to keep black children uninformed and uneducated.

Despite massive economic and social obstacles in the 1930s, many black children were hungry for an education. More than three million school-age black American children lived in the 17 Jim Crow states that operated segregated schools. Those states stretched from Texas to Delaware, and local school boards generally spent three times as much on each white student as they did on blacks. For example, in 1930, Georgia spent $32 on each white child and just $7 on those that were black. In South Carolina, the disparity was even greater— $53 spent for each white child and $5 for each black child.

Interest in the plight of black children in the Deep South began to rise in the late 1930s. Reports of systemic violations of child labor and compulsory education laws prompted key governmental agencies to launch investigations. One agency, the American Council on Education, sent a team of investigators to the Jim Crow South to assess the legally-segregated, state-supported public schools for black children. The investigative report compiled by the team that visited the black grade school in Dine Hollow, Alabama, reflected the widespread findings across the 17 Jim Crow states (also known as the "Black Belt"). The investigators reported:

> A typical rural Negro school is at Dine Hollow. It is in a dilapidated building, once whitewashed, standing in a rocky field unfit for cultivation. Dust-covered weeds spread a carpet all around, except for an uneven, bare area on one side that looks like a ball field. Behind the school is a small building with a broken, sagging door. As we approach, a nervous middle-aged woman comes to the door of the school. She greets us in a discouraged voice marked by a speech impediment.

Escorted inside, we observe that the broken benches are crowded to three times their normal capacity. Only a few battered books are in sight, and we look in vain for maps or charts. We learn that four grades are assembled here. The weary teacher agrees to permit us to remain while she proceeds with the instruction. She goes to the blackboard and writes an assignment for the first two grades to do while she conducts spelling and word drills for the third and fourth grades. This is the assignment:

> *Write your name ten times.*
> *Draw an dog, an cat, an rat, an boot.*

The scenario described at Dine Hollow is a sad reminder of the deplorable separate-and-unequal conditions that prevailed for black Americans in education during the Jim Crow era. Most teachers in black schools like the one at Dine Hollow did not have the benefit of decent books or a written curriculum. In fact, there was limited training and professional development for black teachers.

Typically, there was no real teaching and learning in the classroom. The children were simply given "busy work" to keep them occupied. The so-called education for most black children did not extend beyond the rudiments of literacy and figuring. One can only imagine the "achievement gap" that existed between children in the all-black school in Dine Hollow and their counterparts in the neighboring all-white schools.

The pedagogy at Dine Hollow or almost any all-black school in the Deep South in the early 1900s was sorely lacking in quality.

Figuratively speaking, trying to find quality instruction at schools like Dine Hollow would be like trying to find a four-leaf clover in Brooklyn, NY. Although it's possible, the challenge would be daunting. The absence of a standard curriculum was especially crippling. Essentially, a curriculum refers to the lessons and content taught in a school for a specific course or program. Even the most capable and creative teachers depend on a well-written curriculum. Although a teacher's abilities and personality will affect how materials are delivered, the development of a consistent instructional plan is critical for student success.

Only a small number of black children who finished grade school in the 1930s had the opportunity to attend high school. This was due in large part to the fact that very few states in the so-called Black Belt had black high schools with a curriculum that would allow them to receive state-accreditation to pursue four years of study in a college or university. A report on secondary education for blacks in 1933 showed that, collectively, the states of Florida, Louisiana, Mississippi, and South Carolina had a grand total of only 16 black high schools that were accredited for four-year study.

In addition to having teachers with minimal training, very few of the black high schools offered science courses, foreign languages, music, or art. Moreover, many of the students did not have access to labs or musical instruments. Unquestionably, the schooling for black children was substandard.

RESISTANCE TO DESEGREGATION

The resistance to the *Brown v. Board* decision was fierce. Almost immediately after Chief Justice Earl Warren finished reading the Supreme Court's unanimous opinion in the early afternoon of May 17, 1954, white political leaders in the Deep South condemned the decision and vowed to defy it. Senator Harry Flood Byrd of Virginia said, "If we can organize the Southern States for massive resistance to this order, I think that, in time, the rest of the country will realize that racial integration is not going to be accepted in the South."

In February 1956, Senator Byrd issued the call for "Massive Resistance"— a collection of laws passed in response to the *Brown* decision. The purpose of the laws was to aggressively obstruct and prevent school integration. For instance, the Massive Resistance doctrine included a law that punished any public school that integrated by eliminating its state funds and eventually closing the school. This manifesto for massive resistance led many school officials in the Deep South to close their doors to black children that sought admission.

The Little Rock Nine

Despite vitriolic opposition, nine students (six females and three males) registered to be the first African Americans to attend Central High School in Little Rock, Arkansas. The students were recruited by Daisy Gaston Bates. She was the president of the Arkansas NAACP and co-publisher of the *Arkansas State Press*, an influential African American newspaper. Collectively, those students became known as the Little Rock Nine and included:

- Minniejean Brown
- Elizabeth Eckford
- Ernest Green
- Thelma Mothershed
- Melba Patillo
- Gloria Ray
- Terrence Roberts
- Jefferson Thomas
- Carlotta Walls

Keenly aware of the animus related to school desegregation, Daisy Bates and others from the Arkansas NAACP carefully vetted the group of students and decided they all possessed the strength and determination to face the resistance they would encounter. In the weeks prior to the start of the new school year, the students participated in intensive counseling sessions to prepare them for what to expect once classes began and how to respond to anticipated hostile situations.

On September 2, 1957, two days before school opened, Governor Orval Faubus announced that he would call in the Arkansas National Guard to prevent the African American students from entering Central High. He claimed this action was for the students' own protection. In a televised address, Faubus insisted that violence and bloodshed might break out if black students were allowed to enter the school.

On September 4, 1957, the Little Rock Nine arrived for the first day of school at Central High. Eight arrived together in a carpool coordinated by Bates. Since Elizabeth Eckford's family did not have a telephone, and Bates could not reach her to let her know of the carpool plans—she arrived alone.

Under Governor Faubus' orders, the Arkansas National Guard prevented any of the Little Rock Nine from entering the doors of Central High. One of the most enduring images from that day is a photograph of Elizabeth Eckford walking alone with a notebook in her hand; stoically approaching the school while a crowd of hostile, screaming white students and adults surround her. Eckford later recalled that one of the women spat on her. The image was printed and broadcast widely in the United States and abroad. The photo of Eckford being taunted by white students and adults brought national and international attention to the controversy in Little Rock.

During the following weeks, federal judge Ronald Davies began legal proceedings against Governor Faubus, and President Dwight D. Eisenhower attempted to persuade Faubus to remove the National Guard and let the Little Rock Nine enter the school. Eventually, the President deployed 1,200 federal troops to Little Rock to restore order. On September 25, 1957, troops escorted the Little Rock Nine to attend their first full day of classes at Central High School.

According to a report in the *New York Times* on September 25, 1957, several of the black students had fairly positive experiences on their first day of school. All of them, however, experienced routine harassment and even violence throughout the rest of the year. Melba Patillo, for instance, was kicked, beaten and had acid thrown in her face. Gloria Ray was pushed down a flight of stairs; Minniejean Brown was expelled from Central High in February 1958 for retaliating against the racial attacks; and the Little Rock Nine were barred from participating in extracurricular activities. The 101st Airborne and the National Guard remained at Central High School for the duration of the year.

On May 25, 1958, Ernest Green, the only senior among the

Little Rock Nine, became the first African American to graduate from Central High. Martin Luther King Jr. attended the ceremony to witness the occasion. The rest of the Little Rock Nine opted to complete their high school careers via correspondence courses or at other high schools across the country.

Governor Faubus never ceased his expressed desire to have the Little Rock Nine removed from Central High. In September 1958, four months after Ernest Green graduated, Governor Faubus closed all of Little Rock's high schools for the entire year, pending a public vote to prevent African American attendance. Little Rock citizens voted 19,470 to 7,561 against integration and the schools remained closed.

The story of the Little Rock Nine is a sobering reminder of what public education was like for blacks in many parts of America shortly after the repeal of legal segregation. The overt racism that black students faced during the decades after the *Brown v. Board* decision is just as prevalent today, albeit in a more covert format. The explicit racial bias of the past has simply reemerged in the form of implicit racial bias. In either form (explicit or implicit), racial bias in public education continues to have a deleterious effect on children of color in America.

Ruby Bridges

The violent resistance to integration was not restricted to high school settings in the Deep South. Despite repeated attempts in federal court to stall the desegregation of public schools, the state of Louisiana eventually accepted the *Brown* decision as the nation's rule of law. In 1960, the NAACP informed Abon and Lucille Bridges that their daughter—Ruby Nell Bridges—would be the first black child to attend all-white William Frantz Elementary School in New Orleans. The school was only a few blocks from Ruby's house.

On the morning of November 14, 1960, escorted by four white court-appointed federal marshals to protect her, six-year-old Ruby Bridges became the first black child to attend an all-white elementary school in the South. The image of this innocent little black girl being escorted to school by four large white men inspired Norman Rockwell to create his famous painting—*The Problem We Must All Live With*. This painting subsequently appeared on the cover of *Look* magazine in 1964.

Despite the presence of four federal marshals, Ruby was subjected to many episodes of deliberate racism from members of the Frantz School community. On her second day of school, a woman threatened to poison Ruby and, on another occasion, she was antagonized by a woman displaying a black doll in a wooden coffin. There was also resistance from adults inside the school. For a while it looked as if Ruby would have to withdraw from school because no teacher would teach her. Fortunately, a new teacher—Mrs. Barbara Henry from Boston—accepted Ruby with open arms and agreed to teach her.

Ruby was the only student in Mrs. Henry's class because parents either withdrew or threatened to withdraw their children from her class. For the entire school year, Mrs. Henry and Ruby sat side-by-side at two desks completing assignments. Mrs. Henry was very nurturing and supportive of Ruby, and she helped the six-year-old cope with some of the social and emotional stress she experienced in the school's hostile environment.

Things took a dramatic shift for Ruby during her second year at Frantz School. Most noticeably, Mrs. Henry was no longer there. Her contract was not renewed; consequently, she and her husband returned to Boston. In addition, there were no more federal marshals, and Ruby walked to school every day by herself. There were other students in her second-grade class, and the enrollment at the school started to increase again. It seemed as if the Frantz community wanted to put the experience of the previous school year behind them. Some things, however, cannot be swept under a rug and simply disappear. Ruby's story has been memorialized in Rockwell's painting and etched in America's history of public education for upcoming generations to review.

A possible silver lining in the Ruby Bridges story lies in its alignment with a popular education axiom—good teachers matter! As an adult, Ruby gleefully applauded the role her nurturing teacher, Mrs. Henry, played on her ability to cope with the stress and turmoil she experienced during her first year at Frantz Elementary School. In 1996, Ruby and Mrs. Henry were reunited on an episode of the *Oprah Winfrey Show*. That reunion touched the hearts of millions of viewers and served as a reminder of the vitriol and hatred that was directed at an innocent six-year-old black girl who simply wanted to attend the school near her home in 1960.

KERNER COMMISSION

Nearly ten years after the Little Rock Nine had integrated Central High School, President Lyndon Johnson stood before a national television audience on July 27, 1967, to announce the creation of the National Advisory Commission on Civil Disorders (NACCD). The speech was precipitated by deadly and destructive riots in Newark and Detroit, which marked the culmination of four consecutive summers of racial unrest in American cities. The 11-person bipartisan commission consisted of two African Americans; two Republican and two Democratic members of Congress; representatives from both business and labor; and one woman. New York's liberal Republican mayor, John Lindsay, served as vice chairman and Illinois' Democratic governor, Otto Kerner, was selected as the chairman. Hence, the group became known as the Kerner Commission.

Since there were no radicals or young people appointed to the 11-person group, Johnson assumed that this mainstream commission would produce a mainstream report that would endorse his domestic agenda and shield him from attacks from both the right and from the left. The new commission, however, failed to follow the White House script. The commissioners were determined to assert their independence, and they wanted to take a deep dive into the problem. So, they hired a team of investigators; visited riot-torn areas; and held hearings with activists and public officials. Their report was by no means a "rubber stamp" of approval of the President's domestic agenda; it was more of a rude awakening to the realities that existed in America's society.

The final report was released in March 1968. It used stark language to conclude that the riots occurred because white society had denied opportunities to African Americans living in poor urban areas. The commission also identified conditions which stemmed from decades of racism and oppression that triggered the incidents of unrest in the 1960s. Those conditions included racially segregated communities; poor housing; high unemployment; insufficient or inadequate governmental responses and attention to community needs; and inferior schools. That last condition bears repeating—inferior schools.

Two lines in the summary of the report are especially profound and significant. Borrowing language from the *Brown v. Board* decision (which declared that "separate educational facilities are inherently unequal"), the Kerner Commission concluded: "Our nation is moving toward two societies, one black and one white, separate and unequal." The report also blamed "white racism" for problems in urban communities. The report further asserted: "What white Americans have never fully understood—but what the Negro can never forget—is that white society is deeply implicated in the ghetto. White institutions created it, white institutions maintain it, and white society condones it."

The Kerner Commission's report did not present any new information to America; it merely amplified what everyone already knew. Poverty and institutionalized racism were, indeed, forming a divided society in America— "one black, one white; separate and unequal"— and inciting civil unrest. The commission called for an end to job discrimination and school segregation.

The country has certainly seen much progress since publication of the Kerner Commission report in 1968. Today, in the year 2020, many black Americans enjoy relatively high social and economic status. Overt racism and efforts to exclude or constrain where they live, work, or attend school have greatly diminished. Yet, the report outlined concerns that are still relevant today. Racial segregation remains the defining feature of many U.S. cities; blacks face higher unemployment and lower wages; many public schools have difficulty engaging their black students; and huge disparities in wealth persist at levels near those described by Kerner and his colleagues over five decades ago.

Fifty-two years after the Kerner report, children's race and their parent's income are still the primary predictors of their success (or lack thereof) in school. It does not matter how it is manifested—explicitly or implicitly—racial bias is a disease that continues to infiltrate many classrooms in public schools. Like any disease, racism will continue to spread in our schools until a vaccine is created.

SUMMARY

Very few blacks received any education at all until public schools were established during the Reconstruction Era from 1865–1877. Public schools for blacks were segregated at the outset and were at the mercy of the white-controlled state government for funding. Many whites did not want blacks to become educated because they feared educated blacks would not be content with jobs working in fields or in domestic service. Black schools, therefore, received far less financial support than white schools. Black schools had fewer textbooks, worse building facilities, and poorly-paid teachers.

In light of the dreadful history of "separate and unequal" educational opportunities for blacks in America, no one should be surprised that their achievement in school has lagged behind their white counterparts'. Decades, perhaps even centuries, of challenges related to poverty and racial bias (both explicit and implicit) have stunted the educational growth of generations of black children. The findings in the Kerner Commission's report in 1968 are just as relevant today; specifically, "white racism" is creating two "separate and unequal" societies in America.

The answer to the essential question is "yes." The stain of racism in America's educational-past *does* pose a problem for its educational-future.

"Education has enhanced my senses. It
has allowed me to hear voices
from the past; feel the winds of change in the present;
and see a true post-racial America in the future."

— Dr. James "Jim" Taylor

Educator

★ ★ ★

CHAPTER 2

THE CULTURE GAP

─────────────────★─────────────────

ESSENTIAL QUESTION

What is the nature of the culture gap between teachers and their
students, and what can be done to mitigate its impact on students?

─────────────────★─────────────────

Both learning and communication are hampered when disconnects
or gaps occur. This is especially true in public education. It is well
documented that the rapidly shifting demographics in the United
States are creating a culture gap in K-12 (kindergarten through 12th
grade) public education. In 1996, data provided by the Pew Research
Center indicated that over 63 percent of the 46.1 million students in
our nation's public schools were white. Today, white students account
for just 49.5 percent of the 50 million students enrolled.

Although the complexion of student populations in America's
public schools has undergone a dramatic shift in the twenty-first
century, the profile of teachers in the classroom has remained virtually

unchanged during the past three decades. In 2019, the National Center for Education Statistics released a report indicating that 82 percent of all teachers in public schools were white, English-speaking, and middle class; and 76 percent were white females. In quantitative terms, this suggests that the culture gap in America's public schools is roughly 31.5 percentage points; that is, the percent of white teachers (82) minus the percent of nonwhite students (50.5) equals 31.5 percentage points.

These changes in the racial make-up of America's public schools are reflective of the direction the overall population is headed. The U.S. Census Bureau estimates that by 2060 the white population in this country will decrease by more than 20 million people, while the Hispanic population is projected to double. Black and Asian populations are also expected to increase but at rates slower than Hispanics. By 2043, the nation as a whole is projected to become predominantly nonwhite, which will make our society one of the most culturally diverse on the planet.

Public education in America has a well-documented pattern of serving (and failing!) certain student groups more than others based on cultural demographics, especially race. America must guard against having a repeat of its ugly Jim Crow past. We cannot allow any form of racism or discrimination to spread into our schools and cause harm to our children. As a society, we must acknowledge our past transgressions and make a commitment to educate all children equitably, inclusive of every race, ethnicity, gender, religion, and socioeconomic status. We must adapt to the influx of different cultures into our nation's schools, and we can begin in the classroom by building a bridge to close the culture gap between teachers and their students.

WHAT IS CULTURE?

If we hope to have any measure of success with building that bridge, we must have a clear understanding of the concept. So, what is culture? All of us have a perspective, and there is wide variation among those perspectives. Undoubtedly, it would be helpful to have a common perspective of what constitutes a culture before we are able to engage in a meaningful discussion of the concept. Although cultures (and perspectives) vary across different parts of the globe, they share seven characteristics and their basic elements remain the same. Culture is learned, shared, developed, transmitted across generations, subject to change, not isolated, and essential for life.

Culture is Learned

Culture is not inherited. It is not genetic. It is, however, taught and learned through one's experiences and social environment. The members of a given culture share certain values and beliefs (e.g., language, literature, and biases) that shape their lives. Those cultural values are sustained because they are passed from one generation to another. The future generations learn to follow the same beliefs and traditions, and they adopt them as part of their culture. Thus, no individual is born with a sense of culture; it is a learned behavior.

Culture is Shared

Every culture is shaped by a group of people that usually inhabit the same part of the world. A people's culture consists of the geographical conditions around them, their country's past, their belief system and values, and the heritage they adopt. Since these elements are common to a given group, the people of that group embrace them in a sense of unity, identity, and belonging.

People in the same community tend to share the same values, beliefs, and traditions. The language, mannerisms, and the way the people in that community communicate are similar. Since these aspects of a community are shaped by the people's belief system, their personalities share certain traits. Their roles in the family and society are defined by their culture. This gives the people a collective identity. Thus, culture belongs to a community and not to any single human being; it is shared.

Culture Takes Time to Develop

Not only does culture influences us, but we also influence culture. Culture evolves over time and takes years to develop. It is not static, it is fluid. As time passes, culture even changes in the process. Some traditions are created with a cultural or political purpose or in the interest of the nation. They are passed down from one generation to another. These include holidays, festivals, beliefs, and rituals. Similarly, art and literature are also passed down through generations and, consequently, shape the culture of that community and take years to form.

Culture is Transmitted across Generations

Cultural values are transmitted across generations in the form of symbols and stories that make them easier to understand. When the older generations pass cultural values to forthcoming generations, sometimes information gets lost in translation and sometimes information may be removed on purpose. Moreover, during the process of transmitting, some aspects of the culture are not correctly or completely understood or are simply not accepted. This may even lead to the end of old cultures.

In order to take pride in one's culture, it is important for people to know their past; know how it has shaped their present; and know how it is going to influence their future. This is why it is important for African Americans to know about their cultural past during the Jim Crow era, especially in the area of education. It is important for the older generation to teach the younger generation about that oppressive era in America and how blacks were typecast as being intellectually inferior to whites. This should instill a sense of pride in their heritage and motivate young blacks to rise above the insidious myth regarding their intellectual potential.

Culture Changes

Cultures are not static; they undergo a gradual change. As time passes, some beliefs are transformed, certain traditions or rituals are eliminated, language and mannerisms of people are modified; thus, their culture changes. Migration and globalization have led to a mixing of cultures. When people from different parts of the world come together, they influence each other and each other's cultures. These factors contribute to the formation of a multicultural society and, in some cases, even new cultures develop.

Due to their exposure to various cultures across the globe, people adopt some aspects of other cultures. This affects what they teach their children, which can influence the culture of their future generations and, conceivably, lead to a cultural change. When social thinking undergoes a transition, so does culture. Social mores and gender roles may change. For example, in Pakistan, which is a patriarchal society, men are the primary authority figures and women are subordinate. As the women became more exposed to other cultures, they became more vocal and demanded more equality.

In March 2018, women marched through the streets of Karachi, Pakistan, with clenched fists raised shouting, "Aurat aiee, aurat aiee, tharki teri shaamath aiee!" (Women are here, harassers must fear!) And, in an act of overt defiance to traditional cultural norms, many of the women protesters wore jeans, designer shades, brightly embroidered skirts, and baggy pants. Unquestionably, these women were influenced by western cultures, and they demanded a change in their culture.

Culture Cannot be Isolated

Studies reveal that no culture can remain in isolation. Every culture is mostly influenced by cultures of the surrounding regions. Years ago, there were tribal societies that stayed in seclusion, unaware of the world outside. Today, most of those once-secluded groups are connected to the rest of the world. Thus, there is hardly any social community or culture that is totally isolated from the rest of the world.

The Awá tribe in Brazil, for example, was labeled the "world's most endangered tribe." They still live nomadically in the Amazon forest. They have lived under constant fear of being uprooted by illegal loggers or the possible devastation of wildfires. This inspired other tribes in the region to rise up and protect the Awá, which ended their years of social isolation.

The cultural values of people in a particular country are affected by those of the people from neighboring countries. When people from different geographical locations come together (like the Awá and neighboring tribes), they influence each other's cultures. Trade between two countries, migration of people to different parts of the world, and travel for educational or recreational purposes are some examples of how cultures cannot stay separated. Cultures that evolve around the same time show similarities because they have developed together. Some blend aspects of their beliefs to create shared cultures. No culture can make itself immune to external influences.

Culture is Essential

Culture gives us an identity. Our personalities are shaped by the art and history that give us pride, the literature we learn from, and our upbringing. For example, the Kente cloth is a symbol of West African culture and a source of pride in the African American community. Many college students typically march across commencement stages to receive their degrees while wearing a Kente cloth stole. This college ritual is a visible sign of students connecting with their African heritage.

The things we observe around us and the folk tales our elders share with us are deeply ingrained in our minds. Our cultural values and system of beliefs dictate our thinking and behavior. Rituals and traditions are a part of our daily living. The way we conduct ourselves in society is highly influenced by the culture we belong to. Culture is essential toward making us feel a part of a group and giving us the guiding principles of life.

In short, there are several elements of culture. Collectively, one's language, symbols, religious beliefs, customs, traditions, values, and norms are the key elements of a person's culture. They give meaning to the concept of culture and are important for our overall development as individuals.

WHAT IS A CULTURE GAP?

A culture gap is any systematic difference between two cultures that hinders mutual understanding, communication, or building relationships. Some differences may include the values, religion, behavior, education, and customs of the respective cultures. These cultural differences may lead to conflicts and misunderstandings within a society. Most cultural differences in America are manifested as gaps in generations, the workplace, or in school settings.

Generation Gaps

A generation gap commonly refers to differences between generations that cause conflict and complicate communication. Due to increased life spans, four distinct generations have lived side-by-side in the United States since the middle of the twentieth century. Over time, they have earned names based on how they behave and the historical events that influenced them. Those generations are *Baby Boomers, Generation X, Millennials,* and *Generation Z.*

Baby Boomers. This group is a generation of Americans who were born between 1946 and 1964. They are perhaps the most influential generation in history and are known for their pivotal roles in the civil rights movement, Woodstock, and the Vietnam War. The term "Baby Boomers" was coined due to the dramatic increase in birth rates following World War II. Soldiers came home from the war and had more time to spend creating babies. At approximately 75 million strong, this is the second largest generation group in the United States today.

This generation values relationships, as they did not grow up with technology running their lives. Baby Boomers grew up making phone calls and writing letters, solidifying strong interpersonal skills. As they got older, however, they actually became fluent in technology and now use cell phones and tablets. They tend to use these technologies as productivity tools as opposed to connectivity or social tools.

Generation X. This group is also known as the "lost generation" and consists of Americans who were born between 1965 and1980. Currently, members of this generation are 40 to 55 years of age, and they make up the largest generation group in America. Unlike the Baby Boomer generation, members of Generation X (or Gen Xers) are focused more on balancing work and life rather than following the straight-and-narrow path of Corporate America.

Dubbed by the media as "latch-key kids," Gen Xers are considered the first "daycare" generation because many were raised by two parents who worked or by a single divorced parent. This generation often delayed marriage and childbearing to focus on developing themselves first. They are the first generation to value the balance between work and life. This is possibly in response to what they experienced as a consequence of their parents' workaholism or their broken homes.

In her essay titled *Generation X Goes Global: Mapping a Youth Culture in Motion*, Christine Henseler summarizes this generation as "a generation whose worldview is based on change, on the need to combat corruption, dictatorships, abuse, AIDS; a generation in search of human dignity and individual freedom, the need for stability, love, tolerance, and human rights for all."

Millennials. Members of this group are also known as Generation Y (or Gen Y) and were born between 1981 and 1996. They have also been dubbed as the narcissistic tech gurus, and they are the first generation to reach adulthood in the new millennium. Millennials are the young technology gurus who thrive on new innovations, startups, and working out of coffee shops. These 20-something to early 30-year-olds have redefined the workplace. *Time Magazine* called them the "Me-Me Generation" because they want it all. They are known as confident, entitled, and depressed.

This blog-savvy generation was raised by parents who were not authoritative but saw themselves as partners. The Millennials grew up making the rules rather than having their parents tell them what is right. Their lives are now run by their smart gadgets, their third appendage.

These people date through on-line websites, as opposed to the Baby Boomers who met their spouses through friends or at social outings. The Millennials may be known as successful and driven, but their marriage to technology has nearly destroyed their interpersonal skills. As a result, depression is rampant in this generation.

Their stressors are probably multifaceted, driven by the hardships of society, the obsession with technology, and the "I am smarter-than-you mentality." In the workplace, contrary to Baby Boomers, Millennials strive for flexibility rather than a higher tax bracket. They want more vacation time, casual dress, and the flexibility of working from home rather than the office. They are all about working smarter, not harder.

Generation Z. This is the "evolving" generation. They represent people born roughly between 1997 and the present. Only a sparse amount of data is published about this generation because, currently, the average age is somewhere between five and 23 years old. However, we do know that toddlers are already hooked on technology. Also, given the recent "diversity explosion" in the United States, Generation Z (or Gen Z) is the most racially and ethnically diverse generation with 49 percent identifying as nonwhite. A breakdown of the four generations by age and population is presented in Table 1.

Table 1

Breakdown of the Generations by Age and Population in America in 2020

Domain	Baby Boomers	Generation X	Millennials (Generation Y)	Generation Z
Age	56–74	40–55	24–39	5–23
Population	75 million	82 million	73 million	74 million

A "diversity explosion" is driving this generational gap in the United States. The year 2011 marked the first time in the history of the country that more minority babies than white babies were born in a single year. Soon, most children in the U.S. will be racial minorities; that is—Hispanics, African Americans, Asians, and other nonwhite races. Further, in about three decades, whites will constitute a minority of all Americans. This milestone signals the beginning of a transformation from the mostly white baby-boom culture that dominated the nation during the last half of the twentieth century to the more globalized, multiracial country that the United States is becoming.

Table 2

Ideologies Held by the Four Generations

Domain	Baby Boomers (1946-1964)	Generation X (1965-1980)	Millennials (Gen Y) (1981-1996)	Generation Z (1997-2015)
Media Consumption:	Highest consumers of traditional media.	Heavy television and Facebook users.	Cutting cable in favor of streaming options.	Heavy users of mobile devices.
Shaping Events:	Post-World War II optimism and the Civil Rights Movement.	The Cold War and rise of personal computing.	Explosion of the Internet and the Great Recession.	Internet access at a very young age.
Financial Habits:	Managing retirement pensions.	Carrying the highest debt load while raising children.	Major student debt causes a delay with major life purchases.	Want to avoid debt after seeing Millennials struggle.

In summary, as the younger, more diverse part of America's population reaches adulthood, clear gaps will develop between their economic and socio-political interests than those of older, mostly white generations. This divide will result in disputes over local expenditures (for example, over whether to spend money on schools or senior health facilities), and those disputes may evolve into culture clashes. Table 2 provides a snapshot of disparities in certain ideologies held by the various generations. If the current trajectory in demography is a true indication of America's destiny—her workforce, politics, and place on the world stage will soon be changed forever.

Workplace Gaps

For decades, the business world has recognized the relationship between culture and productivity. In the early 1900s, for example, the Nordstrom Company was among the first business organizations to put forth an intensive effort to create a culture in the workplace that was conducive to productivity and consumer satisfaction. This company built a business model for customer service that is still used by many in the business world today.

Researchers have studied many businesses, both large and small, to identify the essential elements of a great workplace culture. Based on comprehensive surveys and interviews, it has been determined that employees want:

- *Purpose*, which is the need to understand how their work specifically contributes to the organization's goals.
- *Opportunity* to grow, develop, and contribute.
- *Success* or know what it looks like through continuous performance management.
- *Appreciation* for the work they do.
- *Well-being* or having employers focusing on all aspects of their being (i.e., the physical, social, financial, and emotional).
- *Leadership* from supervisors who mentor, advocate for employee development, and establish strong relationships with them.

Today, diversity is typical in most workplaces. With the advancement of technology, it is not uncommon to deal with clients and customers from all over the world. While this may be the new norm, the possible challenges of diversity cannot be ignored. Language barriers may make it difficult to communicate effectively, or cultural differences may inhibit internal and external customers from being comfortable enough to open up, socialize or bond.

In the multicultural workplaces that are typical of doing business in a global economy, cultural barriers to communication are quite common. Besides the obvious difficulty in understanding people whose language is different, there are other factors that challenge people who are trying to work harmoniously with others of a different background. People from different parts of the world have a different frame of reference, and they may display emotions differently and display different behaviors. These potential issues may hinder relationships as well as productivity in the workplace.

Consequently, if organizations plan to do business on a global level, they will need to find solutions to break down barriers that create cultural gaps. Those barriers include (a) language, (b) stereotypes, (c) behaviors, and (d) emotions.

Language is a very complex phenomenon, and communication between people speaking different languages is difficult. Language is a way of looking at the world. Even skilled translators can find it tricky to convey complex emotions and concepts, which can lead to misunderstandings. When you think about how often you misunderstand someone speaking to you in your own language, you can imagine the level of misunderstanding that can occur from someone speaking to you from a different cultural background.

Inaccurate and hostile *stereotypes* of people from other places can be a barrier to communication in the workplace. Stereotypes are assumptions people make about the traits of members of a group. For example, a stereotypical Hispanic person is thought to be Mexican and mostly uneducated. During an interview for ABC News, Mexican Diplomat Claudia Ruiz Massieu stated: "In fact, Mexico has the second largest professional diaspora in the United States. We are talking about lawyers, we're talking about designers in Silicon Valley, we're talking about medical professionals, we're talking about Oscar winners." This data not only applies to Mexico but also other Latin-American countries that contribute professional human capital to the American economy.

The danger in entertaining stereotypes is that an individual is thought to possess characteristics that are ascribed to the entire ethnic group. This is often referred to as painting everyone with the same broad brush. Obviously, not all Hispanics are uneducated nor are they all Mexicans. Prejudging an individual can lead to misconceptions and barriers to communication.

Behavioral differences between employees of different cultures can also cause misunderstandings. Every culture has guidelines about what is considered appropriate behavior. In some cultures, looking someone in the eye when they are talking to you is considered rude, while in other cultures refraining from doing so is considered disrespectful. Getting right to the point at a business meeting may be considered impolite by some, especially for those who expect to "socialize" before the business discussion begins. Likewise, in some cultures, people in face-to-face dialogue give each other space, while in other cultures they stand close. These differences can be barriers to effective communication if they are not recognized.

What is considered an appropriate display of *emotion* can differ from culture to culture. In some countries, displaying anger, fear or frustration in the workplace is considered inappropriate in a business setting. People from these cultures keep their emotions hidden and only discuss the factual aspects of the situation. In other cultures, participants in a discussion are expected to reveal their emotions. Invariably, misunderstandings can arise if a businessperson displays strong emotion in the company of employees who feel that such behavior is inappropriate.

While cultural communication barriers do exist, overcoming these barriers is possible through training in areas such as cultural sensitivity and cultural awareness. Ultimately, this training can lead to a stronger workforce. Multiple cultural perspectives allow for better understanding of the customer, and it encourages creative solutions to problems. Learning to communicate and draw on the positive aspects of each culture benefits everyone.

In summary, diversity is typical in most workplaces. Advancements in technology have made it possible for businesses to deal with clients and customers across the globe. While this may be the new norm, the challenges of diversity cannot be ignored. Language barriers and the presence of negative stereotypes may create cultural gaps that inhibit communication and productivity in the workplace. These gaps can be mitigated through proper training and by implementing strategies that promote the appreciation and awareness of cultural differences.

Gaps in School Settings

Schools are businesses that focus on teaching and learning. As such, many of the principles that apply to culture in corporate workplaces can also apply to school settings, especially with building relationships. The same explosion in diversity that has created cultural gaps in the corporate sector has created virtually the same gaps in the classroom. These gaps are due in large part to challenges teachers encounter from students that do not look like them. This often triggers an implicit racial bias in teachers that lowers their expectations of diverse students, and the students often "fulfill" the low expectations by underachieving in the classroom.

While the nation's school-aged children are becoming more diverse, the teaching corps is not. Of the 3.3 million teachers in the U.S. public school system, slightly more than 80 percent are white. This represents little change since 1990 when 87 percent of teachers were white. There is not a single state in the nation with a teacher population that is as diverse as its students and in some states that gap is huge. In California, for example, only 40 percent of the teachers are nonwhite, while nearly 75 percent of students are nonwhite.

Some schools and families have struggled mightily with their attempts to accommodate the vast and quick changes they have seen over the last few years. In February 2020, a community meeting was held at Saline Area Schools in Michigan after offensive and inappropriate racist comments using derogatory terms about African Americans were posted on social media by some high school students in the community. While the intent of the meeting was to promote diversity, it ended in tension after a white parent yelled out racist comments.

Racial tensions are not restricted to high school settings; they also occur in elementary schools. In 2019, an incident at Key Elementary School in Northwest Washington, D.C., created emotional unrest within in the school's mostly-white, affluent community. In that incident, a white fifth-grader at the school used a racial slur against three black classmates when he became upset during a football game at recess. The white fifth-grader unashamedly proclaimed that he was, indeed, a racist.

And, yes, racism continues to fester on many college campuses. Recently, the campus police at Colgate University in central New York were called with reports of a black male carrying a gun. This prompted school officials to put the campus on lockdown. In reality, the black male was a Colgate student carrying a glue gun for a school project. In a message to the university's students and staff, President Brian W. Casey wrote, "It is important that we understand the role that implicit racial bias had in the initial reporting of and responses to the events of last night."

These are just a few examples of the effects that racism and prejudice have on the perspective of many people in our society. Children aren't born bigots; racial prejudice is something we learn. Since children are very impressionable at a young age, the people who raise them and various media can easily instill ideas about a certain group of people. As these children grow older, they begin observing individuals from these different groups to find traits that support these stereotypes; thus, forming more prejudice and implicit bias toward people that don't look like them.

African Americans have learned to expect bias in their lives from an early age, and very little has been done to counteract the effects associated with implicit biases. If black students experience the effects of implicit bias from the first day they step into a school, how can we expect them to develop healthy or positive attitudes toward authority figures later in life? While we may think of ourselves as unbiased, it is important for educators to recognize and purposefully counteract any effects of implicit bias by beginning with staff and then spreading understanding beyond schools and into the public mindset.

The public mindset is reflected in the biased children's books that are written by educators and non-educators today. Researchers at the University of Wisconsin at Madison found that the characters in children's books are overwhelmingly depicted by white children. Furthermore, animals are more often the main characters than children from any other ethnic group.

As presented in Table 3, some progress has been made with the diversity in children's books from 2015 to 2018. The fact remains, however, that children of color are far more likely to see a caricature of a white child or an animal as a main character in a book as opposed to one that looks like them. While some progress has been made more is needed.

Table 3
Diversity in Children's Books: 2015 vs. 2018

Main Character	2015	2018
White	73.3%	50%
Animals/Other	12.5%	27%
African/African American	7.6%	10%
Asian Pacific Islander/American	3.3%	7%
Latinx	2.4%	5%
American Indians/First Nations	0.9%	1%

Source: School of Education, University of Wisconsin-Madison

Classroom teachers, especially in public education, have a unique responsibility and opportunity to provide optimal learning for the diverse groups of students that are entering our schools. This can be challenging for teachers who are unfamiliar with their students' backgrounds and communities. Their success as teachers will depend upon their ability to mitigate their implicit biases and engage the diverse student populations in their classrooms. Implicit bias and the disparate treatment of children by race starts at an early age.

A study by Dr. Walter Gilliam at Yale University found that when preschool teachers were looking to prevent behavioral problems, they focused on black male students significantly more than on other students. National data sets show that black students in K-12 schools received expulsions at rates higher than students of all other races. They also received out-of-school-suspensions nearly four times more often than white students. This disparate treatment of children of color in classroom discipline leads to higher rates of juvenile incarceration, lower graduation rates, lower academic achievement, higher incidences of future poverty, and extended time in the K-12 public school system.

The essence of learning in the classroom is a function of what is known as *student engagement*. In its most basic definition, the Glossary of Education Reform refers to student engagement as "the degree of attention, curiosity, interest, optimism, and passion that students show when they are learning or being taught." Simply stated, when students are engaged with their teacher, they are learning. When they are not engaged, they are not learning.

Jenny Fulton provides a more comprehensive definition that encompasses three different types of student engagement: emotional, behavioral, and cognitive. *Emotional* engagement refers to students' feelings about their teachers and school experience in general. *Behavioral* engagement includes how active the students are in both extracurricular and cocurricular activities. *Cognitive* engagement refers to how motivated the students are in the learning process.

When barriers are created between teachers and their students, the various dimensions of student engagement are negatively impacted. Students begin to become emotionally disengaged from their teachers;

they become less motivated to participate in school activities; and they become detached from the learning process. In other words, as previously stated, when students become disengaged with their teacher—learning is suppressed.

Perhaps the greatest suppressor of teaching and learning occurs when there is a cultural gap between teachers and their students. This gap is stimulated by implicit biases related to race, language, and negative stereotypes. While many teachers are able to overcome some of the cultural barriers in their classroom through training, hard work, and creativity—most teachers find it overwhelming to make their classrooms places where differences become strengths. These teachers do not recognize the creative ways that students express themselves. They are not able to see students' perspectives; they do not nurture and support competence in both home and school cultures; and these teachers do not seek out ways to make their instruction compatible with the cultural learning styles of minority students.

To begin lessening the effects of implicit bias, schools must provide professional development opportunities to make teachers aware of their implicit biases and the different ways they might impact students. Data collection and analyses in the form of equity audits provide clear information as to where implicit biases most severely impact students. Schools must implement policies that allow adequate time for teachers to react and respond to the academic, disciplinary, and social needs of students. Recognition of culture must become an integral part of a school's climate and be allowed to grow and change based on the population of students served by the school.

SUMMARY

Educators today hear a lot about various gaps in public education, such as achievement gaps, funding gaps, and school-readiness gaps. Yet, there is another gap that often goes unexamined; namely, the cultural gap between teachers and their students. Most classroom teachers in K-12 public education are middle-class, English-speaking white females. But the majority of the faces in their classrooms do not look like them.

To engage students effectively in the learning process, teachers must know their students and their academic abilities individually. They cannot rely on implicit biases that paint distorted pictures of students based on racial or ethnic stereotypes. Many teachers, for example, admire the perceived academic prowess and motivation of Asian American students. But they fail to recognize how even a so-called "positive" stereotype isn't positive if it pressures some students into molds that are not built for them individually. In other words, there is an inherent danger involved in typecasting all Asian American students (or any other group) as possessing an all-inclusive trait or characteristic.

As the nation's public schools become more and more diverse, teachers and other school personnel will be looked upon as the flag-bearers for change. An area in dire need of change is mitigating the effects of implicit racial bias, which is spreading through our schools like an epidemic. In response to the essential question at the beginning of this chapter, schools must develop strategies and create opportunities to make teachers aware of their implicit biases and the different ways they might impact students. Until, and unless, a bridge is built to mitigate the culture gap between teachers and their students— the spread of implicit racial biases will continue to plague America's education system.

"It is not our differences that divide us. It is our inability
to recognize, accept, and celebrate those differences."
—Audre Lorde

★ ★ ★

CHAPTER 3

TEACHER PREPARATION

---★---

ESSENTIAL QUESTION
What is the most effective approach toward preparing
teachers to teach in culturally diverse classrooms?

---★---

Nearly everyone accepts the premise that teachers make a difference in the lives of their students. A plethora of research on teacher quality supports the fact that effective teachers not only make students feel good about school and learning, but their work actually results in increased student achievement and self-esteem. Though she is best known as a poet and author, the late Dr. Maya Angelou was also a professor at Wake Forest University, and she offers a brilliant perspective of an effective teacher:

> "This is the value of the teacher, who looks at a face
> and says there's something behind that and I want to

reach that person, I want to influence that person, I want to encourage that person, I want to enrich, I want to call out that person who is behind that face, behind that color, behind that language, behind that tradition, behind that culture. I believe you can do it. I know what was done for me."

As the virus of implicit racial bias continues to spread in America's public schools, educators continue to scramble for an antidote. Actually, Dr. Maya Angelou has already given us a blueprint that can be used to mitigate the culture gap between teachers and students which, in most cases, is fueled by implicit bias. Teachers matter! An effective classroom teacher can bridge the gap between themselves and their students and, ultimately, improve academic outcomes for students that don't look like them.

If the key to bridging the culture gap rests with having effective, culturally competent teachers in classrooms, then where do we find them? Are they born or are they made? To complicate matters even more, there is a national shortage of teachers. For various and sundry reasons, people are either leaving or shying away from the profession.

Fortunately, teachers can be taught the skills they will need to be successful in the classroom. In response to this growing need, public school districts across the nation have begun to explore ways to make aspiring and practicing teachers better prepared to reach their culturally diverse students. This is accomplished through one of three preparation programs—alternative certification, pre-service, or in-service.

ALTERNATIVE CERTIFICATION

Alternative or non-traditional teacher certification was initially introduced to fill critical teacher shortages, and that process is still used today. Alternative certification programs are also used as a way to recruit talented people who don't have a background in education but do have a passion for teaching. In light of ongoing shortages in the teacher workforce, many states have been forced to use this process to recruit people with less-than-stellar credentials to fill vacancies.

The 2018-19 school year was a tumultuous one for teachers. Hundreds of thousands of teachers participated in walkouts across the nation involving pay disputes, and a record number decided to quit the profession. Moreover, a recent Gallup poll shows that almost half of the teachers in the U.S. said they are actively looking for another job now or watching for other opportunities. Nearly 44 percent of new teachers leave the profession within five years, primarily because of the low pay.

The heartbreaking disputes related to teacher pay remind us of this old African proverb: "When elephants fight, it's the grass that suffers." In this proverb, the grass represents the students and the elephants are the combatants; namely, teacher unions and school officials. This battle is bad news for public education. The high turnover of qualified teachers impacts student performance and can be costly to school districts.

It is within this context that we are reminded of teachers like Sheldon Davis. Sheldon was a fifth-grade teacher in a highly-diverse elementary school in the metropolitan area of Seminole County, Florida. During his career as a teacher, he was widely recognized by his colleagues and peers as extraordinary; a teacher who truly cared about his students and nurtured their academic growth. By all accounts, Sheldon was a "rock star" in the classroom.

Unfortunately, Sheldon had to leave the teaching profession at the conclusion of his third year in the classroom. As a young black man with a pregnant wife, he felt an obligation to better support his growing family by pursuing a career that paid a higher salary. Sheldon will be difficult to replace because only seven percent of the teacher workforce is comprised of blacks. This is really bad news for black children. That's because recent research shows that by having just one—just one—black teacher in elementary school, black children are more likely to graduate and go to college. The importance of having teachers of color in elementary schools cannot be overstated.

Each state has its own laws and policies on how teachers get their certification. Although some states have unique requirements, they all typically follow this four-step process:

1. Obtain a bachelor's degree in education, teaching, or a specific subject from an accredited institution.
2. Adhere to the state's licensure requirements and, if necessary, complete a teacher preparation program.
3. Take and pass the state's required basic skills exam.
4. Submit an application to the state's department of education to receive a certificate to teach.

For people with a degree in a non-education field, there are alternative pathways to achieve certification as a teacher. These alternative pathways to certification can be used to fill shortages in the teacher workforce as well as to recruit people of color into the profession. Four of the most popular alternative programs are (1)

Teach for America, (2) American Board for Certification of Teacher Excellence, (3) Teach-Now, and (4) iTeach.

Teach for America is a nonprofit organization that recruits college graduates and professionals to teach for a minimum of two years in low-income areas across the U.S. The organization provides all the classroom training, curriculum coursework, and support a corps member would need to become a fully certified teacher. In addition, all corps members are required to attend an intensive summer program to prepare them for the rigors of teaching. All applicants for admission into this program must have a bachelor's degree with a minimum grade point average of 2.5.

The *American Board for Certification of Teacher Excellence* allows a person to complete a teacher certification program entirely online. The primary area of study is elementary education and, on average, most students take 10 months to complete the certification process. The American Board is accepted as an approved alternative route for full certification as a teacher in 11 states, which include Arizona, Idaho, Florida, Mississippi, Missouri, New Hampshire, Oklahoma, Pennsylvania, South Carolina, Tennessee, and Utah.

Teach-Now is another online program that offers an alternative pathway to teacher certification. The curriculum for this nine-month post-baccalaureate program involves comprehensive modules and virtual classes with 10 to 15 students in each cohort. Graduates of the program earn a renewable teaching license that, purportedly, is recognized all over the world.

iTeach is yet another online program that offers an alternative pathway to teacher certification. Participants are expected to complete their coursework in six months. After completing their coursework, the students complete an internship as a fulltime teacher for a full year with a salary and benefits.

A recent Gallup study found that "recruiting" and "retaining" skilled teachers is the number-one concern among public school officials. Alternative teacher certification programs offer a quick and fairly easy way to stockpile the dwindling teacher workforce. While this would increase the quantity in that stockpile, the quality or effectiveness of many of those teachers would be suspect. That's because it seems as if Teach for America is the only alternative certification program that provides instruction in culturally responsive teaching strategies. These strategies are absolutely essential to engage the diverse student populations in K-12 public schools today.

PRE-SERVICE

Although agencies such as the National Council for Teacher Education and some state departments of education require teachers to complete some course work in multicultural education prior to obtaining their certification, recent research indicates that many teachers believe they had not been adequately prepared to teach students from cultural backgrounds different from their own. A recent survey of over 15,000 teachers across America was conducted in which they were asked to examine their own level of competence for teaching black, Latino or low-income children. Nearly 40 percent of the white teachers said their college programs left them "completely unprepared" or "mostly unprepared." The majority of the participants felt they had to develop their own skills through trial-and-error or by observing other teachers.

The National Education Association cites additional evidence of teachers entering classrooms without the skills needed to engage their culturally and ethnically diverse students. In a study of teachers in New Jersey, researchers found that the majority of teachers surveyed indicated that they did not have adequate preparation to teach children who came from homes in which English was not the primary language spoken. They described their course work in the area of cultural and linguistic diversity as being too general and less than adequate to prepare them for the context of their current classrooms.

Also, researchers in a school district in Kansas found that the majority of the teachers (kindergarten through 12th grade) felt underprepared to teach students from cultural backgrounds that were different from their own. Invariably, they felt that their college course work and student teaching lacked the depth to adequately prepare them for the challenges they faced in their classroom.

"Diversity in the classroom was not a topic of discussion when I was in college in the 1980s," said Barbara Thompson, a white elementary school teacher with 31 years of experience. "Only recently have administrators in my school even begun to talk about culture and cultural awareness. I think I've been fairly successful teaching and reaching all of my students, but I had to use my common sense and experience."

While Ms. Thompson's efforts in the classroom seem well-intentioned and worthy of praise, common sense is merely the tip of the iceberg. Teachers need more sophisticated utensils in their toolkits to maximize their ability to engage the vast array of cultures represented in their classrooms. Despite their instincts and experience, there is a stark reality for teachers like Ms. Thompson. Through no fault of their own, they are not fully prepared to teach racially and culturally diverse groups of students.

Brianna McGagin's story is slightly different. This biracial 25-year-old teacher graduated from San Diego State University in 2016. After graduation, she received training in multicultural education through the Teach for America program. As part of her two-year agreement with Teach for America, she was assigned to teach in an inner-city high school in Atlanta, Georgia.

Despite her age and inexperience, Miss McGagin was a highly successful classroom teacher, and she engaged the diverse student population with minimal difficulty. She attributed much of her success to the training in multicultural education she received through Teach for America. Pre-service made a difference for her.

"I think the training I received at Teach for America prepared me well for the challenges I faced," Miss McGagin's reported. "Many of my peers at [the high school] struggled a bit because of their lack of training. Although they are good teachers, they get frustrated a lot because they have difficulty connecting with certain groups of students." It is fairly apparent that Miss McGagin's peers struggled because of a lack of pre-service training in multicultural education.

The lack of preparation that aspiring teachers have received in the area of multicultural education raises two questions: (1) Are the college professors providing sound instruction? (2) Are the students giving due diligence to their course work in this area? Although many teacher education programs claim to promote and celebrate diversity, many traditional teacher preparation programs rarely focus on multicultural courses. Instead, these courses are either added-on to or disconnected from the rest of the program

In many universities, typical courses related to multicultural education are focused on helping prospective teachers understand the underlying cultural forces that shape the education system in America and those that seriously affect students' achievement. The hope is that factors in the classroom (i.e., race, language, and religion) that could trigger a teacher-student culture gap can be examined and mitigated without implicit bias. If the ultimate goal of multicultural education is to raise personal awareness about differences in culture and how they may hinder or enhance the way students and teachers interact—then one single course alone cannot accomplish this.

During college, many teachers approach their coursework with a preconceived notion that effective multicultural education is mostly about teaching cultural highlights or how other countries celebrate their holidays. Many of them are often inexperienced in their understanding of what it means to value diversity when teaching for equity. Instead of making an effort to see the world from different perspectives, many of them either deny the existence of "white privilege" or they take a defensive position by claiming to be colorblind; which, to them, translates to valuing diversity. On the contrary, to many people of color the term "colorblind" can denote invisibility; that is— "If you don't see my color then you don't see me."

Colleges and universities should stress the importance of "self-efficacy" as part of the curricula in their preparation programs for teaching culturally and linguistically diverse children. This concept refers to teachers' beliefs in their ability to effectively handle the tasks, obligations, and challenges related to their instructional activities in the classroom. This plays a key role in influencing important academic outcomes and well-being in the classroom environment.

Regardless of their course work in college, teachers' personal beliefs about students of color will have a direct impact on their students' achievement and motivation. Without genuine understanding, the teachers would be more apt to create lesson plans based on a subjective or biased belief about students' experiences. This does a disservice to students.

In the midst of this is the fact that enrollment in teacher preparation programs nationwide has declined by more than one-third since 2010. According to a recent analysis from the Center for American Progress, nearly 340,000 fewer students are enrolled in teacher preparation programs. Enrollment declines in Oklahoma, Michigan, Pennsylvania, Delaware, Illinois, Idaho, Indiana, New Mexico, and Rhode Island have hovered around 50 percent. Moreover, enrollment in New Jersey, New York, Ohio, and California dropped by more than 10,000 students.

Perhaps the most daunting aspect of the decline is the fact that the number of black and Latino students enrolled in teacher preparation programs has decreased by 25 percent. The ramifications of this are fairly obvious. The overall teacher workforce, which is already a little more than 80 percent white, will become even less racially diverse. This is not good news for children of color, because they will begin to see less teachers that look like them. This speaks to an even greater need for multicultural education in K-12 public schools.

Unfortunately, many education courses regularly produce teachers who can recite the politically correct tenets of multicultural education without having the personal beliefs to back them up. The implications of this are clear. Teacher preparation programs should require courses that promote teacher self-efficacy prior to working with children, especially when working with children of color. This would address the disconnection between teachers' culture and the culture of their students.

Teachers probably can get a better gauge of their self-efficacy when they are actually involved in ongoing contact with culturally and linguistically diverse students. Therefore, it would seem plausible that staff development or in-service initiatives would offer better opportunities for them to address their self-efficacy. The next subsection will discuss how in-service can be used to develop more culturally competent teachers.

IN-SERVICE

As former principals in large school systems, we are keenly aware that it takes extensive training to develop and nurture a good teacher. Laws are passed, students change, and new instructional strategies are always being developed. All of these require educators to remain current on best practices, teaching methodologies, and laws. Thus, effective schools and school districts must establish in-service (or professional development) programs to meet the needs of their students and staff. As stated throughout this book, those challenges are related to improving teachers' ability to engage the students in their culturally diverse classrooms. A variety of in-service activities can be planned to address those challenges.

It is reasonably safe to conclude that many prospective teachers leave college feeling somewhat unprepared to teach K-12 classrooms with culturally and linguistically diverse students. So, it becomes the responsibility of school leaders (i.e., superintendents and principals) to provide appropriate professional development or in-service. The number one challenge faced by these school administrators is to provide in-service that is both relevant and effective. The goal of the in-service must be to create learning opportunities that are meaningful to teachers, sustainable, and designed to increase teaching and learning.

The most common types of teacher professional development or in-service are periodic workshops and peer-assisted learning.

School administrators generally offer a series of on-site, *periodic workshops* to introduce concepts or strategies that are not aligned to the actual needs of the faculty. Too often, the workshops employ a "sit-and-get" format with a guest speaker using a PowerPoint to present information. This format is not ideal for teachers because they are adult learners. There is usually not enough time for teachers to discuss ideas, nor adequate follow-up to implement and sustain new strategies. To be effective, workshops should be relevant, engaging, active, and ongoing.

Peer-assisted learning is an effective approach to teacher professional development. Essentially, it involves peers learning from and with peers. One teacher serves as a coach to another teacher. For example, a veteran teacher could be used as a mentor to help a new teacher learn how to better engage the culturally diverse students in her classroom. Finding the right mentor is critically important. Ideally, the mentor should be a colleague who is willing to commit to weekly meetings for up to two years. Of course, the effectiveness of this approach hinges on the level of training the mentor has received in multiculturalism.

It is important to understand that peer-assisted learning should be based on expertise, not age. There are situations in which a younger teacher with a specific area of expertise can assist an older teacher with acquiring a skill. For example, a second-year teacher like the aforementioned Miss McGagin can serve as a peer-assistant to help a veteran teacher become more proficient with multiculturalism. The key to successful peer-to-peer learning is to establish a relationship that is built on mutual respect and a willingness for teachers to learn from each other.

There are no "silver bullets" or panaceas in education. Ongoing support is a critical component of any form of in-service. Teachers must be constantly reminded of the importance of having high expectations for their students, inclusive of every race, gender, language, religion, socioeconomic status, and culture. Unfortunately, too many teachers in public education are in denial. They choose to deny the presence of a debilitating culture gap in their classrooms, as well as the devasting effects of their own implicit biases.

Dr. Wandy Taylor witnessed teacher-denial while serving as a principal in Gwinnett County, Georgia, in 2015. Her school, Lilburn Elementary, was highly diverse with the following student demographics: 67 percent Hispanic, 13 percent black, 12 percent Asian, 6 percent white, and 2 percent "other" ethnicity. Eighty-nine percent of those students received a free or reduced price for meals, which is an indication that the vast majority of them came from high poverty households.

Brookwood Elementary, which is located in an affluent community less than five miles from Lilburn Elementary, had a student population that was not as diverse. Roughly 44 percent of the students in that school were white, 25 percent black, 16 percent Asian, 11 percent Hispanic, and 4 percent "other" ethnicity. Only 30 percent of those students received a free of reduced price for meals, which is an indication that the majority of them came from middle-class households.

Dr. Sharon Smith, a master teacher at Brookwood Elementary, contacted Principal Taylor during the spring of 2015 after reading a news article in the *Gwinnett Daily Post* about a proposal she had submitted to the school board on behalf of a 25-person committee that consisted of principals and district-level administrators. In that proposal, all teachers and staff in the school district would have been required to undergo training in cultural competence. Although the school board rejected the proposal, Dr. Smith, who was the district's Teacher of the Year at that time, recognized the urgent need for cultural competence, especially since her school was undergoing a dramatic shift in demographics.

Therefore, she approached Principal Taylor with a proposal to have the teachers in their respective schools participate in joint-training in cultural competence. Dr. Smith, who is Cuban-American, felt that an emerging culture gap was beginning to impede the ability of her colleagues at Brookwood to engage the students of color in their classrooms. Principal Taylor agreed to confer with her fellow principal to discuss the possibility of having a joint-training session.

After conferring, the principals of the two schools (Brookwood and Lilburn) agreed to hire consultants—Anderson & Ward Consulting Services—to provide a joint-training workshop in cultural competence for their respective faculties. While the session was fruitful, Brookwood's principal conceded that most of her teachers were in denial, and they did not see the value in cultural competence. Principal Taylor and the consultant made the same observations.

Ostensibly, the Brookwood faculty felt comfortable knowing that they were able to engage the majority of the students; namely, the ones that looked like them—white middle-class Americans. Perhaps the main reason for their apparent lack of interest in cultural competence stemmed from the actions (or inactions) of their school board. Since the board had rejected Principal Taylor's recommendation the previous month for the districtwide implementation of training in cultural competence, the teachers at Brookwood followed their lead.

Since the school board did not deem it a priority, neither did they. Leadership matters.

This is by no means an indictment against Brookwood Elementary; it is a high-performing school with a solid faculty. One could only imagine how well the students would perform if the teachers were more culturally competent. Their state of denial only served themselves, not the children of color they served. This is a reality that exists in far too many schools across the nation.

SUMMARY

Currently, K-12 public education is faced with a major challenge. While student diversity is increasing, the teacher workforce is decreasing. This has made the recruitment of new teachers a national crisis. Alternative teacher certification programs offer a quick pathway to recruit individuals with non-education degrees into the teaching profession. Once those teachers are recruited, it is absolutely essential to provide the training they will need to engage the racially and culturally diverse students in their classrooms.

In light of increased student diversity, teacher preparation has become crucial. Pre-service and in-service training programs are typically used to prepare teachers for challenges related to cultural diversity in their classrooms. Pre-service refers to the training or coursework prospective teachers receive in college *before* they enter the workforce as classroom teachers. The effectiveness of pre-service is inconclusive. Based on a national survey, roughly 40 percent of white teachers reported that their college program did not adequately prepare them to teach black, Hispanic, or children from low-income households.

In-service is the ongoing training or professional development teachers receive *after* they enter the workforce as classroom teachers. The results of this approach to teacher preparation are encouraging. School districts in Florida, North Carolina, California, and Arizona have used sound evidence-based best practices to develop plans to make their teachers more culturally competent.

While it is important to use sound principles to design an effective in-service plan, it is equally as important to use sound practices to deliver the plan. Several methods for delivering in-service activities include but are not limited to the use of technology, peer-assisted learning, collegial learning, integrated learning, and presentations from experts.

So, as presented in the essential question: *What is the most effective approach toward preparing teachers to teach in culturally diverse classrooms?* All teacher preparation programs or initiatives should begin by adopting the premise that good teachers are made, not born. Ideally, teachers should receive their foundation for teaching culturally diverse students through their college coursework in undergraduate school. Afterward, teachers should receive ongoing professional development in culturally responsive teaching strategies at their work sites to keep their skills honed and current. Through effective and ongoing training, teachers' behaviors can change.

"What you know matters.
What you do with what you know matters more."
—Dr. Wandy W. Taylor
Educator

★ ★ ★

CHAPTER 4

MULTICULTURAL EDUCATION

———————————★———————————

ESSENTIAL QUESTION
*How are Culturally Responsive Teaching, Cultural
Competence and Multiculturalism connected, and
which one is most desirable in education?*

———————————★———————————

As discussed in the preceding chapter, better teacher preparation (i.e., pre-service and in-service) can play a major role in bridging the culture gap between teachers and their students. This gap, along with the implicit racial biases held by many teachers, inhibits the achievement of many children of color. It would seem plausible to only hold teachers accountable for student outcomes if they are adequately prepared to teach them. As educators, it is our responsibility to prepare teachers to be *culturally responsive* to their students' learning styles and needs, regardless of their race, gender, language, or family's socioeconomic circumstance. We cannot gamble with any child's ability to reap the full benefits of a free K-12 public education in America.

So, how can school systems better prepare their teachers to meet the challenges related to the ever-growing cultural and ethnic diversity in their student populations? Leading scholars in the field of *multicultural education* such as Gloria Ladson-Billings and James Banks have postulated that the underachievement of black, Hispanic, and Asian Pacific students is due to the lack of *culturally competent* teachers in K-12 classrooms across America. It has been argued that a key component to learning is an understanding of culture. Many education-scholars believe that in order to meet the educational needs of linguistically and ethnically diverse groups of children, teachers must use *culturally responsive teaching strategies* to better understand the social, cultural, and emotional experiences of their students.

Before presenting a model that can be used to address the pink elephant in many classrooms (i.e., racially biased and cultural incompetent teachers), let's discuss the italicized terms in the preceding paragraph. Although the terms appear to be ingredients in a word-salad; in reality, they are the key ingredients in a model that can be used to bridge the culture gap between teachers and their students. The next three sections will present a more in-depth overview of multicultural education, cultural competence, and culturally responsive teaching strategies and how they are interconnected in a practical model.

MULTICULTURAL EDUCATION

Multicultural education evolved out of the civil rights movement in the United States. Although it began with the African American community, the movement soon expanded to include other cultural groups who were subject to discrimination. Essentially, multicultural education is a pedagogy or method of teaching a curriculum to children.

As a pedagogy, multicultural education is predicated on the principle of educational equity for all students. It strives to remove barriers to the educational opportunities and success for students from different cultural backgrounds. In theory, educators may modify or eliminate educational policies, programs, materials, lessons, and instructional practices that are either discriminatory toward or insufficiently inclusive of diverse cultural perspectives. In other words, if it is a school system's desire, they can make it a priority to remove barriers to effective teaching and learning.

Multicultural education also assumes that the ways in which students learn and think are deeply influenced by their cultural identity and heritage. This type of pedagogy also requires teachers to use educational approaches that value and recognize the cultural backgrounds of their students. In this way, multicultural education aims to improve the learning and success of all students. This is especially true for students from cultural groups that have been historically underrepresented or that suffer from lower educational achievement. The goals of multicultural education are to:

- Create a safe, accepting and successful learning environment.
- Increase awareness of global issues.
- Strengthen cultural consciousness.
- Strengthen intercultural awareness.
- Teach students that there are multiple historical perspectives.
- Encourage critical thinking.
- Prevent prejudice and discrimination.

CULTURAL COMPETENCE

The formula for any winning-team is to have a roster filled with polished, enthusiastic players. Sports writers and pundits generally consider the 1995-96 Chicago Bulls basketball team as one of the most dominant in sports history. That team, which was led by hall-of-famers Michael Jordan and Scottie Pippen, compiled a record of 72 wins and only 10 losses. Coach Phil Jackson routinely developed brilliant game plans that were executed with precision by a host of competent players on the team. Because of these savvy and competent players, the Bulls were able to successfully adjust to the diverse strategies and game plans the various teams in the National Basketball Association (NBA) devised to defeat them.

Educators can learn valuable lessons from the 1995-96 Chicago Bulls. A key to the Bulls' success was the organization's ability to develop "competent" players that were able to adjust to the barriers the other 28 teams in the NBA created to beat them. The other teams used tactics such as increasing the pace of the game; slowing the pace of the game; and using physical intimidation. Nothing worked. The competent players on the Bulls' team made the necessary adjustments to secure many victories. As a result, and by anyone's metrics—the Chicago Bulls were a competent, high-performing championship team.

Likewise, educators can secure many victories against barriers or challenges that occur in classrooms. As classrooms in America have become increasingly more ethnically and culturally diverse, a one-size-fits-all approach to instruction has become obsolete and ineffective. In order to secure victories against challenges related to barriers created by the ever-increasing diversity in K-12 schools and to become high-performing organizations, educators must develop culturally competent teachers.

Cultural competence is a key factor in enabling educators to be effective with students from cultures other than their own. For teachers, it involves having an awareness of one's own cultural identity and views about differences. It also involves the ability to learn and build on the varying cultural and community norms of students and their families. It is the ability to understand the differences within a specific group that make each student unique. This understanding informs and expands teaching practices in the culturally competent teacher's classroom.

Teachers are not born with cultural competence; those skills are acquired through proper training and professional development. Gaining cultural competence is a lifelong process of increasing self-awareness, developing social skills and behaviors around diversity, and gaining the ability to advocate for others. It goes beyond tolerance, which implies that one is simply willing to overlook differences. Instead, it includes recognizing and respecting diversity through one's words and actions in all contexts. The key aspects for a high degree of cultural competence are:

- *Awareness.* Being aware of your own individual biases and reactions to people whose culture or background are significantly different from your own. By being aware of your own internal biases, you can begin to work toward other aspects of cultural competency.
- *Attitude.* The significance of attitude in cultural competence is to outline the difference between just being aware of cultural differences and actively analyzing your own internal belief systems.

- *Knowledge.* Research into human behavior has shown that our values and beliefs about equality may not always line up with our actual behaviors. We often are ignorant as to the degree of difference between our beliefs and our actions. It has been shown that people who may test well in regards to having low prejudices may in fact act with great prejudice when actually interacting with other cultures. Understanding this disconnect is why knowledge is considered a key aspect of developing one's own cultural competence.

- *Skills.* This component is about actually taking practices of cultural competency and repeating them until they become integrated into one's daily behaviors. The most important aspect of the skills component is having an excellent grasp of effective and respectful communication with students and parents whose culture are different from yours. An often-overlooked aspect of communication is body language. Effective communication occurs when spoken words and body language are in sync.

This is good news for educators because teachers can be taught the aspects of cultural competence. Through a process of comprehensive training, schools can become high-performing teams like the Chicago Bulls.

CULTURALLY RESPONSIVE TEACHING

For clarity, we will begin this section by highlighting the distinction between cultural competence and culturally responsive teaching, which are two interrelated concepts in education. As previously stated, cultural competence refers to a skill; that is, a teacher's ability to teach students from cultures other than their own. On the other hand, culturally responsive teaching (CRT) refers to the process or training whereby teachers acquire and implement those skills. In other words, CRT is the *process* and cultural competence is the *product*.

Most proponents of culturally responsive teaching will point to Gloria Ladson-Billings (1994) as the pioneer in this field of study. In her landmark book—*The Dreamkeepers: Successful Teachers of African American Children*—she coined the term "culturally responsive pedagogy." Ladson-Billings provided a classic definition of culturally responsive teaching as "a pedagogy that empowers students intellectually, socially, emotionally, and politically by using cultural and historical referents to convey knowledge, to impart skills, and to change attitudes."

More recently, in his article on The Edvocate—a website devoted to advocating for education equity, reform and innovation—Matthew Lynch provides a very comprehensive and descriptive definition of the concept as follows:

> "Culturally responsive pedagogy is a student-centered approach to teaching in which the students' unique cultural strengths are identified and nurtured to promote student achievement and a sense of well-being about the student's cultural place in the world. Culturally responsive pedagogy is divided into three functional dimensions: the institutional dimension, the personal dimension, and the instructional dimension.

The *institutional* dimension of culturally responsive pedagogy emphasizes the need for reform of the cultural factors affecting the organization of schools, school policies and procedures (including allocation of funds and resources), and community involvement. The *personal* dimension refers to the process by which teachers learn to become culturally responsive. The *instructional* dimension refers to practices and challenges associated with implementing cultural responsiveness in the classroom."

So, what does CRT look like in the classroom? What are the key components of the concept? Leading scholar-educators have identified several principles that are key to effective *culturally responsive teaching*. They seem to agree that seven principles must be in place in order to meet the educational needs of students in culturally and ethnically diverse classrooms. These principles include (1) knowledge of learners' cultures, (2) student-controlled discourse, (3) positive parent partnerships, (4) high expectations, (5) culturally mediated instruction, (6) teacher as a facilitator, and (7) reshaping the curriculum.

1. Knowledge of learners' cultures. Effective teachers use knowledge of their students' culture as another means of accommodating the cultural diversity in their classroom. This requires that teachers are able to interpret their students' behavior within the cultural context of the homes from which they come. One key to developing cultural sensitivity is to become familiar with the nuances and customs of a particular culture.

    For example, Asian cultures typically value a collectivist

orientation that emphasizes family needs over individual ones. Thus, the Asian student who may appear to be shy to the uninformed teacher, in reality, may be setting a cultural mindset by not wanting to call attention to himself or otherwise diminish the abilities of classmates. This specific knowledge could be used by teachers to help them adjust their instructional strategies to facilitate engagement of their students.

2. Student-controlled discourse. In this type of instruction, students are given the opportunity to control some portion of the lesson. This allows the teacher to see how speech and negotiation are used in students' homes and communities. Children who experience a lack of continuity in the use of language at home are often misunderstood in classrooms.

   For example, in some homes, the rules may encourage multiple speakers to talk at the same time. This, however, may create conflict in schools that encourage one person to speak at a time. Thus, students' prior experiences cannot form the basis of new learning if their ways of communicating and making sense of new material are not considered acceptable in school. Once teachers understand home and community norms, they can help students expand their discourse repertoire.

3. Positive parent partnerships. This principle of culturally responsive teaching involves school teachers having the ability and willingness to participate in an ongoing dialogue with students, families, and community stakeholders on issues that are important to them. When this occurs, the classroom becomes a place where students from different cultures can feel comfortable, see themselves represented in the curriculum

and classroom environment, and engaged with materials that provide connections to their home and community experiences.

4. Communication of high expectations. Teachers' expectations have a powerful effect on students' performance, especially when the student's ethnicity is different from the teacher's ethnicity. Findings from a research review conducted by the Education Commission of the States indicated that negative teacher expectations account for approximately five to 10 percent of the variance in student achievement. The commission concluded that negative expectations from teachers contribute to the ongoing achievement gap between culturally diverse and white students.

    Effective teachers hold high, realistic expectations for themselves and all students. They believe in their ability to create a caring classroom climate and in their students' ability to succeed. If teachers act as though they expect their students to be on-task, interested, and successful in class, they are more likely to be so. Researchers have found that students who feel they have supportive, caring teachers are more motivated to be engaged in academic work than with unsupportive, uncaring teachers.

5. Culturally mediated instruction. This type of instruction is characterized by providing students with culturally rich learning environments and culturally valued knowledge. In this type of classroom environment, students gain an understanding that there is more than one way to interpret a statement, event, or action. By being allowed to share their different points-of-view and perspectives in a given situation

based on their own socio-cultural experiences, students become active, hands-on participants in their learning. Educators believe that culturally mediated instruction provides the best transmission of learning to all students because it may help decrease unacceptable behaviors from students who are frustrated with classroom instruction that does not meet their needs.

6. Teacher as a facilitator. The role of teachers in the twenty-first century has evolved. They are no longer the source of all knowledge in the classroom. Within the confines of an active learning environment, the teacher's role is to inspire all students to take ownership in their own learning. Their role is to provide opportunities for students to learn key concepts and discover the tools that they will need to become life-long learners. Ultimately, teachers are the facilitators for learning. They engage, lead, inspire, and encourage the students in their classrooms.

7. Reshaping the curriculum. A culturally responsive curriculum is authentic, child-centered, and connected to the child's real life. It employs materials from the child's culture and history to illustrate principles and concepts. Researchers in this area strongly advocate for the use of resources other than textbooks in order to make lesson plans in the curriculum more culturally relevant and engaging.

A MODEL FOR MULTICULTURAL EDUCATION

A common myth or misconception about multicultural education is that teachers must teach the "white way" or the "black way." People often get intimidated by concepts such as culturally responsive or culturally competent because of the vast number of cultures in today's classrooms. Too often, teachers embrace the misguided notion that students of different races need to be taught differently, and they waste a lot of effort in the process. Another result is that teachers usually appear fake when they go overboard or try too hard to impress (instead of teach!) students that don't look like them.

Shaminy Manoranjithan, a biracial member of Generation Z who teaches in an urban high school, provides a great perspective of what she describes as "being authentic with your students." She recounted how one of her fellow teachers tried to connect with his black students by playing random rap music. He also attempted to "imitate the way the students spoke" during his conversations with them.

Despite the teacher's best efforts, Shaminy reported that he did not earn the students' respect. They perceived him as being disingenuous and fake. It was also reported that many of the students did not perform well in his classes. The teacher's lack of authenticity, ostensibly, prevented him from making meaningful connections with his students. Ultimately, both the teacher and the students suffered because of the disengagement.

While the actions of many teachers are well-intentioned, their lack of cultural competence can impair their ability to effectively connect with students that don't look like them. The key point from Shaminy's report is that we don't need a different teaching method or curriculum for students based on race or culture. Teachers simply need to have high expectations for all students and engage them in meaningful dialogue and instruction. The principles of culturally responsive teaching strategies can be used to create those outcomes.

In the absence of cultural competence, which is acquired through training in culturally responsive teaching, teachers are more apt to use a trial-and-error approach to connect with diverse groups of children. This is often a recipe for failure, both for the teacher and the entire school community.

The community of Bell Manor Elementary School learned this lesson the hard way. The school, which is located in the Dallas-Fort Worth area of Texas, has an enrollment of nearly 800 students—36 percent are white, 27 percent Hispanic, and 24 percent are black. The *Raw Story* newspaper featured an article about an incident involving a racial slur at the school.

As reported in the article, a white female teacher divided her sixth-grade class into small groups to engage them in a team-building exercise. Each group was assigned a nickname. One group was given the name "Dream Team" and another was dubbed the "Jighaboos." The names for the various groups were prominently displayed in the teacher's classroom for any and everyone to see.

Yes, you guessed it! After one student's father discovered this, he became furious. The parent contacted the local television and openly questioned how a teacher could be so oblivious to the fact that the word "Jighaboo" is commonly used as a racial slur for a black person? School officials investigated the father's complaint, confronted the teacher, and removed the posters. The school released a statement alleging the teacher was visibly shaken and remorseful because she was not aware that Jighaboo (correct spelling is Jigaboo) was a racial slur. While she attributed her misdeed to ignorance; in reality, it was due to her cultural incompetence and deep-rooted implicit racial bias.

Studies conducted over the course of the past 25–30 years have provided evidence that, with proper training or professional development, teachers can become culturally competent and use culturally responsive teaching strategies to improve outcomes for diverse student populations. The Taylor Model in Diagram 1 depicts the flow of the key components of multicultural education.

Diagram 1
Taylor Model for Multicultural Education

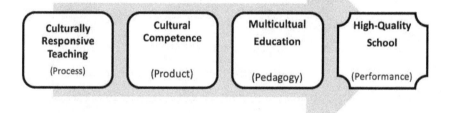

The Taylor Model begins with the *process* of training teachers in the seven key principles of culturally responsive teaching. After completing their training, a polished *product* emerges—culturally competent teachers. These teachers are then equipped to use multicultural *pedagogy* to engage the diverse groups of students in their classrooms. Finally, when educators make the commitment to implement multicultural education schoolwide, they achieve high-quality *performance* from both teachers and students.

SUMMARY

Because culture strongly influences the attitudes, values, and behaviors that students and teachers bring to the instructional process—it is incumbent upon educational systems to prepare teachers to teach students with diverse learning styles. With proper training or professional development, teachers can be taught the skills they will need to bridge the culture gap between them and their students. Multicultural education can provide the structure for effective teaching and learning in K-12 public education.

Multicultural education is not a task to be done or even an end goal to be accomplished. Instead, it is an approach to education that aims to include all students, promote learning of other cultures, and teach healthy social skills in a multicultural setting. The Taylor Model provides a framework for developing teachers to meet the challenges of multicultural classrooms. The *process* begins with providing the faculty with ongoing training in the principles of culturally responsive teaching. The essence of the training is that educators (i.e., teachers, administrators, and support staff) must be willing to embrace children of color, reshape curricula, adjust instructional strategies, and have high expectations for all children under their care, inclusive of every race, gender, religion, and socio-cultural background.

The primary goal of comprehensive training in culturally responsive teaching strategies is to create polished *products*, which are culturally competent teachers. These teachers are aware of their implicit biases and stereotypes, and they have the ability to understand, communicate with, and effectively teach students across various cultures.

The third step in the model is to implement a school-wide approach to *pedagogy* (i.e., instruction) known as multicultural education. This will elevate the *performance* of the schools, and both students and teachers will begin to perform at higher levels. It is not enough to simply be tolerant of the diversity in our school communities; we must embrace it. We must truly love each student who enters our schools.

The Taylor Model provides a perspective for answering the essential question posed at the beginning of this chapter. The three concepts—*culturally responsive teaching, cultural competence* and *multiculturalism*—are interconnected and equally desirable. They work in tandem to improve outcomes for both students and teachers.

"Great teachers have high expectations for their students.
But higher expectations for themselves."
— Todd Whitaker

★ ★ ★

CHAPTER 5

EARLY CHILDHOOD EDUCATION

───────────────────★───────────────────

ESSENTIAL QUESTION
Should universal preschool be provided to
all three and four-year-olds?

───────────────────★───────────────────

While public schools in America are more diverse today than ever, the teachers are still mostly white. This dynamic, coupled with the spread of implicit racial bias, has created a culture gap between teachers and their students. This gap has impaired many teachers' ability to engage students of color in their classrooms, which is essential for meaningful teaching and learning. As discussed in the previous chapter, multicultural education is a viable approach toward bridging the gap between teachers and the culturally diverse groups of students in their classrooms.

Once a decision is made to implement any systemwide innovation, central questions must be addressed: Where is the starting point?

Where do you begin? With multicultural education, a case can be made to begin implementation with a focus on early childhood education. In this chapter, we will try to make the case for universal pre-kindergarten (Pre-K) with an infusion of multicultural pedagogy for all 4-year-olds.

HISTORICAL PERSPECTIVE

October 4, 1957, marked a pivotal moment for public education in America. On that date, the Soviet Union (USSR) launched Sputnik, the world's first artificial satellite. This launching caught the U.S. government under President Dwight D. Eisenhower off guard, shook the country's confidence, and marked the beginning of the race for space. Americans began to question whether the country's educational system was adequate, especially for training scientists and engineers.

The space race caused a revolution in American education. The federal government encouraged school systems to include more math and science courses in their curriculum. Elementary schools began to provide second language instruction and baby-boomer families started buying educational toys such as chemistry sets. Moreover, school systems started to place more emphasis on using standardized testing programs to help identify gifted students to help America reclaim its superiority over the USSR in technology.

While America's reaction to the launching of Sputnik was somewhat praiseworthy, its response plan did not encompass all children in the education system. Since most schools were segregated in the 1950s and 1960s, especially across the 17 Jim Crow states known as the Black Belt, many black children did not have access to the nation's initial STEM (science, technology, engineering and mathematics) curriculum. Moreover, at that time, only a handful of states funded kindergarten and universal Pre-K was nonexistent. America missed a golden opportunity to implement a high-quality PK-12 (pre-kindergarten through 12th grade) STEM curriculum to develop young minds across the four corners of our nation.

Some interest in preschool education emerged during President Lyndon B. Johnson's (LBJ) administration. In 1965, Project Head Start was introduced by the federal government to address the social, emotional, health, nutritional, and psychological needs of preschool children from low-income families. The original intent of the program was to serve as a "catch up" summer school or enrichment program that would teach low-income children in eight weeks what they would need to know to start elementary school.

The program was well-received by educators, child development specialists, community leaders, and parents across the country. However, since Head Start was federally-funded, the program typically operated independently from local school districts. Thus, the programs were most often administered through local social services agencies. Classes were generally small and individual programs developed their own curricula.

The cold car with the USSR was in full force during Ronald Regan's first term as President of the United States. On April 26, 1983, he appeared on national television and presented a comprehensive report titled *A Nation at Risk*. He proclaimed that the cold war against the USSR was still in progress, and America was losing because of its floundering system of public education. The report—which was written by the blue-ribbon members of the National Commission on Excellence in Education at the request of Secretary of Education

Terrel Bell—stated: "If an unfriendly foreign power had attempted to impose on America the mediocre educational performance that exists today, we might well have viewed it as an act of war. As it stands, we have allowed this to happen to ourselves."

The commission painted a bleak picture of public education in America. According to the report, which took 18 months to compile, test scores were rapidly declining; low teaching salaries and poor teacher training programs were leading to a high turnover rate among educators; and other industrialized countries were on the verge of surpassing America in technology. The report provided mounds of statistical evidence to support the bleak picture it had painted. For example, it indicated that 23 million American adults were functionally illiterate; the average achievement for high school students on standardized tests was lower than before the launching of Sputnik in 1957; and only 20 percent of 17-year-old students had the ability to write a persuasive essay.

A Nation at Risk captured huge media attention and triggered a call for another series of reform. The report recommended that schools become more rigorous, adopt new standards, evaluate teacher preparation programs, and review the salary scale for teachers. The report appeared to be influenced by partisan politics, such as the emergence of campaign posters with slogans to re-elect Reagan to win the cold war against communism. Furthermore, the recommendations lacked specificity. What does it mean for schools to become more rigorous? With only limited guidance from the federal government, it became the responsibility of each individual state to infuse "rigor" into their schools.

Despite making people aware of defects in America's system of public education, the response by many states to the *A Nation at Risk* report in the 1980s was lukewarm and lacking a sense of urgency. For the most part, the status quo remained; it was business as usual. States continued to focus on K-12 programs and very little attention was given toward funding Head Start or universal early childhood education programs. Although public schools were beginning to become more ethnically and culturally diverse at that time, many states ignored the trend. They apparently did not deem it necessary to reshape their "rigorous" curricula to meet the instructional needs of their growing diverse student populations.

In 2002, President George W. Bush signed the No Child Left Behind Act (NCLB) into law to hold states more accountable for their schools' performance. Under the NCLB, states were required to use more standardized testing as a way to measure the success of their students in grades 3–8 annually. Schools that did not meet test targets ran the risk of losing funding or even being shut down. Consequently, many school administrators began to prioritize test scores over almost everything else. They adopted the mindset that the best way to boost test scores was to have teachers use more direct, rote instruction to drill students on topics covered in the standardized tests. In other words, teachers spent more time on "test prep" instead of rigorous, curiosity-driven lessons.

The NCLB was a definite step in the right direction toward holding schools accountable for the reading and math scores for all student subgroups in grades three through eight. Schools that did not make adequate yearly progress with black, Hispanic, or poor students faced the threat of losing funding or being shut down. While outcomes for students of color were viewed with greater importance under NCLB, outcomes for our youngest, most vulnerable children appeared to be of little (if any) significance. Once again, America had the opportunity to shine a light of support onto early childhood education programs and failed to do so.

On December 10, 2015, President Barack Obama signed Every Student Succeeds Act (ESSA) into law, which was good news for public education in America. A few highlights of ESSA are listed below. That law:

- Requires—for the first time—that all students in America be taught to high academic standards that will prepare them to succeed in college and careers.
- Ensures that vital information is provided to educators, families, students, and communities through annual statewide assessments that measure students' progress toward high standards.
- Advances equity by upholding critical protections for America's disadvantaged and high-need students.
- Maintains an expectation that there will be accountability and action to effect positive change in our lowest performing schools.
- Sustains and expands the administration's investments in increasing access to high-quality preschool!

The really good news in ESSA is the authorization of the Preschool Development Grant Birth through Five (PDGB-5) program, which provides states with significant funding to develop and coordinate comprehensive early childhood education initiatives. The purpose of these initiatives was to ensure that all children and their families can have equitable access to high-quality programs. Twenty-three states were awarded three-year PDGB-5 grants for 2020. The funding ranged from $3,721,584 (Georgia) to $13,414,500 (California).

As a nation, America is taking incremental steps toward having a system of universal early childhood education. Under President Eisenhower, we fought a "race for space" war with the Soviet Union that resulted in school systems adopting more technology-infused curricula. That focus, however, was directed primarily toward improving outcomes for high school students. Virtually no attention was directed at preschoolers.

During LBJ's presidency, some attention was given to early childhood education, albeit on a limited scale. Programs such as Head Start attempted to achieve equity in education by giving preschoolers from low-income families a chance to start kindergarten at the same level as their middle and upper-class peers. Although some federally-funded Head Start programs were opened in urban cities across America, they operated independent of local school systems. States at that time expressed little interest in or willingness to fund a preschool program.

Under President George W. Bush and the NCLB, schools were held accountable for outcomes for students in all subgroups (e.g., black, Hispanic, Asian, special education, poverty). While black and brown students received more equal learning opportunities in schools during that era, the instruction they received was questionable. Teachers frequently spent an inordinate amount of instructional time teaching children of color how to take a standardized test. This created a limited range of knowledge for an entire generation of students. And, as previously stated, educational opportunities for preschoolers in public education were limited.

Finally, under President Obama, major steps were taken toward states having universal programs for early childhood education. Many states have expressed a desire to have these programs, but they often cite the lack of funding as a deterrent. This dynamic has led states to implement the programs contingent upon receiving funding from the federal government. If states were more aware of the effectiveness of early childhood education programs, they would realize that the benefits far outweigh the costs. The next sections of this chapter will delve deeper and provide information to help states conduct their cost-benefit analyses of early childhood education programs.

CURRENT STATE OF ACHIEVEMENT IN AMERICA

The United States entered the twenty-first century as the world's premier superpower after the collapse of the Soviet Union on December 25, 1991. Ever since then, the U.S. has garnered tremendous accolades on the world's stage. Our country is recognized as having the world's largest economy, the most powerful military, and second to China as having the world's largest higher education system. Despite these global accomplishments, the country faces many challenges at the national level, especially in the area of public education.

For decades, America promised a quality public education for all children, regardless of their ethnicity, race, zip code, or income. However, critics of public education argue that many children do not have equal opportunities to learn and are not likely to attend a quality school. In fact, some critics suggest that the education system has discriminated against poor or disadvantaged schools by providing more support to their rich counterparts. This has created a stark contrast in the learning environments and physical surroundings between the two categories of schools. Furthermore, children of color seem more likely to attend lower-quality schools where teachers have low expectations regarding their academic potential. These factors have produced an achievement gap that still persists in public education today.

National Achievement Gap

As mandated by the Civil Rights Act of 1964, the U.S. Office of Education was given two years to produce a report that was expected to describe the nature of inequities in public education across America. In 1966, Sociologist James S. Coleman released a controversial report titled *Equality of Educational Opportunity* (otherwise known as the "Coleman Report") that introduced the phrase "gap in achievement" to describe the variance in achievement between white and minority students. Shortly thereafter, researchers began to conduct studies to explore and explain the nature of the "achievement gap" in public schools.

Researchers seem to agree that the achievement gap in public education involves a disparity in academic performance between groups of students. The comparison of grades, standardized test scores, course selection, dropout rates, and college-completion rates are the primary measures of success that have been used as evidence of this gap. While the phrase seems to apply to all student subgroups, it really does not. Typically, discussions of the achievement gap are reserved mostly for Hispanic students, black students, and students from low-income backgrounds. Frankly, it is a phrase that attempts to describe why those students are not performing as well academically as white students.

The National Center for Education Statistics (NCES) is the primary office in the federal government that collects, analyzes, and publishes statistical data related to education in the United States. This process is mandated by congress, and the NCES administers an instrument called the National Assessment of Educational Progress

(NAEP) to 4th and 8th grade students across America. The students are assessed biennially in Reading and Math, and the scores from the NAEP are published in a report referred to as "The Nation's Report Card." Data from this biennial report are most frequently used to gauge the achievement gap in public education.

In its comprehensive 2020 report, the NCES indicated that from 1992 through 2019 the average Reading scores for white 4th graders were consistently higher than those for their black and Hispanic peers. However, some achievement gaps had narrowed over time. For example, the white-black gap at grade four narrowed from 32 points in 1992 to 26 points in 2019. Table 4 presents the average Reading scores on the NAEP for 4th graders by ethnicity.

Table 4
2019 NAEP Reading Data for Grade 4

Ethnic Group	2019 Score	2017	2009	1998	1992
White	230	232	230	225	224
Black	204	206	205	193	192
Hispanic	209	209	205	193	197
Asian/Pacific Islander	237	239	235	215	216
Asian	239	231	NA	NA	NA
Native Hawaiian	212	212	NA	NA	NA
Am. Indian/Alaska Na.	204	202	204	NA	NA
Two or More Races	226	227	NA	NA	NA

SOURCE: U.S. Department of Education, National Center for Education Statistics, National Assessment of Educational Progress (NAEP). Maximum score = 500.

At grade eight in 2019, white students scored 28 points higher in Reading than black students, and 20 points higher than Hispanic students. Asian students scored 12 points higher than white students. The white-Hispanic achievement gap narrowed from 26 points in 1992 to 20 points in 2019, while the white-black gap in 2019 (28 points) was slightly lower than the corresponding gap in 1992 (see Table 5).

Table 5
2019 NAEP Reading Data for Grade 8

Ethnic Group	2019				
	Score	2017	2009	1998	1992
White	272	275	273	*271*	*267*
Black	244	249	246	*243*	*237*
Hispanic	252	255	249	*245*	*241*
Asian/Pacific Islander	281	282	274	*267*	*268*
Asian	284	284	NA	*NA*	*NA*
Native Hawaiian	252	255	NA	*NA*	*NA*
Am. Indian/Alaska Na.	248	253	251	*NA*	*NA*
Two or More Races	267	272	NA	*NA*	*NA*

SOURCE: U.S. Department of Education, National Center for Education Statistics, National Assessment of Educational Progress (NAEP). Maximum score = 500.

In 2019, the average Math scores for white 4th and 8th graders were higher than those of their black and Hispanic peers (see Tables 6 & 7). Some achievement gaps have narrowed over time. The white-black achievement gap in Math at grade four narrowed from 32 points in 1990 to 25 points in 2019. The gap between white and Hispanic students in 1990 and 2019 remained virtually the same.

We certainly do not intend to overwhelm you with statitical data, especially for those of us who have a more qualitative than quantitative perspective. What we do want to make clear is that the numbers in

The Nation's Report Card gives evidence that there is a persistent gap between ethnic groups in both Reading and Math. Black and Hispanic students continue to lag behind their white couterparts, on average, by roughly 23.75 points in Reading and 24.25 points in Math. Asian students continued to score highest in all the academic areas that were assessed.

Table 6
2019 NAEP Math Data for Grade 4

Ethnic Group	2019 Score	2017	2009	*1996*	*1990*
White	249	248	248	*232*	*220*
Black	224	223	222	*198*	*188*
Hispanic	231	229	237	*207*	*200*
Asian/Pacific Islander	260	258	255	*NA*	*NA*
Asian	263	260	NA	*NA*	*NA*
Native Hawaiian	226	229	NA	*NA*	*NA*
Am. Indian/Alaska Na.	227	227	225	*217*	*NA*
Two or More Races	244	245	NA	*NA*	*NA*

SOURCE: U.S. Department of Education, National Center for Education Statistics, National Assessment of Educational Progress (NAEP). Maximum score = 500.

Table 7
2019 NAEP Math Data for Grade 8

Ethnic Group	2019 Score	2017	2009	*1996*	*1990*
White	292	293	293	*281*	*270*
Black	260	260	261	*240*	*237*
Hispanic	268	269	266	*251*	*246*
Asian/Pacific Islander	310	310	301	*NA*	*NA*

Asian	313	312	NA	*NA*	*NA*
Native Hawaiian	266	274	NA	*NA*	*NA*
Am. Indian/Alaska Na.	262	267	266	*NA*	*NA*
Two or More Races	286	287	NA	*NA*	*NA*

SOURCE: U.S. Department of Education, National Center for Education Statistics, National Assessment of Educational Progress (NAEP). Maximum score = 500.

In addition to disparities between racial and ethnic groups, gaps continue to exist between students who are eligible and ineligible for the National School Lunch Program (NSLP). This federally-assisted program provides low-cost or free meals for students in school each day and is used as a key indicator of poverty. Nationally, students who were NSLP-eligible (poverty) achieved an average score of 208 on the 2017 fourth-grade Reading and 207 on the 2019 assessment. Students who were NSLP-ineligible (affluent) scored 236 and 235, respectively, on the same Reading assessment. Thus, the current gap between poverty and affluent students in 4th grade Reading = 28 points.

The results for the eighth-grade Math assessment are equally as troubling. Nationally, students who were NSLP-eligible (poverty) scored an average of 267 in 2017 and 266 in 2019 on the eighth-grade Math assessment. Students who were NSLP-ineligible (affluent) posted average scores of 297 in 2017 and 296 in 2019. Thus, the current gap between poverty and affluent students in 8th grade Math = 30 points.

The National Center for Education Statistics tested nearly 294,000 fourth and eighth-grade students across the nation in 2019 to compile data for the national report card. It would be difficult to look at the results and not conclude that the last decade has been a disappointment for student achievement in schools across America.

The current achievement gap between white and black students continues to hover around 27 points and 20 points between white and Hispanic students. The gap between children from poor and affluent families is just as troubling.

Clearly, achievement gaps related to a student's ethnicity and family's socioeconomic status continue to fester within the walls of public schools in America. Everyone claims to care about education. If the NAEP's report is a true indication of the current status of public education in America, then we don't seem to care as much as we should—because we haven't made any gains in ten years!

International Achievement Gap

Another achievement gap that has received considerable attention in recent years is the lagging performance of American students on international tests in comparison to students from other developed countries. The Program for International Student Assessment (PISA) is the tool used to measure students' academic skills in about 80 industrialized countries. The PISA is coordinated by the Organization for Economic Cooperation and Development (OECD), an intergovernmental organization of industrialized countries. Testing is conducted in the United States by NCES. The test is administered every three years to 15-year-old students to measure their performance in reading, math, science, and problem solving. The first international assessment was conducted in 2000 and the most recent in 2018.

The United States, for the most part, was disappointed with the results of the 2015 international assessment. As in previous years, the country fell below the OECD average in Math. The U.S. ranked 38th out of 71 countries in Math and 24th in Science. This caught the attention of educators across the country and caused many people to question the quality of public education in America. The hopes and expectations were that our 15-year-olds would perform much better on the PISA in 2018.

After three years of angst and anticipation, the 2018 rankings on the PISA were released in December 2019. The narrative was essentially the same as in previous years. The U.S. now ranks 37th out of 79 countries that participated in the assessment. Table 8 provides a summary our students' performance.

Table 8
U.S. Performance on 2018 PISA

Domain	OECD Average	US Score	U.S. Rank
Reading Literacy	487	505	13th
Math Literacy	489	478	37th
Science Literacy	489	502	18th

SOURCE: U.S. Department of Education, National Center for Education Statistics, Program for International Student Assessment (PISA). Maximum score = 1,000.

The PISA figures are not all-inclusive; they only provide a snapshot of how America's 15-year-olds are performing on the international academic stage. Undeniably, 15-year-olds in East Asia and Europe are performing well. Perhaps there are some things the U.S. could glean and implement from their educational systems. However, before we draw any hard conclusions—it would seem prudent to review other cross-national data that are not restricted to 15-year-olds.

The Trends in International Mathematics and Science Study (TIMSS) provides an opportunity to collect international data from a population of students not limited to 15-year-olds. This tool has been used to collect science and math data from students in grades four and eight across the globe every four years since 1995. In addition, TIMSS Advanced (TIMSS-A) is used to measure the achievement of 12th grade students in advanced math and physics. Both assessments (TIMSS & TIMMS-A) are sponsored by the International Association for the Evaluation of Educational Achievement (IEA) and, as usual, testing in the United States is coordinated by the NCES.

The most recent TIMSS data collection was in 2015, and students from the United States fared better than they did on the PISA. On the fourth-grade tests, 13 countries (out of 48) had higher Math scores than the U.S. and only nine out of 47 countries had higher Science scores. On the eighth-grade tests, nine out of 37 countries had higher Math scores than the U.S. and nine out of 37 also had higher Science scores (see Table 9).

Table 9
U.S. Performance on 2015 TIMSS

Domain	OECD Average	US Score	U.S. Rank
MATH (Grade 4)	507	539	14th out of 48
MATH (Grade 8)	487	518	10th out of 37
SCIENCE (Grade 4)	506	546	10th out of 47
SCIENCE (Grade 8)	492	530	10th (tie) out of 37

SOURCE: U.S. Department of Education, National Center for Education Statistics, Trends in International Mathematics and Science Study

The data from the 2015 administration of the TIMSS-A, however, gave further evidence of an achievement gap between students in the U.S. and their counterparts in other countries. The average score for U.S. 12th graders in Advanced Mathematics was 485, which was slightly higher than the average score (476) for the test. The U.S. 12th graders ranked tied-for-third out of the ten countries that participated in this assessment.

Relative to their performance in Advanced Mathematics, the U.S. 12th graders performed terribly on the Physics portion of the TIMSS-A. Their average score in Physics was 437, which is lower than the average score (451) for the test. The U.S. 12th graders ranked sixth out of the nine countries that participated in this assessment.

Nearly 600,000 students across 60 countries participated in the most recent (2015) TIMSS data collection. The 2019 results are scheduled to be released in December 2020. Until and unless improvements are made in America's system of public education, the results of the looming international testing will probably yield the same troubling narrative. We are destined to see a continuation of the "international achievement gap" between U.S. students and their counterparts in most industrialized countries.

MAKING A CASE FOR EARLY CHILDHOOD EDUCATION

While analyzing and disaggregating the PISA data, a recurring theme became apparent—students in Singapore are high-achievers! Singapore is consistently among the top-rated countries for math and science; others being Finland, Canada, Estonia, and Ireland. So, why is Singapore's school system the best globally?

A key foundation of Singapore's education system is its emphasis on early childhood education. Children between the ages of three to six attend rigorous preschools. The curriculum for these preschools consists of one year of nursery learning and two years of kindergarten education. During this period, children learn the basics of language and writing skills.

The success of early childhood education is well-documented, both nationally and internationally. So, why isn't every state in the United States implementing a comprehensive preschool or pre-kindergarten (Pre-K) program to provide early learning for our children? Currently, a few states offer universal Pre-K (available to everyone) and some offer targeted Pre-K (available to families below a certain income). Most do not offer any Pre-K education. In this section, we will present the facts and let you decide the merits of early childhood education.

Brain Development

For decades, coaches across the globe have recognized the importance of developing children at an early age to maximize their potential in the sport of gymnastics. Nadia Comaneci began her formal training as a gymnast in Romania at the age of six. During the 1976 Summer Olympics in Montreal, media outlets across the globe blasted headlines informing the world that Nadia was the "first woman to score a perfect 10" in any Olympics event. The media outlets were wrong. Nadia Comaneci was not a woman—she was only 14 years old.

Today, coaches in sports like tennis, gymnastics, and swimming are keenly aware of the importance of introducing children to concepts and basic skills during their early years of development. Serena Williams started playing tennis at the tender age of three, and most babies have the physical and mental capacity to learn the art of swimming as early as the age of six months. So, the pivotal question to educators and policy makers is: When are children developmentally ready to learn reading, writing, and math?

Medical professionals identify the period from birth to age five as the most important years for children because their brains develop more than at any other time in life. Also, early brain development has a lasting impact on a child's ability to learn and succeed in school and life. The quality of a child's experiences in the first few years of life—positive or negative—helps shape how their brain develops.

At birth, the average baby's brain is about a quarter of the size of the average adult brain. Incredibly, it doubles in size in the first year. It keeps growing to about 80 percent of adult size by age three and 90 percent—nearly full grown—by age five. That statement bears repeating—90 percent of a child's brain development occurs before kindergarten!

The early years are the best opportunity for a child's brain to develop the connections they need to be healthy, capable, successful adults. The connections needed for many important higher-level abilities like motivation, self-regulation, problem solving, and communication are formed in these early years, or not formed. It becomes much harder for these essential brain connections to be formed later in life.

Research shows that some disparities in children's early brain development can be linked to their economic background, particularly in vocabulary skills. This "vocabulary gap" is evident in toddlers. By 18 months, children in different socio-economic groups display dramatic differences in their vocabularies. By two years of age, the disparity in vocabulary development between the two groups is even more dramatic. By three years of age, there is a 30-million word-gap between children from the wealthiest and poorest families.

Led by Dr. Anne Fernald, researchers at Stanford University conducted a study to evaluate the vocabulary gap between toddlers from high and low socioeconomic families. In that study, they tested the language processing of 18 and 24-month-old toddlers using pictures, verbal instructions, and eye responses. Each toddler sat on his or her caregiver's lap as images of two familiar objects were shown on a screen. A recorded voice identified one of the objects by name and used it in a sentence ("Look at the doggy"). The researchers filmed the child's eye movements to track which picture was selected (vocabulary) and how long this took in milliseconds (processing time).

The results of the study indicated that children from higher economic backgrounds looked at the identified object faster and spent more time looking at the correct image. A six-month performance gap existed between the two groups. At 24 months, children in the low economic group performed at the same level as 18-month-old children in the high economic group.

The ramifications of research in the area of early brain development are twofold. First, the capacity of a child's brain to absorb new learning is remarkable. At birth, a child's brain has nearly all the neurons it will ever have. The brain doubles in size in the first year. By age three, it has reached 80 percent of its adult volume and, by age five, the brain has reached 90 percent of adult size.

Second, socioeconomic inequalities in America create significant gaps in the cognitive development of many children. These gaps can be measured as early as the age of 18 months. Poverty and lack of exposure to early learning experiences can negatively impact a child's early brain development and school readiness.

Inequalities in our society can (and do) create barriers to success in education as well as in the workforce. Eliminating inequality will require early interventions that directly address the problem. Education is the great equalizer in America, and it is incumbent upon us to prepare each child for success as early as possible. In the words of Frederick Douglass: "It is easier to build strong children than to repair broken men."

Lasting Effects of Early Intervention

In the field of medicine, researchers routinely conduct experiments to determine the effects of an intervention, usually a drug. For example, after a series of controlled experiments, medical researchers discovered that antihistamines could be used to treat common allergy symptoms such as sneezing, watery eyes, and a runny nose. The effects of the intervention (i.e., taking an over-the-counter antihistamine pill), however, are short-term and users often experience temporary drowsiness.

Similarly, in the field of education, researchers often examine interventions (i.e., new innovations and concepts) to determine their effectiveness on student outcomes. Educators continue to express an interest in the effects of early interventions and whether they have long-term effects. Let's look at a few studies to shed some light on this subject.

The Perry Preschool Project. The landmark Perry Preschool Project was conducted from 1962 to 1967 in Ypsilanti, MI, to determine the effects of a high-quality preschool program. The participants were African American children ages 3–4 who were living in poverty and assessed as being at a high risk for school failure. The program was evaluated in a randomized control trial with a sample of 128 children. Sixty-four of the children were placed in a "program" group that received the preschool intervention and 64 were placed in a "non-program" group that did not receive the intervention.

The children in the preschool (or early childhood intervention) program received 2.5 hours of intervention each weekday morning taught by state-certified teachers. The child-teacher ratio was 6:1. The curriculum emphasized active learning in which the children engaged in activities that involved decision making and problem solving. Teachers also made weekly visits to each child's home for a 90-minute interaction with the parents. The purpose of these visits was to get the parents involved in the educational process and to help implement the preschool curriculum at home.

The results of the Perry Project provide evidence of both short-term and long-term benefits of preschool education. At age five, 67 percent of the children in the program group (i.e., those who received the preschool intervention) achieved an IQ score of 90 or higher. Conversely, only 28 percent of the children in the non-program group received a score in that range. It should be noted that an IQ score is not necessarily a measure of intelligence but rather a measure of academic potential. These results suggest that the early intervention stimulated the academic curiosity of the preschoolers.

Perhaps the most noteworthy findings were related to how the children performed during their four years of high school. At ages 15 and 19, the program group had significantly better attitudes toward school than the non-program groups, and their parents also had better attitudes toward their children's schooling. And, most significantly, 77 percent of the children in the program group graduated from high school as compared to only 60 percent in the non-program group.

A unique aspect of the Perry Project was that it was a longitudinal socio-educational study. Staff collected data annually on both groups from ages three through 11 and again at ages 14, 15, 19, 27, and 40. The missing data rate across all measures was only six percent. This means the researchers were able to locate 94 percent of the participants for follow-up interviews. After each period of data collection, staff analyzed the information and wrote an official report. Key findings related to the participants' economic performance and crime prevention at ages 27 and 40 are presented in Table 10.

Table 10

Perry Project: Key for Ages 27 & 40

Domain	Program Group	Non-Program Group
	Age 27	Age 27
Arrested for property felony by 27	14%	26%
Females employed at 27	80%	55%
Out-of-wedlock births by 27	57%	83%
	Age 40	Age 40
Served time in jail or prison by 40	28%	52%
Median monthly income at 40	$2,712	$1,911
Arrested for violent crimes by 40	32%	48%

SOURCE: Laura and John Arnold Foundation: Social Programs that Work

The Perry Preschool Project was designed to provide experimental evidence of the effects of a preschool program on young children living in poverty. While it began as a study to examine the short-term effects of preschool, it serves as a testament to the long-term effects and return on investment of high-quality preschool education for three and four-year-olds. Program participants surpassed non-participants in achievement throughout schooling; high school graduation rate; adult employment and earnings; and reduced adult crime and incarceration. Also, the program's return on investment was seven times as great as its operating cost.

The latest results from this ongoing, longitudinal study were released on May 14, 2019, and indicated that the children of the Perry participants (who are now 50 to 55 years old) have reaped the same benefits. Sixty-seven percent of the adult children of Perry participants completed high school without a suspension, compared to just 40 percent of the children of non-participants. Also, 59 percent were employed full-time or self-employed, compared to 42 percent of the children of non-participants.

Researchers for the Perry Preschool Project concluded that this high-quality preschool program for three and four-year-old disadvantaged children facilitated their intellectual, social, and academic development in childhood. They further concluded that the benefits of the preschool experience extend into adulthood in areas such as economic performance and reduced commission of crime. Overall, the study yields strong evidence in support of the need for Pre-K programs in our nation's public schools.

The Abecedarian Project. The Abecedarian Project was another program that used longitudinal data to determine the benefits of high-quality early childcare and childhood education. The program was initiated in 1972 at the Frank Porter Graham Child Development Institute on the campus of the University of North Carolina. The sample for the experimental program involved 111 children age 0–5 from very low-income families. Ninety-eight percent of the children were African American.

The children were randomly assigned as infants to either an experimental (or early education) group or a control group. The Abecedarian Project differed from other childhood intervention projects, such as the Perry Project, because it began in early infancy and exposed children to a high-quality child care setting for five years. This means they were in a high-quality program the entire period from birth through school entry (0–5), instead of the shorter durations typical of other projects. Researchers monitored the children's progress over time with follow-up data collected at ages 12, 15, 21, 30, and 35.

Children in the Abecedarian (or experimental) group received full-time, high-quality educational intervention in a childcare setting from infancy through age five. These children received child care for six to eight hours a day, five days a week. Each child also had an individualized prescription of educational "games" incorporated into the day. These early childhood activities focused on social, emotional, and cognitive areas of development but with a heavy emphasis on language. The activities were designed to support age-appropriate development across the children's infant, toddler, and preschool years. The control group was provided with nutritional supplements, social work services, and medical care to ensure that these factors did not affect the outcomes of the experiment.

The results of the Abecedarian Project provided evidence that high-quality early programs can have a positive effect on children that is sustained through adulthood. When compared to students in the control group, students in the Abecedarian group had (1) significantly higher scores on cognitive tests due to enhanced language development and (2) higher achievement in both reading and math. In addition, (3) at the age of 30, they were almost four times as likely as to have graduated from college (23.1 percent for the Abecedarian vs. 6.1 percent for the control group).

The researchers concluded that high-quality educational childcare from early infancy is of utmost importance. The early childhood interventions enhance school readiness, increase the likelihood of success in K-12 education, and the socio-educational benefits extend into adulthood. The results of the Abecedarian Project strengthen the case for having Pre-K programs in our nation's public schools.

The Chicago Project. In the mid-1960s, three major problems plagued Chicago's west side neighborhoods of North Lawndale and West Garfield Park. Those problems included low rates of school attendance, family disengagement with schools, and low student achievement. For example, nearly 92 percent of six-graders in the area schools scored below the national average in reading achievement. In response to this crisis, the Chicago Public School District established Child-Parent Centers (CPC) in four sites in May 1967 to serve the most disadvantaged areas of the city.

The school district used federal Title I money from the Elementary and Secondary Education Act of 1965 to fund their preschool initiative. The objective of the CPCs was to provide early childhood education to disadvantaged children from pre-kindergarten through primary grades to ensure their success in school. The program's model includes six core elements:

- Effective learning experiences.
- The Creative Curriculum˚ for Preschool, which enables children to develop confidence, creativity, and lifelong critical thinking skills.
- Collaborative leadership.
- Ongoing professional development.
- Parent involvement and engagement.
- A support system that provides continuity and stability to participating students.

Each CPC site had physical space dedicated solely to host Pre-K and kindergarten classes and a staffed Parent Resource room. Each site also had a Head Teacher to lead the program and coordinate delivery of the curriculum. CPC students in grades one through three received their instruction in the program's partner school facility, but they maintained smaller class sizes and retained the additional support. The Head Teacher worked with a School Facilitator to ensure continuity in the delivery of the curricula and support services to students through their third-grade year.

All staff that worked with the CPC's students received on-going professional development focused on improving student outcomes. Parents were deeply engaged in the program. They worked with CPC staff to develop an involvement plan and calendar, and they committed to regular conferences to monitor their children's (and their own) progress. Parents also actively participated in Parent Resource programming such as health and nutrition services, medical screenings, school events, and classes in parenting and other life skills.

While the original four CPC sites in Chicago Public Schools in the late 1960s fit the definition of a "high-quality" early childhood education program, the school district did not compile comprehensive statistical data to substantiate whether their programmatic goals were achieved. School officials did, however, keep anecdotal data to provide evidence of improved outcomes for students that participated in the program. This propelled the school district to create additional sites. By 1970, there were 25 sites in Chicago; however, budget cuts over the next 40 years reduced that number to just 10.

In the absence of statistical data, a federally-funded investigation of the CPCs was led by Arthur Reynolds of the University of Minnesota and was called the Chicago Longitudinal Study. The study began in

1985, and the researchers tracked 1,539 CPC participants and a group of non-participants over two decades. They found that participation in just the Pre-K portion of the program had the following benefits for students at age 35:

- 41% reduction in special education services
- 40% reduction in grade retention (when a child must repeat a grade in school)
- 29% increase in high school completion by age 20
- 33% reduction in juvenile arrests
- 51% reduction in court-reported child maltreatment

The researchers concluded that participation in the CPCs early childhood education program had substantial academic, health, and economic benefits. Moreover, an analysis of the costs and benefits of the program indicated that, discounted at 3% annually, it yielded a $7.10 return per dollar invested. In his 2013 State of the Union speech, President Obama stated that "every dollar we invest in high-quality early education can save more than seven dollars later on." This led the City of Chicago to announce in 2014 that it would finance expansion of CPCs to an additional 2,600 children with a $16.9 million social impact bond.

In 2011, Reynolds and his research team examined the education attainment of 1,398 participants (90.8%) of the original sample at age 35. The study was performed from January 2002 through May 2015. The results indicated that the disadvantaged children who received an intervention in the CPC preschool program were more likely to have earned a college degree than their counterparts (see Table 11).

Table 11

Percent of Original CPC vs. Non-CPC Preschool Students
Who Earned a College Degree by Age 35

Degree	% CPC Students	% Non-CPC Students
Associate's Degree	15.7	10.7
Bachelor's Degree	11.0	7.8
Master's Degree	4.2	1.5

The results of the Perry, Abecedarian, and Chicago preschool projects provide evidence that the social and educational gains achieved from participating in early childhood education programs extend into adulthood. President Barack Obama provided an eloquent summary of the benefits of early childhood education with more words from his State of the Union speech on February 12, 2013:

> "In states that make it a priority to educate our youngest children, studies show students grow up more likely to read and do math at grade level, graduate high school, hold a job, and form more stable families of their own. We know this works, so let's do what works, and make sure none of our children start the race of life already behind."

CHALLENGES RELATED TO ESTABLISHING QUALITY PROGRAMS

When it comes to early childhood education programs, quality is critical. High-quality preschool gives children a strong start on the path that leads to college or a career. Research shows that all children benefit from high-quality preschool, with low-income children and

English learners benefiting the most. A substantial number of studies demonstrates the benefits of high-quality Pre-K programs.

After a thorough evaluation of 21 public preschool programs, the Learning Policy Institute released a report in 2019 indicating school districts that invest in quality preschool programs bolster student success. Students who attended preschool programs were more prepared for school and were less likely to be identified as having special needs or to be held back in elementary school than children who did not attend preschool. The report also identified the evidenced-based elements of *quality*, which include:

- Sufficient learning time and small class sizes with low student-teacher ratios.
- Well-prepared teachers who provide engaging interactions and classroom environments that support learning.
- Ongoing support for teachers, including coaching and mentoring, with program assessments that measure the quality of classroom interactions and provide actionable feedback for teachers to improve instruction.
- Research-based, developmentally appropriate early learning standards and curricula.
- Assessments that consider children's academic, social-emotional, and physical progress and contribute to instructional and program planning.
- Meaningful family engagement.

Therefore, school districts that aspire to serve their children in a quality preschool program must factor two very important variables into their action plans—funding and teacher training.

Funding

In America, funding for public education comes from a variety of sources at the local, state, and federal level. Approximately 48 percent of a school's budget comes from *state* resources such as income taxes, sales taxes, and fees. Another 44 percent is contributed *locally*, primarily through the property taxes of homeowners in the school's area. The final eight percent of a school's budget comes from *federal* sources, which are primarily in the form of grants for specific programs and services for students that need them (e.g., special education).

Each state has its own formula for how funds are allocated to schools. This means states have a responsibility to make sure their schools have sufficient funding to operate and to ensure every student has access to a quality education. Currently, New York spends the highest of all states at $23,091 per-pupil; Utah spends the lowest at $7,179 per pupil. States may also allocate funding based on specific programs, in some cases using federal money for programs that are implemented at the federal level (e.g., Title 1).

So, given the figures related to states' funding for public education, can we assume that funding for early childhood education is included in those figures? To answer that seemingly simple question, we must take a quick glance at the map. Some states, such as Florida, provide universal pre-kindergarten for all children. Others, such as Idaho, provide zero state-funding for early childhood education. Only 10 states use models that are similar to K-12 funding programs, and several other states lean heavily on block grants and federal programs like Head Start to fund preschool.

Ideologies and perspectives regarding funding for early childhood education are by no means uniform across the various states and territories. At almost any given time in any given geographic region of the United States, activists and lawmakers are squabbling and debating about the best model for funding early childhood education. This makes it painfully clear that America does not have anything resembling national consensus regarding how to implement early childhood education programs. States, however, do seem to agree that the programs significantly improve the social and academic development of three and four-year-olds.

Research studies provide conclusive evidence that preschool gives children a stronger neural network that makes them lifelong learners. Yet, the U.S. government spends only $37 billion annually on early childhood programs. That's less than a half percentage of the American Gross Domestic Product (i.e., the monetary value assigned to goods and services), which puts the spending lower, by percent, than Mexico, Japan, and most of Europe.

In its most recent comprehensive report titled *The State of Preschool 2019*, the National Institute for Early Education Research (NIEER) gives a wealth of information regarding funding for student enrollment in early childhood programs across the nation. According to the NIEER, state-funded Pre-K has changed markedly since its first survey in 2002. States have added more than 930,000 seats since then, the vast majority of these at age four. Enrollment of 4-year-olds has expanded by 20 percentage points to 34 percent since 2002. Enrollment of 3-year-olds increased only three percentage points to six percent during the same period (see Graph 1). State financial investments in preschool have more than doubled since 2002 when adjusted for inflation. Quality standards have generally improved, too.

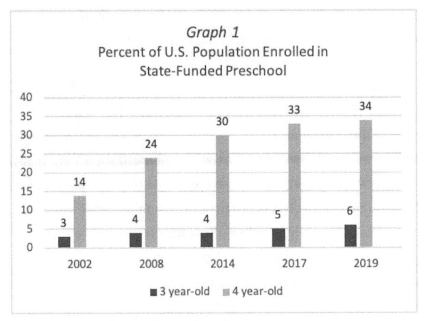

Graph 1
Percent of U.S. Population Enrolled in
State-Funded Preschool

SOURCE: NIEER *The State of Preschool 2019* Report

About a third of the nation's 4-year-old children were enrolled in state-funded preschool programs nationwide during the 2018-19 school year, an increase of about 37,000 children from the previous year. At the current rate of growth, it would take 20 years for state preschool programs to have enough seats to enroll half of the nation's 4-year-olds. For 3-year-olds, the number enrolled was much lower. About 228,000 children were enrolled in state-funded programs or about six percent of the 3-year-old population overall.

Only a handful of states provide state-level funding or match funds with federal dollars for preschool education for children of all socioeconomic backgrounds. This is done primarily through what is known as the annual budgetary appropriations. During this process, lawmakers get together and decide how much money of the budget they will move to early education, based on budget surplus and money in the coffers or reserves. Shamefully, the educational needs of children are often not a part of the math. Decisions are frequently made along political party lines.

In 2013, President Obama announced his bold *Preschool for All* proposal to establish a federal-state partnership that would provide high-quality preschool for all 4-year-olds from low and moderate-income families. After the President's clarion call for action, many states took action and, today, all but six states (Idaho, Indiana, New Hampshire, South Dakota, Utah, and Wyoming) offer some level of preschool to young children. As a nation, we must re-examine our Gross Domestic Product and make funding high-quality early childhood education a top priority. It would be a solid financial, social, and educational investment in America's future.

Training Teachers

Invariably, when educators and policy-makers discuss preschool and early children education, the word "quality" enters the conversation. Quality is critical. The goal is always to have a high-quality early childhood program with the following evidence-based building blocks the Learning Policy Institute has identified:

- Early learning standards and curricula that address the whole child, are developmentally appropriate, and are effectively implemented.
- Assessments that consider children's academic, social-emotional, and physical progress and contribute to instructional and program planning.
- Support for English learners and students with special needs.

- Meaningful family engagement.
- Sufficient learning time.
- Program assessments that measure structural quality and classroom interactions.
- A well-implemented state quality rating and improvement system.
- Well-prepared teachers who provide engaging interactions and classrooms environments that support learning.
- Ongoing support for teachers, including coaching and mentoring.

These high-quality building blocks should be the foundation of any early childhood education system. However, they are only as good or effective as the people who implement them, especially in the classroom. Research shows that effective teachers are the most important factor contributing to student achievement. Although curricula, reduced class size, district funding, family and community involvement all contribute to school improvement and student achievement, the most influential factor is the teacher. In other words—teachers matter!

Despite common perceptions, effective teachers cannot reliably be identified based on where they went to school, whether they are licensed, or how long they have taught. A better way to assess teachers' effectiveness is to look at their on-the-job performance, including what they do in the classroom and how much progress their students make on achievement tests. This has led to policies that require evaluating teachers' on-the-job performance based in part on evidence about their students' learning.

Effective teachers can be molded through relevant professional development. Effective teachers are adept at engaging their students in meaningful instruction that improves student achievement. When students are not engaged with their teacher, they are not learning. Ongoing training in the principles of culturally responsive teaching strategies is critical, especially in light of the increasing diversity in our schools. The Taylor Model for Multicultural Education provides a framework for building a structure to generate a high-quality level of performance for both students and teachers.

SUMMARY

In his best-selling book—*Good to Great*—Jim Collins presents a strong argument that no organization can improve significantly, no matter its tax status, until it confronts its brutal facts. These are three data-demonstrated brutal facts or "gaps" related to public education in America:

1. A shift in demographics has created a "culture gap" in the classroom between students (50.5% non-white) and their teachers (80.1% white, mostly English-speaking, middle-class females).
2. The current "national achievement gap" between white and black students is 27 points and 20 points between white and Hispanic students.
3. An "international achievement gap" exists between U.S. students and their counterparts in most industrialized countries.

Currently, America is risking its global competitiveness and reputation if it fails to invest in the learning and development of the country's youngest children. The "gaps" in student achievement are due in large part to social and economic inequalities that are beyond a child's control. Many children are mere victims of their circumstance. Eliminating this inequality will require early interventions that directly address the problem. As the ole saying goes: "an ounce of prevention is worth a pound of cure."

Research reveals that the effects of high-quality preschool programs for three and four-year-olds are lasting and positively profound. Without high-quality preschool, children are:

- 25% more likely to drop-out.
- 40% more likely to become teen parents.
- 50% more likely to be placed in special education.
- 60% more likely to never attend college.
- 70% more likely to be arrested for a violent crime.

In the United States, primary school usually and arbitrarily begins at age five, even though brain science shows that children are learning long before they enter a kindergarten classroom. High-quality universal Pre-K for three and four-year-olds could significantly reduce the financial burden facing families with young children and help ensure that children are prepared for kindergarten.

Additionally, economists have shown the monetary benefit of early education investments. The programs generate approximately $7.00 for every dollar invested. As educators, we recognize a cross-generational return on investments. That's because even the children of the children who participate in high-quality preschool programs tend to reach higher levels of economic and social success than their counterparts in adulthood.

In response to the essential question for this chapter, we believe a strong case has been made for universal pre-kindergarten. If school systems in America sincerely want to mitigate the spread of implicit racial bias in public education and close the three "gaps" (i.e., cultural, national achievement, and international achievement)—they must allow three and four-year-olds access to publicly-funded high-quality preschool. We rest our case.

EARLY CHILDHOOD EDUCATION
is one the best investments
Our country can make

"The goal of early childhood education should
be to activate the child's own natural desire to learn."
— Dr. Maria Montessori

★ ★ ★

CHAPTER 6

OBAMA VS. TRUMP: TWO DIVERGENT FEDERAL AGENDAS FOR PUBLIC EDUCATION

─────────────────★─────────────────

ESSENTIAL QUESTION
*What is the federal government's role in public
education and what should it be?*

─────────────────★─────────────────

BACKDROP

Prior to the 1960s, the federal government had virtually no involvement
in K-12 public education. The states were (and remain) the entities
that are primarily responsible for the management and operation of
public schools. They are also heavily involved in the selection and
regulation of instructional materials in their schools, as well as setting
standards for hiring teachers. Consequently, each state has different

standards and policies which may determine the quality of education offered in their schools.

Under President Lyndon B. Johnson, the federal government's role in K-12 public education increased when he signed the Elementary and Secondary Education Act (ESEA) into law in1965. ESEA doubled the amount of federal expenditures for K-12 education; worked to change the relationship between states and the federal government in the area of education; called for equal treatment of all students; and attempted to improve reading and math proficiency for children in poverty.

ESEA is still the law of the land today. The law, however, has required periodic reauthorization, which has led to significant changes since 1965. One of the most well-known reauthorizations was President George W. Bush's No Child Left Behind (NCLB) Act of 2001. The NCLB required all schools nationwide to achieve 100 percent proficiency in their math and reading scores by 2014. The law also expanded the role of standardized testing to measure student achievement.

The extent of the federal government's involvement in public education depends almost entirely on the person who is serving as president at that time. In many regards, the president's leadership role in public education is akin to a school principal's leadership role. The primary role and responsibilities of a principal are to manage the daily operation of the school; supervise all staff; ensure that teaching and learning occur in all classrooms; provide training opportunities for all staff; manage the budget; and, most importantly, maintain a safe environment for all students and staff. When these duties are performed at a high level and as a top priority, the students and staff also perform at a high level.

When presidents don't consider their "school" (i.e., the nation's K-12 public education system) a top priority, the outcomes are fairly predictable. Funding for education, which is roughly only 4 percent of the federal budget, would run the risk of being allocated in a haphazard and capricious manner. When someone deems something a high priority it often reflects that person's value system. We will examine the Obama and Trump administrations, two men with divergent leadership styles, to determine whether K-12 was a priority under their respective federal agendas.

BARACK H. OBAMA

Barack Hussein Obama II (born August 4, 1961, in Honolulu, Hawaii) was the 44th president of the United States (2009–17), and the first African American to hold the office. Before winning the presidency, Obama represented Illinois in the U.S. Senate (2005–08). In 2009, he was awarded the Nobel Peace Prize "for his extraordinary efforts to strengthen international diplomacy and cooperation between peoples." He married Michelle Robinson in 1992. They have two daughters, Malia and Sasha.

EDUCATIONAL BIOGRAPHY

Obama received his early years of primary education in elementary schools both in the United States and abroad. He lived in Jakarta, Indonesia, for several years with his mother, half-sister, and stepfather. While there, he attended both a government-run school where he received some instruction in Islam and a Catholic private school where he received his Christian education. Obama completed his public education in 1979 when he graduated from Punahou School, an elite college preparatory academy in Honolulu, Hawaii.

Obama spent his first two years of college on a full scholarship at Occidental College in suburban Los Angeles. He later transferred to Columbia University in New York City. In 1983, he received a bachelor's degree in political science. He experienced great intellectual growth during college. Obama's professors recognized his intellectual gifts and pushed him to continue his studies. Instead of returning to school immediately, he opted to hone his skills as a leader and communicator. He began his career by serving as a writer and editor for Business International Corporation, a research, publishing, and consulting firm in Manhattan. In 1985, he took a position as a community organizer on Chicago's largely impoverished Southside.

Three years later he returned to school and graduated magna cum laude in 1991 from Harvard University's law school. While there, he was the first African American to serve as president of the *Harvard Law Review*. After receiving his law degree, Obama moved to Chicago and became active in the Democratic Party. He lectured on constitutional law at the University of Chicago and worked as an attorney on civil rights issues.

VIEWS ON DIVERSITY

Barack Obama defines himself as African American. His mother (the late Stanley Ann Dunham) is a white American, and his father (Barack Obama, Sr.) is a black African. This irritates some people because they wonder why Obama doesn't use the term biracial to describe his race. Many extremists view this as his rejection of the white race, a baseless position without a kernel of truth to support it.

While serving as Democratic Senator for Illinois, Obama delivered a powerful speech on March 18, 2008, in Philadelphia at the Constitution Center. In that speech, he addressed the role race played in his presidential campaign. Here are some excerpts from the transcript of that speech:

> "I am the son of a black man from Kenya and a white woman from Kansas. I was raised with the help of a white grandfather who survived a Depression to serve in Patton's Army during World War II, and a white grandmother who worked on a bomber assembly line at Fort Leavenworth while he was overseas. I've gone to some of the best schools in America and lived in one of the world's poorest nations. I am married to a black American who carries within her the blood of slaves and slaveowners—an inheritance we pass on to our two precious daughters. I have brothers, sisters, nieces, nephews, uncles and cousins of every race and every hue, scattered across three continents, and for as long as I live, I will never forget that in no other country on Earth is my story even possible. It's a story that hasn't made me the most conventional of candidates. But it is a story that has seared into my genetic makeup the idea that this nation is more than the sum of its parts—that out of many, we are truly one."

In his own words, Obama acknowledges that a respect for "diversity" is in his genes. Furthermore, the words in his speech were not a simple impromptu attempt to talk about race in front of a captive audience. In 1995, he wrote and published his first book titled *Dreams from My Father*. The memoirs tell the story of Obama's search for his biracial identity by tracing the lives of his now-deceased father and his extended family in Kenya.

Obama's book is written in three parts. Part One focuses on the period of his life that covers his birth to his graduation from high school. His earliest memories are of living in Hawaii after his father, Obama Sr., abandon's him and his mother, Ann Dunham. His mother marries Lolo Soetoro, an Indonesian geologist, and the family moves to Jakarta. After witnessing what she perceives as growing corruption in Indonesia, Ann decides to protect her son and sends him to Hawaii to live with his maternal grandparents.

During his years as a student at the prestigious Punahou School, Obama begins to feel somewhat like a misfit. He struggles to claim a racial identity. He becomes increasingly aware of his unusual family and the power that race and racism exercise over the lives of African Americans. Obama experiments with drugs during this time but also makes friendships with other African Americans. He also gains an identity as an athlete when he plays for his high school basketball team.

Part Two of Obama's book focuses on his growth as a scholar and as a man of color. He begins his college career at Occidental College in the suburbs of Los Angeles. While at Occidental, Obama has the new experience of living among a large cohort of African Americans, and he becomes involved in the South African divestment movement. He still feels uncertain about his racial identity. Obama reaches a turning point during his sophomore year and transfers to Columbia University in New York. While there, he makes a promise to himself that he will dedicate his life to serving the African American community.

After completing college, Obama goes to work in Chicago as a community organizer following a brief stint in corporate America. Obama's time in Chicago proves to be pivotal. He is mentored in community activism and politics by Marty Kaufman, and he learns to operate in a city that has elected its first African-American mayor. Obama also commits to Christianity during these years while attending Reverend Jeremiah Wright's Trinity United Church of Christ in Chicago. He becomes convinced that the only way to bring about lasting change is to learn about the law. Thus, Obama applies to and is accepted into the Harvard Law School.

In Part Three, Obama decides to take a trip to Kenya to reconnect with his father's family. His father died in a car accident in Kenya when Obama was 21. While in Kenya, Obama comes to understand how flawed and complicated a man his father was; learns about his family's history from the time of Kenyan colonization; and makes peace with his father's memory. Obama closes the memoir with scenes from his multicultural wedding to Michelle Robinson.

Obama's family history, upbringing, and Ivy League education are distinctly different from those of African-American politicians who launched their careers in the 1960s after participating in the civil rights movement. In response to questions directed at him as to whether he was "black enough," Obama told the National Association of Black Journalists during a meeting in August 2007 that "we're still locked in this notion that if you appeal to white folks then there must be something wrong." With this statement, Obama makes it clear that he embraces diversity, and he does not judge others purely on the basis of the color of their skin.

OBAMA'S EDUCATION PLAN FOR AMERICA

When President Obama took office in January 2009, the country was in the Great Recession that started in December 2007. The country was on edge and in a free-fall. In addition, the federal education law known as No Child Left Behind (NCLB) needed to be updated because of strong bipartisan criticisms from politicians as well as parents and teachers. Obama had a vision for education, which included universal pre-kindergarten and a goal for the United States to produce the highest percentage of college graduates in the world by 2020. He needed an experienced, competent educator to serve as his Secretary of Education. He selected Arne Duncan.

Arne Duncan was confirmed by the U.S. Senate on January 20, 2009, to serve as the U.S. Secretary of Education. He served in this position until December 2015. Prior to his appointment, Duncan served as the CEO of the Chicago Public Schools from June 2001 through December 2008, becoming the longest-serving big-city education superintendent in the country. Duncan graduated magna cum laude from Harvard University in 1987.

Duncan's tenure as secretary was marked by a number of significant accomplishments on behalf of American students and teachers. He helped to secure congressional support for President Obama's investments in education. These investments included funding 325,000 teaching jobs; increasing the amount of money available in Pell grants; and providing interventions to help low-performing schools. Under his leadership, the U. S. Department of Education launched a comprehensive effort to transform the teaching profession.

Since the nation was in the Great Recession when he took office, Obama's education legacy began with his plan to bolster the sagging economy, especially through competitive federal grants that became available to states. During his tenure, Obama signed sweeping education reform into law that gave states more freedom to develop their own K-12 education standards with assistance from his Secretary of Education, as needed.

Race to the Top

Race to the Top was President Obama's signature education reform initiative. It was paid for with $4.35 billion from the American Recovery and Reinvestment Act of 2009, a massive stimulus bill. Through this reform initiative, Obama managed to address two issues concurrently—education and a sagging economy. He and Secretary Duncan used the money to create competitive federal grants for states to use for reforms in K-12 public education.

The administration used the money to encourage states to embrace the President's policies on education, which included charter schools, college and career-ready standards, and evaluation of teachers using test scores. This money became available when many states were in dire straits caused by the Great Recession. Governors and state education agencies didn't simply want the extra money—they needed it! Therefore, they agreed to the big policy changes in hopes of winning a grant. Although the grant program was voluntary, 46 states and the District of Columbia applied.

Teacher Evaluations

By 2011, it was clear that the key requirement of the NCLB act—"that all children be proficient in reading and math by 2014"—was not going to happen. It was unrealistic and virtually impossible to achieve. So, the Obama administration began to offer states a way to navigate the unrealistic expectation of the act. This came in the form of a reprieve from the law in the form of a waiver. States were granted waivers contingent upon making an agreement to evaluate their teachers using student test scores.

This stipulation for receiving waivers infuriated many teachers and their union leaders. It also angered lawmakers on Capitol Hill who considered waivers a way to circumvent their authority. When Congress finally rewrote NCLB in late 2015, renaming it Every Student Succeeds Act, lawmakers noticeably decided not to require states to evaluate teachers using student test scores.

Common Core

Common Core refers to a set of national education standards that evolved after years of discussion between private nonprofit groups and state education departments. The goal of the standards is to better prepare students for college and careers, as well as to ensure that students in different states learn the same academic concepts. The Obama administration used its grant process (i.e., Race to the Top) to encourage states to adopt the new standards. Although states were not required to use Common Core standards, they could earn points toward federal grant money if they had them in place.

Today, the Common Core standards, or something very similar

to them, are still used by the vast of majority states. President Donald Trump, however, has vowed to do all he can to dismantle the standards once and for all.

Preschool

President Obama talked early and often about the importance of high-quality preschool for all children. He often spoke passionately about universal preschool for three and four-year-old children, and he mentioned this in his 2013 State of the Union Address to the nation. Obama even proposed a $75 billion plan to provide universal preschool to the nation's 4-year-olds. Congressional Republicans, however, rejected the way he wanted to pay for it, which was by imposing a 94-cent tax increase on cigarettes.

Ultimately, just as he did with Race to the Top, the President used the promise of federal dollars to entice governors to create or expand the availability of Pre-K in their states. According to the U.S. Department of Education, in 2014, the administration's Preschool Development Grants spread more than $200 million across 18 states. This expanded access to high-quality preschool to 33,000 children.

Improving America's Schools

Obama was passionate about public education, especially as it related to providing an equal opportunity for all children to have access to high-quality schools. That's why he placed his initial focus on fixing America's lowest-performing schools. He wanted all children to leave school with the skills they needed to succeed in the workforce. As part of the American Jobs Act, he proposed investing $30 million dollars to make our education system the best in the world by rebuilding and modernizing K-12 schools. He envisioned this as an investment in our youth, which would maintain American economic power abroad and a strong middle class at home.

The Promise Neighborhoods was an initiative that was designed to improve educational outcomes for students in high-poverty neighborhoods. The program was modeled after the success of the Harlem Children's Zone, which is a ground-breaking program committed to ending generational poverty in Central Harlem, New York. Under the Promise Neighborhoods initiative, communities were awarded up to $6 million in grants to create an infrastructure to improve student outcomes through a strong system of family and community support.

Nation's Graduation Rate

Between 2010 and 2014, the high school graduation rate in the United States fluctuated between 78 and 80 percent. Under the Obama administration, the high school graduation rate hit an all-time high of 83.2 percent in 2014-15. This figure also included an increase across all ethnic groups, as well as for disabled students and students from low-income families.

This increase in the graduation rate created what appeared to be a healthy competition among schools across American, because they all aspired to exceed the new national average. Unfortunately, there was an unintended consequence. Some school systems concocted strategies to artificially boost or inflate their graduate numbers. For example, while the average increase of graduation rates across the country was about four percentage points, Alabama's rate rose by 17 points. This prompted an investigation by federal officials, and they found evidence that many students in Alabama were "given" diplomas they did not earn.

"Zero Tolerance" School Discipline Policies

Obama drew national attention to the issue of "zero tolerance" in school discipline policies and procedures. He argued that such policies unfairly target and expel black and Latino students for minor infractions like truancy, dress code violations, and use of profanity. He vowed to have his administration's Education and Justice departments crack down on states and districts that had gone too far with their "zero tolerance" policies. It's unclear how much of an impact this had on school disciplinary policies across the country. Some advocates (e.g., groups like the school-to-prison pipeline) who have spent years calling for an overhaul of these policies at the state level credit the Obama administration for bringing national attention to the issue.

Every Student Succeeds Act (ESSA)

As previously mentioned, by the time Obama took office, the federal law known as No Child Left Behind had frustrated just about everyone who had a stake in public education. Since there was bipartisan disagreement on how to fix NCLB, and despite the fact that the Democrats were in control of Congress early in his first term—Obama did not prioritize a rewrite. Consequently, the law remained in effect until the middle of his second term.

The rewrite became official when President Obama signed ESSA into law in December 2015. A bipartisan consensus had been reached regarding a few major improvements:

- School systems should continue their annual testing and disaggregating data into specific groups of students.
- The federal government should no longer be involved with how to measure school success or remedy failure.
- States have the sole authority to adopt curriculum standards and metrics for teacher evaluation.

The ESSA is in many ways a rejection of NCLB's unrealistic expectations and heavy-handed tactics. Some civil rights groups, however, worried that the new law transferred too much responsibility back to states. This created some anxiety because, in the past, states sometimes failed to protect the interests of their most vulnerable and disadvantaged students.

America's College Promise Act

From the start of his presidency, Obama viewed the cost of college as an urgent matter that required federal intervention. One of his early proposals for higher education was the America's College Promise Act of 2015, which included a $12 billion dollar increase in community college spending. Under this proposal, responsible students across America would have the opportunity to attend a community college. Obama had a vision that students would be able to either earn the first half of their bachelor's degree or obtain the technical skills needed in the growing workforce—all at no cost to them.

The bill was referred to committee in July 2015 where it languished. Despite this setback, Obama remained vigilant and appointed an independent coalition of supporters of higher education to advocate for the proposal. Senator Tammy Baldwin (D-Wisconsin) and Representative Andy Levin (D-Michigan) re-introduced the bill on July 24, 2019. To date, no vote has been taken. The bill still remains on the Republican senate majority leader's desk.

Student Debt

Soaring college costs and student debt were two major concerns for President Obama when he took office. During his tenure, the total amount of outstanding student loan debt for the first time exceeded one trillion dollars. The administration moved swiftly to bring relief. In 2009, the U.S. Department of Education initiated a "pay as you earn" repayment plan using students' discretionary income after graduation. Students saw their monthly payments drop considerably. The administration also reduced the interest rate on Stafford Loans, the biggest government-guaranteed loan program, and put an additional $50 billion into Pell Grants for low-income college students. This raised the award to its current maximum of $6,345.

These will be remembered as some of the most sweeping changes in the federal government's oversight of higher education. Most notably was Obama's decision to end the federal government's partnership with banks and private lenders who for decades had issued government-backed loans to college students. Instead of having to deal with private lenders and banks, borrowers and schools now deal with only one entity—the federal government. The administration argued that by removing private lenders, the program would save over $60 billion that could be put back into more loans and grants.

College Scoreboard

In 2013, Obama crafted another controversial proposal—a federal "rating" system. This system was designed to help students and parents compare colleges based on cost, financial aid, and academic quality. Colleges would be required to disclose, in a more user-friendly way, things like student default rates, dropout rates, and graduation rates. For the first time, institutions would also have to disclose their students' earnings after graduation.

Despite the pressure to hold institutions of higher education more accountable for the hundreds of billions of dollars they get in federal funds, private and public institutions lobbied successfully to kill the rating system idea. They said the ratings were based on the wrong metrics and, therefore, would result in unfair comparisons. Although the rating idea didn't gain any traction, the administration compromised by creating a "scorecard" that provides a wealth of data on colleges and costs, leaving students and parents to make their own comparisons. The U.S. Department of Education's College Scorecard can be accessed on its website at https://collegescorecard.ed.gov/

Restrictions on For-Profit Colleges

Obama came into office at a time of mounting concern over some for-profit colleges and whether they were giving students their money's worth. The administration worked with Democrats in Congress to create a plan that for the first time tied federal aid to something called "gainful employment." The idea is that if you're going to pay an arm and a leg for a college degree—it should at least guarantee you a job with a living wage. Eventually this led to a crackdown on for-profit colleges that were taking federal aid but, too often, burdening students with enormous debt and worthless degrees.

In the end, President Obama's efforts to expand access, lower college costs, and introduce consumer-friendly reforms to higher education were overshadowed by a growing perception among many Americans that higher education was becoming too expensive.

ANALYSIS OF OBAMA'S EDUCATION PLAN

Obama's education plan went beyond K-12 (i.e., kindergarten through 12th grade), it was more of a P-20 (i.e., preschool through graduate school) plan. Throughout his political career, he continually preached the need for America to invest in education. In his own words, "Countries that out-educate us today will out-compete us tomorrow." The core of his plans for education was to provide the same education opportunities for all students to reach high levels of proficiency, regardless of their race, ethnicity, gender, zip code, or family's income. Through his actions, as well as his words, the President embraced the diversity in our nation's public schools.

As president, Obama continually invested in and supported early childhood education because he knew it was the foundation for future academic success. And his passion for early childhood education was reflected in his federal spending. Under his American Recovery Act, $5 billion were allocated for early childhood programs and $77 billion for reforms to support elementary and secondary education. It was unprecedented for a president to show such passion and commitment toward early childhood, while articulating a deep understanding of its importance.

Most of Obama's sweeping education reform occurred through his signature initiative—Race to the Top. Under this initiative, states received much-needed extra money contingent upon implementing reforms espoused by the Obama administration. Some of those reforms included adopting common K-12 teaching standards and creating performance-based evaluations for teachers and principals. States were also encouraged to create charter schools to allow for more flexibility with instructional practices, curriculum, and hiring. In exchange for flexibility, the charter schools were required to meet strict accountability standards.

Obama also included higher education in his plan. In terms of college access and loans, he made higher education more affordable by doubling financial support for Pell Grants. This resulted in an increase in the number of students who received those grants, from six million in 2008 to over nine million in 2012. Obama accomplished this mostly by cutting out the "middle man" from the college loan program. This action freed billions of taxpayer dollars.

In conclusion, it is important to note that the Obama administration's education agenda began in the midst of one of the worst economic downturns since the Great Depression. The administration aggressively tackled education reform. Those reforms included having a respect for student diversity; placing an emphasis on early childhood education; providing debt relief from student loans; using competitive grants to encourage states to reform their schools; and signing Every Student Succeeds Act to improve K-12 public education in America.

DONALD J. TRUMP

Donald John Trump (born June 14, 1946) was the 45th President of the United States. He was a businessman and television personality prior to entering politics. His father, Frederick Christ Trump, was a Bronx-born real estate developer whose parents were German immigrants. His mother, Mary Anne MacLeod Trump, was born in Scotland and became a naturalized U.S. citizen in 1942.

In 1977, Trump married Czech model Ivana Zelnickova; they have three children. Ivana became a naturalized U.S. citizen in 1988. The couple divorced in 1992 following Trump's affair with actress Marla Maples. Trump and Maples married in 1993 and have one daughter. The couple divorced in 1999. In 2005, Trump married Slovenian model Melania Knauss, and they have one son. Melania gained U.S. citizenship in 2006.

EDUCATIONAL BIOGRAPHY

Trump grew up in the Jamaica Estates neighborhood of Queens, New York. His early childhood was characterized by rude and unruly behavior. This deeply concerned his rich father, Fred Trump, who was worried about his son's future. Thus, Fred took corrective measures to address little Donald's unruliness and enrolled him at the Kew-Forest School, a coeducational preparatory school in Forest Hill, NY. The school serves students from kindergarten through 12th grade.

Trump attended the Kew-Forest School from kindergarten through seventh grade. He exhibited an ongoing pattern of unruly and disruptive behavior throughout his enrollment in the preparatory school. To prevent him from causing further troubles, his dad enrolled him in the New York Military Academy, a private boarding school, to receive more structure and discipline. While at the military academy, Trump's social and academic life moved into a more positive direction. He also participated as a member of the school's soccer and baseball teams.

After graduating from the military academy, Trump enrolled at Fordham University for two years (1964–1966) before transferring to the Wharton School of Business at the University of Pennsylvania (UPenn). Trump claims he transferred to UPenn because he wanted to attend an elite Ivy League school. There are rumors that he left Fordham because of bad grades.

In her tell-all book—*Too Much and Never Enough*—Trump's niece alleges that he cheated to get into UPenn. Mary Trump writes: "Donald worried that his grade point average, which put him far from the top of the class, would scuttle his efforts to get accepted. To hedge his bets he enlisted Joe Shapiro, a smart kid with a reputation for being a good test taker, to take his SATs for him. That was much easier to pull off in the days before photo IDs and computerized records."

While at the Wharton School, Trump worked at the family business, Elizabeth Trump & Sons. He graduated in May 1968 with a B.S. in economics. Profiles of Trump in *The New York Times* in 1973 and 1976 inaccurately reported that he graduated first in his class at Wharton, but he never even made the honor roll while there. In 2015, Trump's legal team threatened Fordham University and the New York Military Academy with legal action if they ever released his academic records.

Trump continues to boast of his intelligence and academic acumen. However, it is difficult to ascertain details of his academic performance because Trump has blocked all access to his academic transcripts, kindergarten through college. Ironically, he constantly questioned President Obama's educational background.

TRUMP UNIVERSITY

Most of you are probably familiar with the old saying— "actions speak louder than words." Perhaps Trump's "actions" with Trump University provide the most telling indicator of his perspective of education. In 2005, he opened Trump University as a real estate training program. The "university" offered courses in real estate, asset management, entrepreneurship, and wealth creation. At the opening ceremony for Trump University, Trump told reporters that he hoped to create a "legacy as an educator" by "imparting lots of knowledge" through this program.

Trump University began by offering online courses but eventually transitioned into offering in-person seminars and mentorship services. Shortly after the so-called university opened, the New York State Department of Education (NYSDE) warned that Trump University was in violation of state law for operating without a valid NYSDE license. Trump ignored the warnings and simply changed the name of this education-business venture to Trump Entrepreneur Initiative, LLC.

The education-business never received accreditation from the NYSDE as a college or university. It did not confer college credit, grant degrees, or give grades to its students. In 2011, the company came under heavy scrutiny and was investigated by the New York Attorney General's Office for illegal business practices, which resulted in a lawsuit filed in August 2013. In addition, two class actions were filed against the education-business in federal court. The lawsuits centered around allegations that Trump University defrauded its students by using misleading marketing practices and engaging in aggressive sales tactics.

Trump University was not an institution of higher learning. The company and the lawsuits filed against it received renewed interest and national attention during Trump's campaign in the 2016 presidential election. Although he boldly insisted that he would not settle, Trump settled all three lawsuits in November 2016 for a total of $25 million after being elected president.

During a presidential debate in February 2016, Republican Senator Marco Rubio of Florida accused Trump University of being a fake school. During a verbal exchange with Trump, Rubio said: "There are people that borrowed $36,000 to go to Trump University, and they're suing him now. And you know what they got? They got to take a picture with a cardboard cutout of Donald Trump." If Donald Trump, indeed, wanted to create his "legacy as an educator" with Trump University—he failed to do so because his so-called school was nothing more than a scam to defraud others in order to enrich himself.

VIEWS ON DIVERSITY

During an impromptu question-and-answer session with reporters on the White House's lawn in 2020, President Trump was asked if he is a racist. He replied saying he is "the least racist person that you've ever encountered." His actual record, however, tells an entirely different story. A brief chronology of times when Trump revealed some of his racial ideology follows.

1973: Department of Justice sues Trump for Housing Discrimination

In 1973, the Management Corporation was run by 27-year-old Donald Trump. He was sued by the Department of Justice for violating the Fair Housing Act. Specifically, Trump's company was accused of refusing to rent to or negotiate with black tenants; changing the terms of leases based on race; and lying to black applicants about whether apartments were available. Trump fought the law suit and accused the federal government of trying to force him to rent to welfare recipients.

As evidence to "prove" that he wasn't a racist, he estimated that roughly 700 of the 16,000 tenants in his buildings were black. That's a little over four percent. Approximately 25 percent of the people living in New York were black at that time. Trump eventually signed an agreement in 1975 vowing to not discriminate against renters of color, without having to admit that he had actually done so.

1986: Accusation made by Kip Brown

Kip Brown was a former employee at Trump's Castle, a gambling casino in Atlantic City, NJ. He accused the Trump-owned casino of racial discrimination. "When Donald and Ivana came to the casino, the bosses would order all black people off the floor," Brown said. "It was the eighties, I was a teenager, but I remember it. They put us all in the back."

1989: The Central Park Five

In April 1989, New York City was gripped by a controversial case that was characterized as a modern-day lynching. Four black and one Hispanic teenager—the "Central Park Five"—were accused of attacking and raping a jogger, 28-year-old Trisha Meili, in New York City. The five teenagers (Antron McCray, Kevin Richardson, Yusef Salaam, Raymond Santana, and Korey Wise) were swiftly arrested and confessions were obtained. Trump immediately went on the offensive and ran an ad in local newspapers demanding (in all caps): "BRING BACK THE DEATH PENALTY. BRING BACK OUR POLICE!" Two prominent black ministers called Trump's ad a "thinly veiled polemic" because he did not express any concerns when white teenagers chased a black man to his death in Howard Beach.

The five teens were all found guilty and served time in prison. In 2002, another man confessed to the crime, and his DNA matched the evidence from the crime scene. All of the Central Park Five's convictions were vacated, and the city paid them $42 million in a court settlement. To date, and despite many requests to do so, Trump has not apologized for having run his fiery ad against the five innocent men of color.

1991: John O'Donnell's Book

Through his position as the former president of Trump Plaza Hotel and Casino, John O'Donnell had frequent interactions with Donald Trump. In his 1991 book—*Trumped! The Inside Story of the Real Donald Trump-His Cunning Rise and Spectacular Fall*—O'Donnell recalls some of Trump's racist comments. He recalls an offhand criticism Trump made regarding a black accountant: "Black guys counting my money! I hate it. The only kind of people I want counting my money are short guys that wear yarmulkes every day... I think that the guy is lazy. And it's probably not his fault because laziness is a trait in blacks. It really is, I believe that. It's not anything they can control." In a 1997 interview with *Playboy*, Trump said, "The stuff O'Donnell wrote about me is probably true."

Trump's bigotry is bold and deliberate. He has an unabashed disdain for blacks. In his world, black people are uniformly inept and untrustworthy when it comes to handling money. He doesn't make any attempts to use the typical bigot's ploy of making a qualifying distinction between so-called "good" and "bad" black people. Trump paints black people with one broad brush—they're all the same and inferior to him.

1993: Native American Reservation

In a congressional testimony, Trump said that some Native American reservations operating casinos shouldn't be allowed because "they don't look like Indians to me." This was a reference to the fact that they were not dressed in buckskins or wore feathers, which is Trump's stereotypical perception of Native Americans.

2004: Trump fires a Black Apprentice contestant for being "overeducated"

In season two of *The Apprentice*, contestant Kevin Allen—who holds degrees from Wharton Business School (Trump's alma mater), Emory University, and the University of Chicago—was given a challenge that involved selling candy bars outside a subway station.

Shortly after that, he was fired for being overeducated. "You're an unbelievably talented guy in terms of education, and you haven't done anything," Trump said on the show. "At some point you have to say that's enough [education]."

2010: Trump hates the "Ground Zero Mosque" proposal

In 2010, there was a huge national controversy over the "Ground Zero Mosque"—which was a proposal to build a Muslim community center in Lower Manhattan near the site of the 9/11 attacks. Trump opposed the project, calling it "insensitive" and offered to buy out one of the investors in the project. While on *The Late Show with David Letterman*, Trump argued, referring to Muslims: "Well, somebody's blowing us up. Somebody's blowing up buildings, and somebody's doing lots of bad stuff."

2011: Birtherism

Trump played a huge role in the "birtherism" conspiracy theory that Obama was not born in the United States. He even sent investigators to Hawaii to look into Obama's birth certificate. Obama later released his birth certificate and called Trump a "carnival barker."

Philip Klinkner, a noted political scientist at Hamilton College in New York, examined the effects of race and racial attitudes on birtherism in a 2014 paper. He concluded that belief in birtherism "is almost completely resistant to factual correction and is strongly related [to] partisanship and attitudes about race." In other words, according to Klinkner—racial resentment is a key driver of birtherism.

Admittedly, none of these incidents taken in isolation should be used to categorized Trump as a person with a racial bias. One could argue that he is simply a bad speaker or perhaps racially insensitive. However, when you put all of these events together, a clear pattern emerges. At the very least, Trump has a history of playing into people's racism to bolster himself socially and monetarily.

The aforementioned incidents occurred before Trump entered the political arena. Instead of suppressing his racially-charged vitriol during his presidential campaign, he unleashed it. While on the campaign trail, he repeatedly made explicitly bigoted remarks, from calling Mexican immigrants criminals and rapists to proposing a ban on all Muslims entering the United States. The trend even continued into his presidency—from stereotyping black reporters to pandering to white supremacists after they held a violent rally in Charlottesville, Virginia.

The tweet Trump posted on July 14, 2019, suggests that there are no limits to his penchant for using race as a weapon. He tweeted that several black and brown members of Congress are "from countries whose governments are a complete and total catastrophe" and they should "go back" to those countries. The tweets were aimed at Representatives Alexandria Ocasio-Cortez (D-NY), Ayanna Pressley (D-MA), Ilhan Omar (D-MN), and Rashida Tlaib (D-MI). This is similar to other race-based responses Trump has used against immigrants and minority groups who criticize U.S. policies. Democrats, including House Speaker Nancy Pelosi, condemned Trump's tweets as racist.

It would be fair to say that Donald Trump does not necessarily embrace diversity; but rather, he uses it as a weapon to ingratiate himself with whites who harbor implicit and explicit racial biases. In America, our strength lies in our diversity and it should unite us. Trump tends to use diversity to divide us.

TRUMPS' EDUCATION PLAN FOR AMERICAN

During their campaigns, presidential candidates typically take pride in lauding their positions on education. It's the next best thing to kissing babies. It was difficult to determine Trump's views on education during his campaign. Education was not among the major "positions" he cited on his campaign website. Much of the attention was devoted to building a wall to prevent Mexican immigrants from entering into the United States; making America great again; draining the political swamp; dismantling Obamacare; and protecting 2nd Amendment rights.

"I'm a tremendous believer in education," Trump said in a campaign ad. "But education has to be at a local level. We cannot have the bureaucrats in Washington telling you how to manage your child's education." Trump's lack of details regarding his education agenda left many educators and policymakers bewildered. No one had any idea what plans he had for public education. On October 18, 2015, Trump told host Chris Wallace of Fox News that, if elected president, he would consider cutting the U.S. Department of Education entirely.

Betsy DeVos

In the absence of a clear plan for education, President Trump decided to appoint Betsy DeVos as his Secretary of Education and follow her lead. Many educators across the nation gasped when he announced his choice, because DeVos has a history of not supporting K-12 public education. She has always supported vouchers for private and religious schools. In addition, she has been a staunch supporter of organizations like Michigan's Mackinac Center for Public Policy, which has lobbied for the privatization of the education system. A chronology of some of the controversy that has surrounded DeVos follows.

Support for privatization (1990s–2000s). For over two decades and before she became the Secretary of Education, Betsy Devos used her family's wealth to privatize public schools. She funded politicians who supported voucher schemes. She also chaired the pro-voucher American Federation for Children. In her home state of Michigan, she was recognized as one of the architects of Detroit's charter school system, one that downplays regulations and accountability while draining resources from public schools. Even some advocates for privatization described it as a major school reform disaster.

Educators denounce Trump's nomination of Betsy DeVos (November 2016). Lily Eskelsen García, elementary school teacher and president of the National Education Association (NEA), declared that DeVos would be the first Secretary of Education with no experience in public education. García is correct because DeVos has never been a teacher, an administrator, nor has she ever served on any public board of education. Moreover, neither she nor her children ever attended a public school.

Confirmation hearing (January 2017). The confirmation hearing raised grave concerns regarding DeVos' qualifications. She could not answer basic questions about the federal Individuals with Disabilities Education Act, including whether states and localities have to adhere to it. She was unfamiliar with the difference between proficiency and growth. DeVos refused to give a definitive answer on whether she believes guns belong in schools. Her answer that raised the most eyebrows was when she stated that a school in Montana might need guns to protect students against a "potential grizzly" bear. That answer went viral on social media and provided fodder for numerous comedians and talk-show hosts across the globe.

Unprecedented and unpopular confirmation (February 2017). There was a public outcry from parents, students, and educators across the nation over Trump's nomination of DeVos. Despite receiving over one million e-mailed letters and over 40,000 phone calls from NEA supporters urging senators to vote "No"—the U.S. Senate still confirmed DeVos. Vice President Mike Pence had to cast the deciding vote, which was the first time in America's history a vice president's vote was necessary to approve a cabinet nominee.

Shortly after her confirmation, DeVos gave us all an indication of her perspective regarding higher education as well as her unpopularity in the African American community. On May 10, 2017, when DeVos stood to deliver the commencement address for historically-black Bethune-Cookman University— many of the students booed and turned their backs to her. A Florida educator had gathered more than 10,000 signatures asking the school officials to cancel DeVos' address because she had referred to historically black colleges and universities (HBCUs) as "pioneers of choice." In reality, HBCUs were founded during the period of segregation when black students were barred from attending white colleges in the South and beyond.

Given her background, we must continue to question Betsy DeVos' qualification to serve as the Secretary of Education. Despite her ineptitude and lack of experience with public education, Donald Trump still embraced her. He was willing to allow DeVos to place her "thumb print" on his education plan for America. Let's take a look at some key components of the Trump-Devos plan.

Local Control

Throughout his campaign for the presidency, Trump shouted his belief that the federal government should not be involved in public education. In his mind, schools are the business of the local community and, historically, the U.S. Department of Education has been an adversary that has imposed overly-rigid rules to make life more difficult for educators, students, and parents. For each of his first three years in the Oval Office, Trump explored ways to slash the U.S. Department of Education's (USDE) budget.

In his proposed budget for fiscal year 2020, he sought a 10 percent or $7.1 billion cut in spending for the USDE. The cuts would include $2.1 billion to eliminate professional development for teachers under Title II; $1.2 billion to eliminate Title IV funding for academic supports and enrichment; and $1.1 billion to cut 21st Century Community Learning Centers that support after-school programs. In total, funding for 29 programs would be eliminated in the federal budget.

Common Core

On February 10, 2016, Trump tweeted: "I have been consistent in my opposition to Common Core. Get rid of Common Core—keep local!" As previously mentioned, the Common Core are learning standards in math and English language arts that were developed through a collaboration between the National Governors Association and the Council of Chief State School Officers. According to the Core's website, they are being used in 42 states and the District of Columbia.

While Trump's disdain for the Common Core is noted, he does not have the unilateral authority to simply "get rid of" the standards. If he is sincere in his desire for states to have control of education, one would think Trump would adopt a laissez-faire or hands-off approach and not get involved with Common Core. Besides, since 42 states and the District of Columbia have already adopted the core, they—not the President—have the option to repeal them. So, Trump's education plan regarding Common Core is much ado about nothing.

Education Freedom Scholarships

During a White House roundtable discussion in 2019 with students, teachers and policymakers, Trump said that children trapped in failing government schools "would be forgotten no longer." He urged Congress to pass his Education Freedom Scholarships (EFS) proposal, which he said would improve education for America's children.

Under Trump and DeVos' EFS proposal, taxpayers could make voluntary contributions to organizations that granted scholarships. These organizations would be identified and approved by states. Subsequently, these organizations would award scholarships to students that could be used for a wide variety of educational options. Taxpayers that make contributions would receive a non-refundable dollar-for-dollar tax credit. Essentially, EFS would not be a mandated federal program because it would allow states to decide whether to participate, how to participate, how to select eligible students, and how to select education providers.

Once you peel away the rhetoric in Trump's plan, a clear picture emerges. Education freedom doesn't really mean providing educational opportunities to "free" students from any restraints. It means something a little more sinister. It allows a pathway for students to leave public schools with the assistance of state and federal dollars. Once they exit, the students can receive scholarships (i.e., vouchers) to attend religious or private schools. This has the potential of weakening public education because, through a discriminatory process of assigning scholarships, states can create "white flight" and *de facto* segregated school systems.

Student Loans Proposal

The Student Loans Proposal (SLP) is Trump's 10-point plan to provide for debt relief on federal student loans. Trump and DeVos believe that previous regulations increased the cost of college and student loan debt. The expressed goals of the SLP are to waive interest payments on student loans and make college more affordable. Although the full details of the proposal are still a work-in-progress, here is a synopsis of the major components of the proposal:

1. Interest payment on federal student loans will be waived temporarily.
2. The proposal applies only to federal student loans, not private student loans.
3. The interest waiver applies only to "student loans held by federal government agencies." Thus, it's possible that some federal student loans may not be eligible.
4. The waiver applies only to interest payments, not to principal payments.
5. The interest waiver will be in effect "until further notice."

6. You don't need to sign up for an interest waiver. The interest is expected to be waived automatically.

7. You still need to pay your student loans. An interest waiver does not mean "no student loan payments."

8. The interest waiver could start as early as one week from the day the proposal is enacted.

9. Borrowers who are enrolled in an income-driven repayment plan or forbearance for federal student loans are expected to be eligible.

10. There is no indication of any interest limit, so borrowers with high-balance federal student loans potentially could save the most.

While the Trump-DeVos plan is a noble effort, it is not the student loan forgiveness plan that Senator Bernie Sanders (I-VT) has proposed. Under the Trump-DeVos plan, a person's student loan balance will not be waived. Be mindful that as of today, Congress has not approved all the components of this plan. It's still a work in-progress. That's why it is critical for people to continue paying their student loans and not skip a payment during the waiver period.

ANALYSIS OF TRUMP'S EDUCATION PLAN

In the purest sense, Trump does not have a comprehensive written document that outlines his education plan. Instead, he often uses a lot of inflammatory rhetoric to express his disdain for Obama's plan, and he formulates proposals to address issues as they emerge. Trump's primary education agenda is to reduce the authority of the U.S. Department of Education. His second priority, seemingly, is to allow his Secretary of Education, Betsy DeVos, to promote her agenda, which is to privatize public schools through vouchers.

The crux of Trump's plan or blurred vision for education is captured in his proposal called the Education Freedom Scholarships (EFS). This proposal appears to focus more on ending the tenets of public education instead of improving or enhancing them. The Trump administration won't publicly admit that its main goal is to end public education because of the political backlash it would receive, including from members of Trump's own base. Instead, Trump and DeVos have carefully focused on dismantling some core aspects of public education without formally announcing their attacks.

However, when you dig deeper into the cryptic language and convoluted tax schemes in the EFS, a picture of an agenda that is incongruous with public education emerges. That cryptic language was on full display in Trump's State of the Union address on February 4, 2020: "American children have been trapped in failing government schools." He said private school choice will "rescue these students." The so-called "government schools" refer to public schools in general.

A central part of our analysis of Obama's education plan was to review his budget. By following the money, so to speak, we are able to pinpoint priorities. Trump's proposed budget for the 2020 fiscal year allows us to gauge his priorities for education. In that budget, he proposed to slash funding for teachers and after-school programs. In effect, Trump was asking Congress to cut teachers' salaries, increase class sizes, and cancel after-school programming to pay for tax cuts for wealthy parents who can already send their children to private schools. Meanwhile, working class families would have to bear the brunt of the depleted funding for public schools and tax breaks for the rich.

SUMMARY

In the words of Maya Angelou, "When someone shows you who they are, believe them the first time." Both Barack Obama and Donald Trump have shown us who they are regarding their morals, values, and education leadership. Barack Obama clearly is a man with family values and a respect for diversity. He was, and continues to be, a huge supporter of P-20 education. His passion for preschool is undeniable, and he understands the importance of getting children involved in high-quality education programs as early as possible.

As an education leader, Obama established Race to the Top to facilitate much-needed reform in public education in America. Governors had the opportunity to compete for federal grants to improve education in their respective states. This resulted in nationwide changes in the way teachers were evaluated and placed even more emphasis on test results.

Donald Trump revealed his perspective of education through his Trump University debacle and, per Maya Angelou, we should believe him. Ronald Schnackenberg, a sales manager at Trump University from 2006–2007, testified during a court preceding that: "Trump University was a fraudulent scheme that preyed upon the uneducated to separate them from their money." That's quite a paradox. As a so-called education leader, instead of trying to teach the "uneducated"— Trump endeavored to take advantage of them for personal monetary profit.

Regarding his vision for K-12 public education, Trump appears fixated on privatization and pandering to the wealthy. Billionaire Betsy DeVos, his Secretary of Education, directs his education plan, and she has dedicated her career to the cause of school choice. The Trump-DeVos Education Freedom Scholarships plan is a veiled attempt to promote school choice and to privatize K-12 public education. Moreover, Trump's disdain for diversity is well-documented, extending back to the early 1970s. During his campaign for the presidency, he often solicited votes from members of the black community using these words: "You're living in poverty, your schools are no good, you have no jobs, 58% of your youth is unemployed—what the hell do you have to lose?"

In response to the essential question at the beginning of this chapter, the answer is multifaceted. The federal government plays a relatively small role in public education. While education is not exactly a constitutional right like free speech or the right to assemble, it is important enough to warrant constitutional protection. Therefore, under the 14th Amendment, students and school personnel are protected against discrimination based on race, gender, religion, disability, or ethnicity. The federal government also allocates funding to school districts that follow federal guidelines. Roughly four percent of the federal budget is spent on education.

Under the 10th Amendment to the Constitution, the states have the primary responsibility for overseeing public education. The federal government has and should employ a support role in K-12 public education. Moreover, states may allow local school boards to govern and oversee the operation of specific school districts in their county or jurisdiction. In terms of numbers, on average, the percentage of revenue for a school's budget comes from three sources of government as follows:

- 47% (State Government)
- 45% (Local Government)
- 8% (Federal Government)

These percentages carry a strong message; that is—the federal government's impact on public education is rather minimal. Ideally, we would love to have someone in the Oval Office who is pro-education, but the real work starts at the state level and trickles down to local school boards. That being the case, we have one tool that can be used to impact education in the various states—the ballot box. Parents and supporters of public educators must pay more attention to the education platforms of elected officials at the state and local level, because they determine approximately 92 percent of the funding that goes into an individual school's budget. When you vote—vote for high-quality PK-12 public education for all children.

"Leadership and learning are indispensable to each other"
— John F. Kennedy

★ ★ ★

CHAPTER 7

THE COLLISION AND ITS IMPACT ON AMERICA

―――――――――★―――――――――

ESSENTIAL QUESTION

*What indelible lessons have we learned from the collision
between the two deadly diseases, Racism and COVID-19, and
how should America move forward during the aftermath?*

―――――――――★―――――――――

On December 31, 2019, the World Health Organization's (WHO)
China office heard the first reports of a previously-unknown virus that
was behind a number of pneumonia cases in Wuhan, a city in Eastern
China with a population of over 11 million people. This SARS-CoV-2
virus spread into more than 200 countries and territories. While it was
popularly referred to as coronavirus, on February 11, 2020, the WHO
announced the official name of the disease as COVID-19.

While COVID-19 was rapidly flowing into America, systemic
racism continued to ravage the nation just as rapidly. Both diseases

were silent killers that left a path of mayhem, death, and destruction. The two diseases collided in Minneapolis, Minnesota, and shook the foundation of America. The public "lynching" of George Floyd on May 25, 2020, unveiled 400 years of racism that were largely "invisible" to many Americans, especially the younger generations.

The collision of the two diseases exposed the evil that lurked within many institutions in America. For centuries, systemic racial disparities existed in health care, employment, criminal justice, housing, and education. Both shock and outrage gripped America after those two diseases collided. People from all ethnicities, genders, and generations bonded together and demanded change under the mantra of "Black Lives Matter." In this chapter, we will explore the impact of the collision between COVID-19 and systemic racism in America.

COVID-19 STRIKES AMERICA

The first recorded case of COVID-19 in America occurred on January 19, 2020, when a 35-year-old man went to an urgent care clinic in Snohomish, Washington, with a four-day history of coughing and a high fever. The man disclosed that he had returned to the United States on January 15 after visiting family in Wuhan, China. One day earlier, Japan, South Korea, and Thailand had reported their first cases of COVID-19.

The Trump administration failed miserably to protect American lives from the wrath of this deadly virus. It was not until February 25, 2020, after local transmission of the virus was established in other states (e.g., Oregon and New York), that the Centers for Disease

Control and Prevention (CDC) warned the American public for the first time to prepare for a local outbreak. The agency also updated its guidance to include testing people who had traveled to China. As suggested by Dr. Anthony Fauci, director of the National Institute of Allergy and Infectious Diseases, the slow response by the federal government at the outset of the COVID-19 crisis was costly because had they started mitigation earlier—they "could have saved lives."

Despite repeated warnings from scientists and the WHO, Trump's immediate response was to politicize the disease, claiming on February 28 that it was a "new hoax" concocted by the Democrats. Two weeks later, after the virus had struck 49 of the 50 states in America, the President declared a national emergency. West Virginia reported its first case on March 17, making the virus present in all 50 states.

Many innocent lives were lost due to Trump's poor leadership and lackluster attitude regarding the crisis. A retro-analysis conducted by scientists at the Columbia University Mailman School of Public Health projected that 55% or 35,927 of the reported deaths up to May 2020 would have been avoided if mitigation measures (i.e., social-distancing and wearing face masks) had been adopted one week earlier. In other words, had the mitigation measures been in place on March 8 instead of March 15, nearly 36,000 American lives could have been saved.

President Trump's failure to respond to the COVID-19 pandemic did not begin in February 2020 with his bungled messaging to downplay the crisis even as it was surging like a tsunami. Nor did it begin in mid-March when he insisted that the country should discontinue its social distancing measures. Trump's failure began in April 2018, more than 18 months before the people in China even realized they were dealing with a new disease.

The Trump administration's failure began when they started dismantling the response team that the Obama administration had assembled to be in charge in the event of a possible pandemic. They fired the team's leadership, disbanded the entire team in the Spring of 2018, and ignored the comprehensive written "pandemic playbook" the Obama administration had prepared. Also, Trump's repeated calls to cut the budget for the CDC made it clear that the government's ability to fight a pandemic was not a priority.

Impact on America's Economy

While pandemics may differ, they always affect economic output in a similar fashion. The Black Death or bubonic plague of 1347–1352 caused more than 75 million deaths around the world and devasted many urban areas. This led to a reduction in the workforce, along with an increase in wages for people who were able to work. The Spanish Flu of 1918–1920 caused the deaths of up to 100 million people and curtailed economic activity that could be traced into the 1980s.

In an early effort to try to stop the spread of COVID-19, cities across the nation started shutting down restaurants, bars, hair salons, gyms, and schools. People were also ordered to "shelter-in-place"— which required residents to remain at home unless they had to leave for essential reasons such as purchasing groceries or medicines, or keeping a doctor's appointment. So, for months, people across America spent the vast majority of their time "locked" in their homes, and they tapped into their limited resources to only purchase essential items. In scenes reminiscent of the Great Depression, some people with no resources stood in long lines to receive much-needed food items.

During the first five months of the COVID-19 pandemic, the U.S. economy went into a tailspin. Stocks collapsed, airlines cut routes, and many businesses closed. Millions of workers were sent home and cautioned to minimize their interactions with friends, neighbors, and even family members. More than 36 million of those American workers filed claims for unemployment insurance, and the Bureau of Labor and Statistics reported that the unemployment rate jumped from less than 4 percent in January 2020 to 14.7 percent with the loss of 20.5 million jobs by the end of July 2020. In addition, the GDP plummeted to 32.9 percent during the second quarter of 2020. America had not seen numbers of this magnitude since the Great Depression.

In an effort to mitigate the economic downturn triggered by the COVID-19 pandemic, Congress passed a $2 trillion stimulus bill called the Coronavirus Aid, Relief and Economic Security Act (CARES). With a possible recession looming on the horizon, the CARES legislation was designed to support large and small businesses, industries, individuals, families, gig workers (i.e., temporary employees), independent contractors, and hospitals. Key components of the act included:

- $367 billion loan and grant program for small businesses.
- Expansion of unemployment benefits to include people furloughed, and gig workers with benefits increased by $600 per week for a period of four months.
- Direct payments to families of $1,200 per adult and $500 per child for households making up to $75,000.
- Over $130 billion to hospitals, health care systems, and providers.

- $500 billion in funds to corporate America (which the Democrats called a slush fund when the Treasury was solely in charge).
- Cash grants of $25 billion for airlines (in addition to loans), $4 billion for air cargo carriers, and $3 billion for airline contractors (caterers, etc.) for payroll support.
- A ban on stock buybacks for large companies receiving government loans during the term of their assistance plus one year.
- $150 billion to state and local governments.

While the CARES Act provided some relief for America's economy, it was only temporary. A report by the Census Bureau indicated that due to pandemic-related restrictions that limited movement and disrupted economic activity—retail sales in the U.S. fell 8.7 percent in March 2020. The drop was the largest month-to-month decrease in retail since at least 1992. For example, overall retail sales, including food services such as restaurants, fell from $529.3 billion in February 2020 to $483.1 billion in March 2020. Table 12 provides a snapshot of declines in the various categories of retails from February 2020 to March 2020.

As indicated in Table 12, the high rate of unemployment, coupled with nationwide mandates to shelter-in-place, significantly changed how Americans lived during the pandemic. During the period between February and March 2020, spending for groceries and health/personal care increased, while spending for clothing and motor vehicles decreased significantly. This paints a picture of a society in which people remained in their homes to sustain their health and welfare instead of traveling back-and-forth from places of work or entertainment.

The massive loss of jobs in America will have a long-term impact on employers as well as their employees. When people lose their jobs, the long-term effects are not just on their income. Unemployment has a negative effect on the workers' skills, education, and even their health. People who are unemployed tend to become sicker. The pandemic placed a large portion of America's human capital (i.e., the skills of the workforce) at-risk of decay over time because of the high rates of unemployment. Most assuredly, one of the main objectives of the CARES Act was to keep businesses afloat in order to boost the economy and help preserve America's human capital—its skilled workforce.

Table 12

U.S. Retail Sales during the COVID-19 Pandemic

February 2020 – March 2020

Category	March 2020 Sales ($ Billion)	Feb. 2020 Sales ($ Billion)	Change b/w 2/2020 and 3/2020
All retail & food services	483.1	529.3	-8.7%
All retail & food services except for automobile-related	403.8	422.7	-4.5%
All retail & food services except for gas	447.7	486.6	-8.0%
All retail & food services except for automobile-related and gas	368.4	380.1	-3.1%
All retail	434.5	463.2	-6.2%
Automobile and other vehicles	71.9%	98.7%	-24.9%
Health & personal care stores	30.8	29.5	4.3%
Clothing stores	11.1	22.4	-50.5%
Grocery stores	74.2	58.4%	26.9%
Food services & drinking places	48.6	66.1	-26.5

SOURCE: Census Bureau 2020.

The pandemic crisis created many shifts in American society. With an economic downturn and a possible recession imminent, many companies and organizations throughout the nation made a paradigm shift from a prosperity mode to an austerity mode. They began to focus on developing plans to cut their budgets and staff in an effort to do more with less. Another shift precipitated by the pandemic crisis was a move to remote services. Some companies began to learn that allowing employees to work from home was suitable and cost-effective.

Finally, as we peer into the future, many slow-burning societal and political shifts will exacerbate underlying issues. The steady rise in inequality will take a sharp increase as poorer communities get hit harder by the financial hardships, potentially leading to greater social unrest. The Occupy Wall Street movement, which was a protest movement against economic inequality, came out of the Great Recession of 2008 when the unemployment rates for black Americans and Hispanics were disproportionately high. Given the already tense political division perpetuated by the Trump administration, it would be foolish to think that similar social uprisings won't occur in America during its post-pandemic period.

Impact on People of Color

Medical professionals have identified several deadly diseases that strike black Americans harder and more often than white Americans. This is not to imply that the diseases are racially-biased; they simply take advantage of inequities that society has imposed on black Americans. Before we discuss those inequities, let's take a look at seven of those deadly, "biased" diseases:

- Diabetes is 60% more common in black Americans than in white Americans.
- Blacks are three times more likely to die from asthma than whites.
- Sarcoidosis (death from lung scarring) is 16 times more common among blacks than whites.
- Despite having lower exposure to tobacco, black men are 50% more likely to get lung cancer than their white counterparts.
- Strokes kill four times more blacks in the 35 to 50 age range than whites.
- Blacks develop high blood pressure earlier in life than whites.
- While cancer treatment is equally successful for both races, black men have a 40% higher cancer death rate than white men. Black women have a 20% higher cancer death than white women.

So, why do these disparities exist between blacks and whites? Are these diseases racially biased? That would be hard to imagine because racism is a learned human behavior. Medical doctors do agree, however, that a person's race and socioeconomic status play a role in inequities. In a statement to WebMD, Clyde W. Yancy, MD, associate dean of medicine at the University of Texas, said:

> "We must recognize there are some arbitrary issues that are present in the way we practice medicine and dole out health care. It forces us to think very carefully about the very volatile issue of race and what race means. At the end of the day, all of us acknowledge that race is a very poor physiological construct. Race

is a placeholder for something else. That something is less likely to be genetic. It is more likely to have to do with socioeconomics and political issues of bias as well as physiologic and genetic issues that go into that same bucket. Some racial differences are more nuanced. But there are issues of disparity and there are issues relative to racism that operate in a very broad context."

The crux of Dr. Yancy's statement is that while genetics may play a role in many blacks' susceptibility to the seven deadly diseases, underlying socio-political issues related to racism exacerbate their disparate attack on blacks. This means America must address race-related disparities in health education and health care before blacks can gain equal protection from the dreaded diseases. These investments will pay health dividends not just for blacks but for everyone.

We can add COVID-19 to the list of diseases that strike black Americans harder and more often than white Americans. In early April of the 2020 pandemic, New Orleans health officials realized their drive-through testing strategy for the virus was not working. Soon it became apparent through census tract data that the hot spots for the virus were located in predominantly low-income African American neighborhoods where many residents did not have cars. In response to this, the health officials sent mobile testing vans into those areas and recorded a significant increase in the number of people who tested positive for the virus.

After New Orleans posted its racial data for COVID-19, many large cities adopted their strategy for testing. Within weeks, 48 states plus Washington, D.C. began to report at least some racial data. Soon the national data began to paint a picture that was all-too-familiar; that is—communities of color were being hit excessively hard by COVID-19.

In many instances, people of color were "essential workers" such as bus drivers and grocery store clerks who were often among the lowest-paid wage-earners. They faced a moral dilemma of having to choose between going to work to secure income for bare necessities or staying at home to protect their health. Many chose to face possible exposure to the coronavirus, which placed them at a greater risk of possible death. This highlights the societal, income, and health inequities that many people of color continue to face today.

The primary focus of the strategies used by the various states was to identify people who tested positive for COVID-19. Testing should not be confused with treatment. A nasopharyngeal swab procedure was often used to test for the virus. For this procedure, a technician would insert a 6-inch cotton swab up both sides of a person's nose and move it around for about 15 seconds. The swab was then sent to a lab to analyze the material on it for the presence the virus.

Not only was the infection rate disproportionately higher for people of color, so was the death rate. Comprehensive data provided by the American Public Media (APM) Research Lab reported that the virus had claimed nearly 112,000 American lives through June 9, 2020. That data revealed continued deep disparities by race, primarily for African Americans and Indigenous Americans. The mortality data were obtained from Washington D.C. and 43 states. While seven states did not publicly post their data by race and ethnicity, they had a legal requirement to report death certificate data to the CDC. Based on their analysis of the nearly 112,000 COVID-19 deaths at that time, the AMP researchers compiled these key findings:

- 1 in 1,625 Black Americans had died
  (or 61.6 deaths per 100,000).
- 1 in 2,775 Indigenous Americans had
  died (or 36.0 deaths per 100,00).
- 1 in 3,550 Latino Americans had died
  (or 28.2 deaths per 100,000).
- 1 in 3,800 Asian American had died
  (or 26.3 deaths per 100,000).
- 1 in 3,800 White Americans had died
  (or 26.3 deaths per 100,000).

According to the AMP report, collectively, blacks make up roughly 14 percent of the population in all U.S. territories that released COVID-19 mortality data, but they accounted for 25 percent of the deaths. The bars in Graph 2 depict a telling picture of the disparity in America. It would be easy to say that the death and economic hardship blacks experienced in 2020 were due entirely to COVID-19. That assertion is not true because inequities related to systemic racism have always played a role in hardships blacks have suffered in America. COVID-19 made us even more aware of the potential long-term consequences of unbridled racism. If left unrestrained, there is a real risk that inequities will continue to create a racial divide in America.

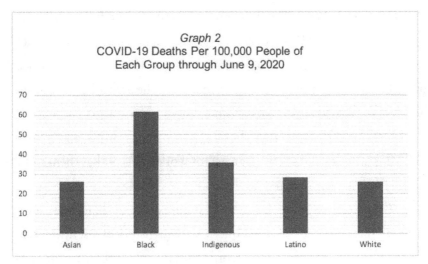

Graph 2
COVID-19 Deaths Per 100,000 People of
Each Group through June 9, 2020

SOURCE: AMP Research Lab June 2020

However, we have a chance to build a better America, and we must do it. To achieve equitable outcomes during the pandemic, we must channel more resources into communities of color to combat the disparate impact of COVID-19. These resources should include communities of color having increased access to free testing and treatment, greater unemployment benefits, and loans for small businesses that do not traditionally have access to capital (e.g., black women in the beauty industry). Most importantly, once a vaccine is developed to treat COVID-19, we must ensure that people of color have ready access to it.

Finally, after this pandemic runs its course, America must resolve systemic racism in two major areas of disparity—wealth and health care. Otherwise, systemic racism will continue to make people of color more vulnerable to future pandemics. A close examination of wealth in the U.S. yields evidence of stunning racial disparities. In 2016, the last year these data were available, the median white wealth

($919,000) was over $700,000 greater than the median wealth for black households ($140,100). In other words, white family wealth was seven times greater than black family wealth. We have learned that economic status matters for reducing the risk of exposure to COVID-19. A lower socioeconomic status means a person is more likely to have to leave their home (or crowded multi-generational housing units in high-density areas) for work. This makes them more exposed and less protected.

While centuries of economic suppression of blacks is well-documented, we tend to forget America's grim history of discrimination in health care. In 1962, Dr. George Simkins, Jr., a black dentist in Greensboro, NC, had a patient with an abscessed tooth who needed surgery. Greensboro's black hospital did not have space to serve him, and the whites-only hospitals refused to treat him. Dr. Simkins and others filed a lawsuit in federal court claiming that having whites-only hospitals was unconstitutional. Although the plaintiffs lost in federal court, they appealed and prevailed in the landmark 1963 U. S. Supreme Court case— *Simkins v. Moses H. Cone Memorial Hospital*— that led to the elimination of segregated health care.

We are keenly aware of what happens when institutions in America receive an order to desegregate. Change comes slowly because many whites stage strong resistance. Recent findings indicate that when compared with whites, members of racial and ethnic minorities are less likely to receive preventive health services and often receive lower-quality care. To combat these disparities, health care professionals must explicitly acknowledge that race and racism continue to factor into health. It is our duty to hold them accountable for the disparities that have existed for years. The coronavirus simply removed the veil to allow America to see her racism in health care more clearly.

Impact on Education

In an attempt to combat the spread of the COVID-19 crisis, over 124,000 schools across America were closed for more than 55 million K-12 students. These closures caused the portion of homeschooled children to soar from around three percent to nearly 100 percent of the school-aged population. Essentially, America's system for K-12 public education had transformed into an unexpected system of homeschoolers. Students, parents, teachers, and school districts were tossed into an extraordinary situation during the pandemic. School systems across the nation experienced growing pains and frustrations as they made the transition to on-line learning on the fly.

There are many components to America's multifaceted education system. The pandemic crisis created challenges for virtually all aspects of the system. Some areas that presented daunting challenges for both K-12 and higher education included technology, learning loss, mental health, meals, and revenue.

Technology for students. Even prior to the pandemic crisis, educators were aware of a digital divide between students with access to home technology and those without it. In a 2018 survey by the Pew Research Center, about 17 percent of teens (ages 13 to 17) said they were often unable to complete homework assignments because they did not have access to a computer or internet connection. Black teens and those living in lower-income households were even more likely to say they could not complete homework assignments for the same reason.

Therefore, as schools closed and made an abrupt shift to online classes and assignments, they had to confront the reality that many of their K-12 students did not have reliable access to computers and the internet at home. For many black students and those from low-income households, a lack of technology suddenly meant a lack of school. When some school officials responded dutifully by handing out laptops, they received another sobering dose of reality—hardware is easy, reliable internet is tough.

School officials learned that while it is possible to close the digital divide by disseminating laptops—affordable, fast internet is not available in many places. The Federal Communications Commission estimates that more than 21 million Americans live in areas without any broadband options. This includes small towns in upstate New York and sprawling counties in Southern California. Even where it is available, a lot of families simply can't afford it.

Technology for teachers. The COVID-19 pandemic forced many teachers and parents into an education experiment. They had to adjust to fluctuating schedules, new methods of keeping students engaged, and navigating challenges related to the digital divide. Teachers turned their homes into classrooms. They used materials like chart paper and poster boards to communicate their lessons over the internet. Many schools also supported staff by providing computer programs.

Brittany McCray, a millennial first-grade teacher in a large racially diverse elementary school in suburban Georgia, shared her perspective of the challenges with technology she faced trying to provide online instruction during the pandemic. "This has been a real challenge. By nature, first-graders are active and need hands-on nurturing. Teaching even basic concepts on-line can be very challenging because it makes it difficult to engage the children. All kids don't learn the same way. Some learn better visually while others learn better auditorily," Brittany detailed.

Brittany further reported that although her school district provided training on how to use Zoom for the video instruction, many teachers felt the training did not adequately prepare them for teaching online. In addition, several of the children did not have an adequate computer device and, on average, only 17 of Brittany's 22 students logged-in each day for instruction. She described the experience as somewhat of a "nightmare" and both she and her students are looking forward to returning to hands-on classroom instruction, when it is safe to do so.

Annette Samuel, a seventh-grade teacher in rural Tennessee, experienced similar difficulty with technology in her school. Her situation was slightly different; she teaches special needs children. Since there was limited access to the internet in many areas of the town, the parents of the few students that had access to laptops were asked to drive nearly nine miles to the nearest Walmart to get free Wi-Fi while sitting in their car. After less than two weeks, Annette suspended her efforts to teach online. Instead, she spent most of the day trying to provide "individualized" instruction over the telephone to each student. It would not be callous to say that the students, in reality, did not receive much meaningful instruction for over two months.

The online learning environment may not be appropriate for all students and all grade levels. While middle and high school students are often familiar with online learning, the challenges of delivering instruction online to kindergarteners or first-graders can be daunting. In addition to primary students, the needs of bilingual, special education, and students that require special accommodations (such as those with hearing and visual impairments) for access need to be considered. This poses two obvious questions for schools: Is an online environment appropriate for these students? What are the alternatives that might better support teaching and learning for them?

Moving school systems to a remote or online learning environment isn't just a technical issue. It is a pedagogical and instructional challenge. Technology is the means for delivery. A successful effort to move school outside of a traditional brick and mortar structure requires a close cross-collaboration between instructional and technology teams. Taking students and teachers out of the classroom is a pedagogical transformation that requires rapid mobilization across the district to transform delivery.

In the event of a future pandemic or crisis, teacher preparation and readiness are absolutely essential. Teaching online requires specialized skill sets that include understanding how to conduct classes in a virtual environment; knowing when and how to use video conferencing; and how to share content and respond to students' submissions. Good teachers are not born, they are made. You can "make" a good online teacher through comprehensive training to improve the specialized skills they will need to manage an online classroom.

Learning loss. The term learning loss refers to the general loss of previously-acquired knowledge or skills due to extended gaps or breaks in a student's education. The most commonly discussed loss in K-12 public education is "summer learning loss" or "summer slide." It is widely understood that, on average, students lose academic ground during the summer. In a 2016 study, data from over 500,000 students in grades two through nine were collected and revealed that students, on average, lost between 25 to 30 percent of their school-year learning over the summer. Furthermore, black and Latino students tended to gain less over the school year and lose more over the summer when compared to their white counterparts.

The so-called faucet theory is typically used to explain the fundamentals of summer learning loss. It theorizes that school is like a faucet that pours out resources during the academic year, enabling all students to make learning gains. When school closes for the summer, the faucet shuts off. Presumably, this means that learning for students from disadvantaged backgrounds stops, while learning for wealthier students continues because they have access to other learning opportunities. These opportunities for learning enrichment can occur through resources such as participating in expensive summer camp programs, visiting aquariums and zoos, or traveling to other cities and countries.

Undoubtedly, the "faucet" was partially shut off for many students during the pandemic. Although the final figures have not been compiled as of September 2020, educators are bracing for a worse "summer slide" this year for students in schools that were shuttered because of the pandemic. Prior research on summer learning loss has found that students can lose somewhere between two weeks and two months of academic growth over the summer. Projections compiled by researchers with the Northwest Evaluation Association (NWEA) caution us that learning loss related to COVID-19 school closures will be anything but typical. According to NWEA projections, if students in primary grades return to school in the fall without continuous instruction during the closures, they probably will retain only about 70 percent of their progress in reading as compared to a normal year.

The pandemic has caused many school systems nationwide to re-think their approach toward mitigating the amount of knowledge students lose during the summer. Some large school systems (e.g., Los Angeles Unified and Clark County, NV) have extended their online programs into the summer months. Other somewhat smaller systems are offering free remedial courses online and/or courses that focus on enrichment and project-based remote learning. Our children are our greatest resource, and it behooves our schools to put forth every effort to regain what the pandemic has taken from them. And it must be done with all deliberate speed and by any means necessary.

Mental health. When the coronavirus slammed into the United States the primary focus was to determine the physical harm it would cause and ascertain what the symptoms would look like. As previously stated, the national response was to close non-essential businesses, prohibit large gatherings, encourage social distancing, and issue a stay-at-home (or shelter-in-place) mandate for everyone except essential workers.

While national, state, and local officials focused on the physical effects of the virus, the mental effects of the disease slowly began to emerge. Social distancing and isolation for weeks can (and did) take its toll on the mental health of both children and adults. A broad body of research links social isolation and loneliness to both poor mental and physical health.

Well over a century ago, in 1904, psychologist G. Stanley Hall characterized adolescence as a period of "storm and stress" or inevitable turmoil. Much of this turmoil was attributed to conflicts with parents, mood swings, and risk-taking behavior. Fast-forwarding to today, recent research shows that adolescence is still a period of storm and stress for many teens. Research by the Henry J. Kaiser Family Foundation (KFF) indicates that from 2016–2018, over three million or 12 percent of adolescents ages 12 to 17 had depression and/or anxiety. Also, suicide was the second leading cause of death for that age group at that time.

The implications of these data are numbing. Although we don't know the full extent of the impact, existing mental health illness among adolescents was probably exacerbated by the pandemic. With long-term school closures, they did not have the same access to key mental health services such as school counselors, their favorite teachers, and opportunities to socially engage with peers.

By nature, kids are social beings who have a need to affiliate with others. When these interactions are disrupted, they often experience periods of stress and anxiety. The pandemic-induced sheltering-in-place disrupted those much-needed interactions. As 13-year-old Taryn Greene puts it: "I used to think school was so boring and some people got on my nerves. Being at home is even more boring. I miss school and even the people who got on my nerves."

The pandemic did not spare parents. Their mental health was impacted, too. With the long-term closure of childcare centers and schools, the daily routines for many parents were disrupted. Data from the KFF during April 2020 showed that nearly half of the parents with children under the age of 18 suffered coronavirus-related stress that negatively impacted their mental health. Thus, in many sheltered-in-place households, the COVID-19 pandemic created a petri dish for conflict between stressed-out parents and their stressed-out children.

Mental health is undoubtedly just as important as physical health and should also be addressed during and after the COVID-19 pandemic. The longer our society goes without social interaction, the more likely mental health decline is going to take place. Most importantly, we should not make any assumptions that our children were unscathed by the long periods of social isolation; they were not. We must pay close attention to them and provide the support many of them will need to assimilate back into their school environments.

School meals. After schools were shut down to keep children safe from the coronavirus, many education officials scrambled to find ways to continue feeding their students. That's because many students throughout the country rely heavily on schools to provide free or low-cost meals. These meals are a necessary staple for many families across the country, especially low-income families. This speaks volumes to the problem of income inequality in America.

On a typical school day prior to the pandemic, the National School Lunch Program provided low-cost or free lunches to nearly 30 million children, and 14 million received a free or reduced-price for breakfast under the School Breakfast Program. That translates to 30 million students who rely on their schools for at least one meal a day. However, when school is not in session, such as during the summer, they struggle to secure enough food. Educators refer to this as the "summer nutrition gap"—which represents another "gap" in K-12 public education between advantaged and disadvantaged students. This gap puts undernourished students at an academic disadvantage when they return to school in the fall after their summer break.

During the pandemic, educators and policymakers across the nation created various strategies to safely deliver meals to their disadvantaged students. Considering the record-shattering spike in unemployment during the pandemic, these meals became even more crucial for disadvantaged students. Some of the strategies that were used for delivering the meals included:

- Grab-and-go meals at designated pick-up-sites.
- Drive-through lanes for meal distribution to limit contact with others during pick-up times.

- Regular school bus routes doubling as meal delivery routes to reach children whose families may be unable to access pick-up sites.
- Partnership with local food banks with additional infrastructure, resources, and prior experience in providing food to children and their families.

The school lunch program is second-only to SNAP (or food stamps) as the largest federal nutrition assistance program in the country. School leaders recognize that healthy nutrition fundamentally improves children's cognitive function and measurable academic achievement. Perhaps the most powerful research findings to support the importance of healthy nutrition can be found in the Abecedarian Project, which were discussed in chapter five. Briefly, when compared to their counterparts, children in the study who were served two healthy meals and a snack daily in the project's daycare from birth to age five had dramatically, sustainable higher levels of achievement. Nutrition matters!

School money. The coronavirus outbreak literally placed a stranglehold on the U.S. economy. The closing of schools and stores, coupled with state-level mandates to stay-at-home, had a massive negative impact on the economy. Although Congress passed the CARES Act to help address the economic crisis, states were faced with having to deal with budgetary shortfalls that came as a result of enormous decreases in tax revenue from all funding streams. Those funding streams include sales taxes, amusement taxes, hotel occupancy taxes, income taxes, and property taxes.

Schools receive nearly half of their funding from state coffers. However, with businesses shuttered in response to the pandemic and the unemployment rate hovering near 15 percent (well above the 10 percent during the Great Recession)—state income and sales tax revenue revenues were crashing. During the first full month (April 2020) of the coronavirus lockdowns, states were reporting significant declines. Some states claimed they lost as much as 25 percent to one-third of their revenues when compared to the same month (April 2019) in the previous year.

"I think we're about to see a school funding crisis unlike anything we have ever seen in modern history," warns Rebecca Sibilia, the CEO of EdBuild, a school finance advocacy organization. "We are looking at devastation that we could not have imagined ... a year ago."

Unlike the federal government, most state governments are required to balance their budgets. Thus, many governors and state lawmakers had to implement deep cuts, including cuts to school funding. Georgia's governor, for example, asked state education leaders to prepare for a 14 percent cut in funding. Wayne Schmidt, a top Republican in Michigan's state senate, warned superintendents that they could see their school funding slashed by as much as 25 percent.

In many states, the impending cuts will hit vulnerable, low-income communities the hardest. That's because of how education is funded in America. As stated, on average, the majority of a school's resources comes from a fairly even spit between state and local funding. Property taxes are the primary source of revenue for local funding. When there are differences in property wealth between individual districts, many states have tried to "adjust" these disparities by allocating extra money to the poorer districts. However, when state funding starts to drop—like the proposed 14 percent cut in Georgia—the budgetary gap between the wealthy and the poor school districts begins to widen.

The COVID-19 crisis has disrupted nearly every aspect of our education system. Our most vulnerable students have been hit hardest by disruptions caused by a virus that appears to prey on the disadvantaged. The federal government has provided $31 billion to support state education systems during the pandemic, but this investment is modest relative to the projected budget shortfalls that are on the horizon. As resources grow scarce, states and districts must prioritize their resources to design emergency response and recovery programs that support our most vulnerable students.

Higher education. Just as it did with K-12 education, the coronavirus pandemic disrupted the day-to-day operations of colleges and universities. Not only did campuses shift to remote learning almost overnight, but most institutions of higher education had to wrestle with grave financial challenges, as both domestic and global economies faced a possible major recession. The most immediate challenge for most institutions involved cash flow. As institutions began to lose parking fees, dining outlet sales, and other auxiliary revenues, they also faced unexpected expenses. Some of those included partial refunds on tuition fees and room-and-board.

Uncertainties surrounding student enrollment further compounded the cash flow challenge. If students were unable to return to campuses for the 2020-2021 fall semester (and beyond), colleges and universities could face unprecedented attrition. It would be conceivable that many students would not re-enroll. Dissatisfaction with their distance-learning experience or their ability to afford tuition during the stagnant economic climate could cause many students to forego re-enrollment. Even institutions with ample financial resources would find it hard to make enrollment projections for the 2020-21 academic year.

For institutions that were already financially stressed or operating from a deficit position prior to the pandemic, short-term unanticipated expenses and longer-term enrollment declines could likely create severe hardships. This is especially true among many struggling historically black colleges and universities (HBCUs). Morehouse College in Atlanta, among the highest-rated HBCUs, is anticipating a decrease in its enrollment for 2020-21 by 25 percent because of the pandemic. Its president, David A. Thomas, announced that the school would implement a reduction in force, furloughs, and pay cuts to offset an anticipated budget deficit due the impact of the virus.

Howard University in Washington, D.C., another highly-rated and financially stable HBCU, will also have to take unprecedented measures to offset its COVID-induced budget shortfall. The university's president, Wayne Frederick, said endowments are not a cure-all and "the situation is 10 times worse" for those institutions that don't have them. He further stated in an interview with CNN: "Even schools with large endowments are suggesting that the crashing economy, and the fact that there's so much restricted money in their endowment, that they can't use those endowments to fix their financial situation."

If we are reading the tea leaves accurately, some colleges will not be able to resolve the financial challenges that the COVID-19 pandemic has dumped on them, especially some HBCUs. It is conceivable that some colleges will go bankrupt. This is especially true for institutions that don't have major donors and a big alumni base to rely on for help. As the president of Howard University stated, the "situation is 10 times worse" for those colleges.

The impact of COVID-19 has forced many colleges and universities to re-think how they do business. The changes and adjustments will be difficult for many of them, especially for HBCUs. According to higher education consultants, most colleges and universities will have to address areas related to student loans and instruction.

"It is too early to predict implications for student loan debt. However, losses in endowments and operating funds may prompt college and universities to reduce merit and need-based aid, which would drive students to take out larger loans," said Allison Vaillancourt, vice president of organizational effectiveness at Segal. "Students who have traditionally relied on on-campus work may have fewer options. Students with outstanding loans who choose not to return to colleges and universities may find themselves challenged to secure the salary levels needed to pay back their debt in a timely manner."

Like their counterparts in K-12 education, institutions of higher education made a huge shift toward online and virtual learning. While their ability to make the shift was impressive, the effects on teaching and learning were inconclusive. Even schools that had a viable online course system before the crisis struggled to adapt to an entirely virtual program. If students become less successful with online courses, schools will see their retention rates and revenues decline. In all likelihood, some universities will go all-in and move entire programs online. Others will put some but not all online courses. Either way, teaching at many colleges and universities will look different in the future and, hopefully, most HBCUs will remain afloat at the end of the crisis.

THE OTHER PANDEMIC—RACISM!

If the COVID-19 pandemic peeled away some of the bandages that hid inequities in America, the murder of George Floyd ripped away the scab on that wound to expose a deep-rooted system of racism that has infected America for centuries. Undoubtedly, many books and articles will be written about the incident that occurred on May 25, 2020. The real-time murder of George Floyd by four policemen in Minneapolis, Minnesota, will go down in history as a tipping-point for the exposure of racism and police brutality in America. Rather than try to capture every detail, which would take an entire book to do so—we will give due diligence to the incident and provide a vivid and accurate portrayal of the global impact of Mr. Floyd's death.

America's History of Police Brutality

In order to have a better grasp of police brutality in America, let's go back to the eighteenth century. During that time, slave patrols—also known as "paddyrollers"—were authorized in many southern states to "police" blacks. The slave patrols were primarily squads of white volunteers who focused on enforcing discipline and policing black slaves. They captured and returned fugitive slaves; quashed slave rebellions; broke up slave meetings; and kept slaves off of roadways. The so-called paddyrollers gleefully performed their duties unabated and with brute force. Some historians believe the transition from slave patrols to police forces in the South was a seamless one.

Understandably, many blacks wanted to flee the racism and brutality that were pervasive in most regions of the South. This led to the Great Migration (1916–1970) of African Americans from the rural South into urban areas of the northern and western regions of the United States. The presence of blacks awakened the slumbering giant of racism in those communities.

Most white communities in the late 1920s, including white police departments, were not accustomed to the presence of African

Americans and reacted to their increasing numbers with fear and hostility, attitudes that were exacerbated by deep-rooted racist stereotypes. Consequently, northern police departments acted upon the presumption that African Americans, especially the men, possessed an inherent tendency toward criminal behavior, one that required constant surveillance of blacks and restrictions on their movements (segregation) in the interests of white safety.

Incidences of police brutality against African Americans became more frequent and more intense throughout the country in the decades following World War II. Many black American soldiers fought in that war to help preserve democracy abroad; therefore—they expected to have greater freedom and democracy at home. As black Americans started to demand local governments and law-enforcement agencies to show more respect for their formal rights and liberties, their demands had the effect of reinforcing the tendency of white police officers to view themselves as gladiators to protect white communities.

Beginning in the 1960s, police brutality created many notable race riots (i.e., large protests caused by racial discord and hatred) in urban America, most notably the Watts Riots of 1965 and the Detroit Riot of 1967. In 1980, the Liberty City section of Miami erupted over the police killing of an unarmed black man. During a three-day period, 18 people were killed and nearly 1,000 arrested, and more than $100 million in property damage was committed.

One of the most horrifying incidents of police brutality was captured on tape in real-time. In March 1991, Rodney King led police on a high-speed chase through Los Angeles. When police finally caught him, King was ordered out of the car. Officers with the Los Angeles Police Department then kicked him repeatedly and beat him for about 15 minutes. The video showed that more than a dozen cops stood and watched the brutal beating. King's injuries resulted in fractures to his skull, broken bones and teeth, and permanent brain damage.

Four officers were eventually charged with excessive force. A year later on April 29, 1992, a jury of 12 residents from a suburban community in Ventura County—nine white, one Latino, one biracial, and one Asian—found the four white officers not guilty. That verdict triggered the Los Angeles Riots of 1992, which still are considered the worst race riots in American history. During a period of six days, more than 50 people were killed, more than 2,300 were injured, and property damage was estimated at about $1 billion.

During the first decades of the twenty-first century, America did not experience any major episodes of race rioting and looting. Police brutality, however, was still prevalent and many people either ignored or became willfully ignorant to the implicit racism that was gnawing at many institutions (e.g., health care, education, law enforcement) in America. Things reached a near boiling-point again in 2013 when a "paddyroller" or so-called neighborhood watchman named George Zimmerman was acquitted of murdering Trayvon Martin, an unarmed 17-year-old black teen. This prompted three black women—Alicia Garza, Patrisse Kahn-Cullors, and Opal Tometi—to start the Black Lives Matter initiative. It started as an online community to combat police brutality and anti-black racism across the globe but evolved into a national organization to serve as a contributing voice for black people.

Colin Kaepernick was inspired by the mantra of the Black Lives Matter movement. He raised eye-brows in 2016 when he made a silent protest to draw attention to police brutality in America. Kaepernick, who is biracial, was the quarterback of the San Francisco 49ers in 2016. During the national anthem before a preseason football game between the 49ers and the Green Bay Packers, he chose to sit on the bench rather than stand to salute the American flag. When asked to explain his actions, Kaepernick replied:

> "I am not going to stand up to show pride in a flag for a country that oppresses black people and people of color. To me, this is bigger than football and would be selfish on my part to look the other way. There are bodies in the street and people getting paid leave and getting away with murder."

Kaepernick's silent protest went largely unnoticed by the medica. At the urging of supporters and some teammates, he opted to take a knee instead of sit on the bench during the national anthem. Although Kaepernick repeatedly indicated that he took a knee to protest police brutality, not the American flag, his actions still created an outrage in many parts of white America. Donald Trump was especially vocal in his disdain for Kaepernick or any black athlete who did not salute the flag. During one of his infamous political rallies, Trump told a group of supporters in Alabama that players who protest during the national anthem should be fired. "Get that son of a bitch off the field right now," Trump bellowed to his frenzied supporters at the rally.

Despite widespread criticism from Trump, Kaepernick continued to take a knee during the national anthem with his teammate, Eric Reid. Soon other players throughout the National Football League (NFL) began to do the same thing. Eventually, NFL owners and officials began to impose fines on players who did not stand for the flag. Kaepernick was "black balled" (no pun intended), and he has not played professional football since 2016.

Police Brutality during COVID-19

After the COVID-19 pandemic struck America in January 2020 there was a period of relative calm between people of color and the law enforcers that wanted to control or discipline them. While many children of color were sheltering-in-place, school referrals for discipline halted dramatically. No longer were little black boys being suspended or expelled from their schools disproportionately for frivolous reasons. The school-to-prison pipeline was shut down, and children of color were nestled in their sanctuaries under the watchful eyes of caring adults who believed in their future.

And those caring adults of color, except for essential workers, were also safely sheltering-in-place. This minimized the possibility of them having an encounter with a racist cop. Unfortunately, not all adults of color were safe from police brutality while in the safety of their homes during the pandemic crisis. In fact, essential workers like Breonna Taylor could not escape police brutality while sheltering-in-place. Breonna's story, along with those of Ahmaud Arbery and George Floyd, are true American tragedies and each will be discussed separately.

Murder of Ahmaud Arbery (The Sizzling Point). We will begin the discussion with the story of Ahmaud Arbery because it was the first video-recorded modern-day "lynching" of a black man during the COVID-19 crisis. On February 23, 2020, an unarmed black man—Arbery (age 25)—was shot to death after being pursued by two white men in a pickup truck while he jogged down a road in a neighborhood outside of Brunswick, GA. A third man followed in a separate pickup truck and video-recorded the entire incident.

Neither of the pursuers—a father (Gregory McMichael age 64)

and his son (Travis McMichael age 34)—was arrested or charged with a crime, even though Gregory admitted to police that Travis was responsible for the shooting. Gregory claimed that Arbery resembled a suspect who had committed burglaries in the area. The local police department claimed that the Brunswick District Attorney's Office advised them not to arrest the two McMichael suspects.

Although this happened in 2020, it seems eerily similar to how law enforcement "policed" black people in 1920. Although local officials tried to keep it hidden, a Jim Crow-like system was very much alive in Brunswick (Glynn County), Georgia. Gregory McMichael, the father, was a former police officer before he worked as an investigator in the district attorney's office. However, according to the *Washington Post*, McMichael's law enforcement certification and power to arrest had been suspended in February 2019 because he failed to complete mandatory training, including firearms training. McMichael was required to give up his badge and weapon, and he retired three months later in May 2019.

Two prosecutors assigned to the case had to recuse themselves because of conflicts related to their ties with the two McMichaels. On April 13, 2020, a third prosecutor took over the case. After reviewing video footage of the incident that had surfaced on May 5, he promptly submitted a formal request for the Georgia Bureau of Investigation (GBI) to look into Arbery's death.

Thirty-six hours later, Travis and Gregory McMichael were booked into the Glynn County Jail, a total of 74 days *after* Arbery's death. Both men were charged with murder and aggravated assault. At a news conference on May 8, 2020, GBI Director Vic Reynolds said their investigation was straightforward. "The video was already out, we saw it, we reviewed the rest of the file, and we made an arrest," he said. "Probable cause was clear to our agents pretty quickly." On May 21, the GBI arrested William "Roddie" Bryan (age 50), the third pursuer in the incident. He was charged with felony murder and criminal attempt to commit false imprisonment.

At the behest of the Georgia State Attorney General, the Arbery case was transferred from Glynn County to the Cobb County (GA) District Attorney's Office, the fourth prosecutor's office to handle the case. This was due in large part to alleged corruption in the Glynn County Police Department (GCPD). According to CBS News, Bobby Christine—U.S. Attorney for the Southern District of Georgia—was actively investigating the state of Georgia, the 74-day delay in the arrest in Arbery's case, and the GCPD's alleged history of civil rights violations.

There should be little doubt that the three men who were arrested for killing Ahmaud Arbery were modern-day paddyrollers who were working with the local "slave owners" (GCPD) to discipline a "slave" (Arbery) and keep him off the roads. In his statement to the GBI, Bryan said Travis McMichael said "f_ _king nigger" while he stood over Arbery's body, as he laid dying in the street. Yes, racism and police brutality were alive in Glynn County, Georgia.

Although Arbery's death did not spark national protests, hundreds of people donned their COVID-protection masks and lodged several huge, peaceful protests in front of the Glynn County Courthouse. During one protest, which was organized by a coalition of groups that included the American Civil Liberties Union, Brunswick NAACP President John Perry said: "As I sit here and I look at you all, I see the beginning of the great awakening. An awakening that acknowledges that there's been a lot of darkness for a long, long time. But Ahmaud's death sounded off an alarm. We've got to wake up right now, and we've got to demand of our justice system to be to us what it promised to be."

While physical protests to Arbery's death were relatively limited in scope, verbal expressions of disgust and dismay resonated across the nation. Highly-respected leaders like former President Obama, House Speaker Nancy Pelosi, Actor Robert DeNiro and many others released statements condemning the murder as a racist hate crime. Despite the fact that most Americans were sheltering-in-place to avoid COVID-19, the disease known as racism had begun to "sizzle" outside of their homes. As John Perry stated, Arbery's death was "the beginning of the great awakening."

Murder of Breonna Taylor (The Boiling Point). If the reaction to racism reached a sizzling point in response to Arbery murder, it reached a "boiling point" with the death of Breonna Taylor, a 26-year-old black woman who worked as an emergency medical technician. After working well over eight hours on a Thursday helping patients fight the coronavirus, Breonna and her boyfriend met for dinner and then drove to their apartment and fell asleep in bed; she was physically exhausted.

Shortly after midnight on that Friday (the 13th of March, 2020), there was a thunderous pounding at the door. While weeping in obvious fear, Breonna's boyfriend, Kenneth Walker, immediately dialed 911 and told a dispatcher that intruders had entered their home. The phone call would, subsequently, be used as proof that he did not know the trespassers were police officers.

Three men, dressed in street clothes, rushed into the apartment brandishing guns. Walker, who was licensed to carry a firearm, fired a shot at what he believed were dangerous intruders; he struck one of them in the thigh. The men responded by shooting over 20 rounds into the apartment, striking objects in the living room, dining room, kitchen, hallway, bathroom, and both bedrooms. Breonna was shot eight times while in her bed. She was pronounced dead at the scene.

The men, whom Walker said he believed were intruders, turned out to be officers with the Louisville Metro Police Department (LMPD). They were serving a "no-knock" warrant at Breonna's apartment in search of a suspected drug dealer. The alleged dealer, who police said had previously picked up a package at Breonna's house, had in fact already been arrested by other officers at his house 10 miles away. On their warrant, the LMPD said a postal inspector told them that the suspected drug dealer had received packages at Breonna's address. Later, the city's postal inspector denied that claim during an interview on a local television station, saying there was no history of Breonna receiving suspicious packages.

Walker was jailed and charged with first-degree assault and attempted murder of a police officer. After a wave of public outrage regarding his arrest and confinement, he was later released from jail, allegedly, because of concerns with the coronavirus and placed under house-incarceration. On May 22, a judge released Walker from house-incarceration. The state's attorney, Tom Wine, dropped all charges against him because, inexplicably, the officers never mentioned Breonna's name to the grand jury or that they had shot her.

In Louisville, a city with a racist and segregationist past, protests against Breonna's death didn't sizzle—they boiled! Thousands of demonstrators gathered in a park near the city and clashed with police officers dressed in riot gear. They fired tear gas and pepper balls at the protesters and two journalists with a local television station. This prompted the general manager of the television station, Ken Selvaggi, to release this statement on May 29, 2020:

"We strongly condemn the actions of the LMPD
officer who tonight repeatedly fired at and hit
our reporter and cameraman, both of whom were
courageously and lawfully covering breaking news
in their community. There is simply no justification
for the Louisville police to wantonly open fire, even
with pepper balls, on any journalists under any
circumstances."

Later that evening, there was sporadic exchange of gunfire. Seven
people were injured and one killed. Over the next two nights, looters
began to break into local businesses. Finally, the mayor said he had no
other choice but to crack down and restore order. He issued a curfew
and asked the governor to send in the National Guard.

Ironically, Breonna's family retained the same attorney, Benjamin
Crump, who was representing the family of Ahmaud Arbery. The
family filed a lawsuit accusing police of wrongful death, excessive
force, and gross negligence. In an interview with the *Washington Post*,
Crump lamented:

"They're killing our sisters just like they're killing
our brothers, but for whatever reason, we have not
given our sisters the same attention that we have given
to Trayvon Martin, Michael Brown, Stephon Clark,
Terence Crutcher, Alton Sterling, Philando Castile,
Eric Garner, [and] Laquan McDonald. Breonna's
name should be known by everybody in America
who said those other names because she was in her
own home, doing absolutely nothing wrong."

June 5, 2020, marked Breonna's 27th birthday. Many head-liners in the entertainment industry paid a special tribute to her. Singer John Legend penned an op-ed in *Entertainment Weekly* in which he wrote, "Now is the time for us to join together and emphatically SAY HER NAME. Black women created this call to action because we continue to wrongly talk about the generations-long crisis of police and vigilante violence in a gendered way, as if it only happens to Black men."

Other famous figures in Hollywood remembered Breonna's birthday with personal posts. Ariana Grande, Lizzo, Kate Hudson, Jada Pinkett Smith, Gabrielle Union, and Janet Jackson were other stars who paid tribute her. But perhaps the greatest tribute to Breonna Taylor did not occur on her birthday, nor was it made by a star in the entertainment world. It occurred on June 11, 2020, when the Metro Council of Louisville voted unanimously to ban no-knock warrants. The legislation was aptly titled—Breonna's Law.

Murder of George Floyd (The Explosion). Like Mount Vesuvius, absolute disgust with racism virtually exploded in America. And like the volcano, it erupted and spewed hot, burning ash across the country. This "explosion" against America's pandemic of racism occurred on a Memorial Day and will be etched in America's history and remembered as a day when people across various diversities, religions, and age groups locked their arms together and said—Black Lives Matter! The murder of George Perry Floyd, Jr. (age 46), occurred on that memorable Memorial Day on May 25, 2020.

We all have heard the all-too-familiar story of how black men had to flee poverty and, during that flight, how systemic racism often pushed them to commit illicit acts out of desperation in order to survive. Floyd was no different. He was born in North Carolina but grew up in impoverished conditions in Houston, Texas. According to the people that knew him, Floyd was a "gentle giant" who simply wanted to escape the bondage of poverty.

In his effort to escape those shackles, Floyd committed several thefts and drug-related offenses between 1997 and 2005. He was arrested on several occasions and, ultimately, sentenced to serve five years in prison. Shortly after his release from prison, he moved to Minneapolis, MN, in 2014 to seek a new beginning. He found work as a truck driver and a bouncer.

Like everyone else, Floyd had to shelter-in-place when the coronavirus pandemic engulfed the state of Minnesota. He contracted COVID-19 that April and recovered after two weeks. On Memorial Day, demons from Floyd's past—the desperate need for money—haunted him again, and he attempted to pass a counterfeit $20 bill at a grocery store. After a verbal exchange, the store clerk called the police.

Four policemen responded to the call and promptly arrested Floyd. He was handcuffed and placed face down in the street. Derek Chauvin, a white police officer, pressed his knee against Floyd's neck the entire time—8 minutes and 46 seconds. Two of the officers pressed their knees in his back to further restrain Floyd, and a fourth officer prevented onlookers from intervening. That officer even barked at 17-year-old Darnella Frazier and told her to quit recording the incident via her cellphone. She didn't. In fact, had it not been for her video recording—the world would not have heard Floyd (the father of five children) pleading for his life. These were the last words in Floyd's plea: "I can't breathe, man. Please, let me stand. Please, man."

Video footage showed that Chauvin kept his knee on Floyd's neck for three minutes *after* his pulse stopped, and none of the officers attempted to revive him. The day after Floyd's death, the police department fired all four of the officers involved. In less than a week, each former officer was arrested and charged with a felony. Chauvin was eventually charged with second-degree murder, and the other three—Thomas Lane, J. Alexander Kueng and Tou Thao— were charged with aiding and abetting second-degree murder.

THE NATIONAL RESPONSE

With a knee pressed on his neck and head pinned against concrete, George Floyd became the face of one of the largest uprisings in modern American history. The protests began in the streets of Minneapolis and rapidly spread across the nation to over 2,000 cities and towns in all 50 states and U.S. territories. While the vast majority of the demonstrations were peaceful, there were instances of rioting, looting, arson, police brutality, and violence. There were even instances of protesters being killed. By June 2020, seventeen people died in incidents stemming from the unrest following Floyd's death.

The wave and intensity of the civil unrest was reminiscent of the race riots in the summer of 1967 and the King assassination riots of 1968. While the protesters in both of those riots were primarily African Americans, the protestors in the 2020 demonstrations were more representative of the diversity in America. Men and women across all age groups, ethnicities, and religions joined together under the mantra of "Black Lives Matter" to speak out against police brutality and racism.

The Floyd-inspired protests shook the foundation of many institutions in America because they could feel the raw emotions. They knew "changes" were imminent and, ultimately, those changes would quash white-privilege and dismantle systemic racism in America. Georgia Congressman John Lewis, one of the original freedom riders in the civil rights movement, said on NBC's Today Show:

> "Men, women, people with different backgrounds from all over America and all over the world, it gives me hope. As a nation and as a people, we're going to get there. We're going to make it. We're going to survive and there will be no turning back."

Congressman Lewis' words were prophetic during an apocalypse. He recognized that "there will be no turning back" because there was a new generation of leaders in the streets of America battling a generational struggle with systemic racism. And it was being done in the midst of a deadly pandemic!

"I'm just as likely to die from a cop as I am from Covid," one organizer said.

The response to Floyd's death was epic. Institutions and corporations across the nation began to openly pledge solidarity toward the "Black Lives Matter" movement to end police brutality and dismantle institutional racism in America. In what could also be classified as "eating crow" regarding Colin Kaepernick, Commissioner Roger Goodell released this statement at the height of the Floyd-inspired protests: "We, the National Football League, condemn racism and the systematic oppression of black people. We, the National Football League, admit we were wrong for not listening to NFL players earlier and encourage all to speak out and peacefully protest."

Along similar lines of "admitting we were wrong," *NASCAR*

(National Association for Stock Car Auto Racing) announced it was banning the display of the Confederate flag. *Quaker Oats* announced that their Aunt Jemima brand of syrup and pancake mix would get a new name and image because the company recognizes the "origins are based on racial stereotype." Shortly thereafter, the *Mars Incorporation* announced that "now is the right time to evolve the Uncle Ben's brand"— a reference to changing the antebellum image of a black man on its packaging.

While some Fortune 500 Companies have used periods of racial unrest to boast about their commitments to diversity, there were signs that the Floyd-inspired protests were spurring meaningful changes in many major corporations. *Apple* pledged $100 million toward a racial justice initiative and said it would improve its hiring practices and work with more black-owned vendors. *Sephora*, a makeup retailer, said it would devote at least 15 percent of its shelf space to black-owned products, and they urged other major companies to take the so-called "15 Percent Pledge." *Amazon* banned the police's use of its facial recognition software for one year, and *IBM* and *Microsoft* said they would not sell the technology to police forces.

Google's "Commitment to Racial Equity" was among the most impressive initiatives to address systemic racial inequity in America. In their six-point strategic plan, this mega company pledged to donate $175 million dollars to improve and sustain racial equity in America. *Walmart* made a commitment to invest $100 million over the next five years to create a center focused on racial equity; *Facebook* pledged to double the number of its black and Latinx employees and increase the number of blacks in leadership; *Target* pledged to donate 10,000 hours of consulting services for small businesses owned by black people in the Twin Cities (Minneapolis and St. Paul) to help with rebuilding efforts; and several companies decided to recognize Juneteenth as a holiday for their workers.

Perhaps one of the most notable changes occurred in the area of police reform. During the more than two months after George Floyd's murder, 31 of America's 100 largest cities enacted policies restricting police officers' use of chokeholds. Overall, 62 of the 100 largest cities now have such policies in place, including New York and Minneapolis.

Collectively, the actions made by these major corporations and law enforcement departments have provided support for Congressman Lewis' optimism about change coming to America. Systemic racism in America can only change when systems in America change. There are signs that maybe—just maybe—systemic change has begun.

THE GLOBAL RESPONSE

Floyd's death globalized the struggle against racism. As news of his death spread across the world, solidarity marches and gatherings took place from Sydney to Beirut to Istanbul to Berlin to London. In Parliament Square in London, tens of thousands of people defied chilly weather and the threat of contracting COVID-19 to lodge a massive protest. They shouted Floyd's name; chanted "Black Lives Matter"; and dropped to one knee for nine minutes (the amount of time Chauvin had his knee pressed on Floyd's neck) with a clenched fist raised to the sky.

In Syria's Idlib province, an artist painted a portrait of Floyd on the side of a bombed-out building to support the Black Lives Matter movement in the United States and draw attention to the plight of

Syrians in an oppressive regime. In Berlin, a mural of Floyd appeared on a remnant of the Berlin Wall. In Belgium, protestors demanded the removal of statues of Leopold II, the genocidal conqueror of what is now the Democratic Republic of Congo. In Bristol, England, protestors were more hands-on with a statue removal. They removed the statue of slave trader Edward Colson and tossed it into the nearby River Avon. They were inspired by demonstrators in the U.S. who dismantled monuments that honored the Confederacy.

Floyd's death also inspired many Australians to protest the persistent oppression of the continent's indigenous communities. Protests in France erupted in anger over police brutality in the country's big cities. And protestors in Germany shouted, "Germany you are not innocent," as they denounced Floyd's murder and the racism that permeates German society.

The civil unrest in America also prompted systemic changes in international sports arenas. Many professional soccer players in the English Premier League began to take a knee prior to each game in support of the Black Lives Matter movement. Moreover, the governing body of professional soccer in England—the Football Association—instituted guidelines that involved imposing a six to 10-game suspension on any player or official who demonstrated any act of racism or racial discrimination.

Statements from the European Union, a political and economic coalition of 27 countries in Europe, offer a measure of the global reaction to Floyd's death. "This is an abuse of power, and this has to be renounced and has to be combatted in the [United] States and everywhere. We support the right to peaceful protest. We condemn violence and racism of any kind and call for a de-escalation of tensions," said Josep Borrell, the union's foreign policy chief. The civil unrest in the United States caused many nations across the globe to examine police brutality and racism in their societies.

SUMMARY

For well over a century, a camouflaged system of racism crept beneath the surface in America. When the COVID-19 pandemic struck, it unveiled that system of racism and pushed it to the surface. On May 25, 2020, George Floyd's death ignited that system of racism and the explosion engulfed America. That explosion awoke many Americans who were either in denial or not fully aware of the depths of the systemic racism that oppressed people of color for centuries.

After weeks of demonstrations by racially diverse groups of outraged people in all 50 states and U.S. territories, officials and decision-makers took notice, and they took action. Mayor Marty Walsh of Boston, for example, declared racism a public health crisis. He reallocated $3 million of the department's budget to address the public health emergency. Walsh said his decision came after he listened to black people—both in the Black Lives Matter movement and in his life—who shared with him "how racism shapes lives and hurts communities."

In a Press Release on May 29, 2020, the American Public Health Association declared that "racism is an ongoing public health crisis that needs our attention!" Councilwoman Natasha Harper-Madison of Austin, Texas, echoed those sentiments by saying:

> "Racism is literally killing black and brown people.
> It's a public health crisis and it's beyond time to treat
> it as such. The inequities are countless and they aren't

because African Americans are inherently inferior. They are the fruits of generations worth of explicitly discriminatory and racist policies, things like housing policies from the federal level on down to the local level, that kept black residents from even reaching the ground floor of generational wealth-building."

Major organizations like Google, Facebook, Apple, Target, Amazon and others made both financial and written commitments to fight racial injustice in America. Police reform also became a reality. While both houses of Congress were drafting bills to address police brutality, some local departments acted quickly to ban no-knock warrants and chokeholds.

And many memorials and statues that were prominently displayed to honor the Confederacy were shoved from their pedestals. Americans across all ethnic, age, religious, and socio-economic groups clenched their fists in solidarity with a pledge to eradicate vestiges of the country's racist past and build a future devoid of racial injustice. Multicultural groups of Americans across the nation re-assembled in solidarity on June 19, 2020. Instead of clenching their fists, they lowered their heads in prayer to celebrate Juneteenth (June 19th)—a holiday to commemorate the end of slavery in the United States.

It is especially worth noting that K-12 public school officials in one of the nation's largest school systems—Fairfax County (VA) Public Schools—seized the moment to make a profound statement to their students, parents, and stakeholders. On July 23, 2020, the school board voted unanimously to rename Robert E. Lee High after the late U.S. Congressman John R. Lewis. "The name Robert E. Lee is forever connected to the Confederacy, and Confederate values are ones that do not align with our community," said school board member Tamara Kaufax in a statement. During that same meeting, the school board voted and renamed Columbus Day as "Indigenous Peoples' Day" for school calendars. Kudos to this school board for providing a powerful history lesson to their students from the "curriculum of life."

Floyd's death also ignited protests across the globe that caused many nations to look at racism and police brutality in their cities. This prompted reforms that promoted inclusivity and a repudiation of police brutality across the globe. From New York to London to Berlin, multicultural crowds of mostly young people raised their clenched fists in solidarity and shouted—Black Lives Matter!

As with most catastrophes, the most vulnerable are hit the hardest, especially in the area of K-12 public education. When schools were shut down and transitioned to online learning, many children from disadvantaged families could not participate in that process due to a lack of access to computers and internet service. Many children also lost access to at least one free meal a day that was provided under the school lunch program.

The exposure of systemic racism in America sends a loud message— destroy it before it destroys you. Some changes have begun to occur. The most important change, thus far, has been the heightened sense of awareness that institutional racism does, indeed, thrive in America. Not only are more people aware that it exists—they acknowledge its destructive impact on our society.

The essential question at the beginning of this chapter is: *What indelible lessons have we learned from the collision between the two deadly diseases, Racism and COVID-19, and how should America move forward during the aftermath?* In response to that question, America must move forward by developing a plan to dismantled systemic racism, and that plan must begin with reforms in K-12 public education. While the current generation is building an ark of systemic reform, we must continue to educate our children. Because leaders in the future generations must keep the ark afloat.

> "If a man like Malcolm X could change and repudiate racism; if I myself and other former Muslims can change; if young whites can change — then there is hope for America."
> — Eldridge Cleaver

CHAPTER 8

ACTION NEEDED: A STRATEGIC PLAN TO ADDRESS RACISM IN OUR SCHOOLS

────────────────★────────────────

ESSENTIAL QUESTION

How can schools mitigate the implicit racial biases that depress academic and behavioral outcomes for children of color?

────────────────★────────────────

SYSTEMIC RACISM EXPOSED

Racism has always haunted America. Most people either denied its existence or chose to look at it through a blind-eye. But the year 2020 has cleared the vision of many people, both home and abroad. With newly-acquired 2020 vision, many Americans have become more aware and vocal about the ugly disease—systemic racism—that has infected our country for centuries.

Joaquin Phoenix (who is Puerto Rican-American) called out systemic racism in the film industry at the 2020 British Academy Film Awards

(BAFTA). During his acceptance speech for the Best Actor Award, he stunned the crowd at that gala in London with these words:

> "I think that we send a very clear message to people of color that you're not welcome here. I think that's the message that we're sending to people that have contributed so much to our medium and our industry and in ways that we benefit from. […] I think it's more than just having sets that are multicultural. I think we have to really do the hard work to truly understand systemic racism. I think that is the obligation of the people that have created and perpetuate benefit from a system of oppression to be the ones that dismantle it. So that's on us."

Actress Viola Davis (who is African-American) and director Lulu Wang (who is Chinese-American) were among the first to applaud him on Twitter. Davis tweeted: "Thank you Joaquin Phoenix. For your honesty, solidarity AND courage. Well done." Wang tweeted: "An uncomfortable silence filled the hall for a long noticeable moment. Thank you, Joaquin."

There are three noteworthy take-aways from this scene at the 2020 BAFTA awards. The first one is Phoenix's willingness to risk his livelihood by calling out the invisible disease in the film industry— systemic racism. It is a clear indication that many people of color are tired of being silent and are ready to speak up. The second take-away is the appreciation expressed by Davis and Wang. Apparently, those two women of color had witnessed the same racism Phoenix exposed. Lastly, the "uncomfortable silence" Wang noticed is a typical reaction from whites when their "privilege" is revealed to them.

The terms institutional racism, systemic racism, implicit bias, and explicit bias are often used interchangeably. This can create confusion. We will present a model to help explain these concepts.

Systemic Racism: A Model Rooted in Biases

There is a complex system of institutions in America that regulates political and economic power in our society. The major parts of that complex system include institutions such as education, housing, employment, criminal justice, and health care. Systemic racism occurs when those white-controlled institutions impose an array of racially-discriminatory practices that are designed to create barriers for the upward mobility and welfare of blacks and other people of color, while removing barriers to enhance the upward mobility and welfare of whites. The model in Diagram 2 provides a depiction of how systemic racism operates to create those outcomes or "equity gaps" between whites and people of color.

Diagram 2
A Model for Systemic Racism

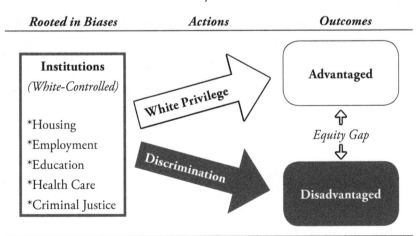

The five major institutions that regulate various forms of social and economic power in America are listed in the first column. These white-controlled institutions are *rooted in biases* or ideologies that are manifested both explicitly and implicitly. Explicit bias is more overt and is rooted in white supremacy. This form of bias is reflected in the hatred spewed by violent extremist groups like the Ku Klux Klan. Implicit bias is more covert and rooted in racial stereotypes. People who harbor this form of bias typically respond to people of color with prejudice and disdain, but not with violence. Explicit and implicit biases have been ingrained in the infrastructure of the five major white-controlled institutions in America for centuries.

The second column in the Diagram 2 depicts the *actions* or standard operating procedures the institutions typically use to provide "service" to their customers. Whites are treated with privilege and the institutions remove barriers to enhance their upward mobility. For example, a bank would approve a $20K loan for white customers despite their poor credit histories or employment status. This is the core of white privilege.

Conversely, blacks with acceptable credit histories and employment would not be approved for the same loan due to race-based discrimination. Hence, instead of removing barriers to enhance the upward mobility of black and brown people, historically, these institutions have used their discriminatory practices to create barriers to depress their upward mobility. This is the core of systemic racism in America.

The last column highlights the outcomes of systemic racism. Systemic racism directed at people of color in hiring, funding for education, lending, housing, adjudicating, and providing health care has created a huge opportunity or equity gap in America's society.

While white privilege has created an "advantaged" group of people that travels along a path of upward mobility, racial discrimination has created a "disadvantaged" group that continues to struggle along a path of socio-economic oppression.

Although it would take a Herculean effort, systemic racism in America can be dismantled. That effort would have to involve action from all levels of government—federal, state, and local. And those efforts must begin by creating systemic reforms in the major institutions.

Systemic Racism: Overt and Hidden

For centuries, systemic racism in America was bold and overt. As time passed, systemic racism camouflaged itself until events in 2020 unveiled it for everyone to see. As indicated in Graph 3, systemic racism was at its peak during the Jim Crow era (1865–1968). The overwhelming majority of bigotry directed at blacks was blatant, legal, and flaunted; very little was hidden from the public.

Things shifted during the 1970s and 1980s. While systemic racism was still prevalent at that time, some of it remained disguised or hidden from society. This was due in large part to the enactment of federal affirmative action policies, which were designed to prevent institutions from discriminating against people based on their race, religion, color or national origin. As many blacks became more educated and economically empowered through these federal policies, systemic racism directed at them became less overt and mostly hidden during the period between 1990 and 2019. However, in May 2020, the death of George Floyd heightened the nation's awareness of the systemic racism that was hidden to the naked eye; people's vision became clear.

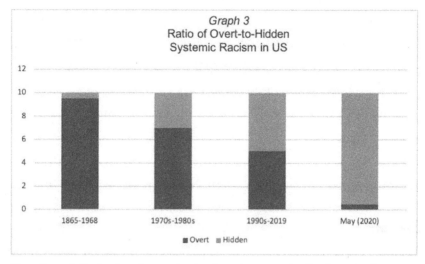

Note: Systemic Racism has always existed and continues to exist. But the ratio of overt- to-hidden racism has varied over time.

Systemic racism is like any other disease. If left untreated, it will fester and cause irreparable damage. Now that this disease has been exposed, America is in an untenable position. The country has two choices: It can maintain its centuries-old culture of systemic racism and risk destroying our representative democracy. Or America can make a commitment to assess the damage and begin the process of making "economic justice and equality" available to all citizens. In the next section, we will take a deep dive into the damage that systemic racism has created in America.

THE DAMAGE CREATED BY SYSTEMIC RACISM

The deep racial inequities that exist today are a direct result of systemic racism. Historical and contemporary policies, practices, and norms were designed to create and maintain white supremacy. Ongoing evidence indicates that the deliberate effort to damage the social and economic growth of black and brown people in America has worked, thus far. Let's examine the damage.

Wealth

Aside from income, the wealth of a family is a key indicator of its financial security. Wealth includes the values of homes, cars, personal valuables, businesses, savings, and investments. Systemic racism has created the unequal distribution of wealth in the United States. The Urban Institute has compiled data from its Survey of Consumer Finances 1983–2016 to reveal that the wealth gap between white families and families of color has persisted across the past four decades. As seen in Graph 4, in 1983, the average wealth of white families was $259,000 higher than the average wealth of families of color. By 2016, the average wealth of white families ($919,000) was over $700,000 higher than the average wealth of black families and of Hispanic families.

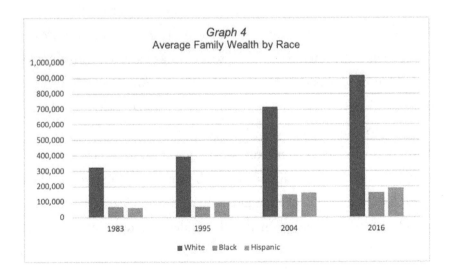

Graph 4
Average Family Wealth by Race

Systemic racism has created barriers along the pathway families of color travel to access many of the building blocks of wealth such as fair banking practices. This has created significant wealth inequality. For every $100 white families earn in income, black families earn $57.30. These dollar figures reek of racism and a system in America that has promoted the economic power of whites, while depressing the economic rise of families of color.

Employment

Historically, employment for blacks has always been described as "the last hired and the first fired." Blacks continue to face hurdles in the labor market related to discrimination and pay inequality. They usually get paid far less than their white counterparts. The typical median weekly earnings for black full-time employees was $727 from July 2019 to September 2019, compared to $943 for whites. This translates to blacks having less economic security and frequently living from paycheck-to-paycheck.

It is extremely difficult, if not next to impossible, to build wealth without steady and rewarding employment. Regardless of the state of the economy, the unemployment rate for blacks has been consistently twice that of whites over the past six decades. And systemic racism has played a key role in that disparity. In some white-controlled institutions, for example, a person's name on an application can determine whether that person is even given an interview. A labor study showed that job applicants with white-sounding names get called back roughly 50 percent more often than applicants with black-sounding names, even when they have identical resumes. In other words, Emily and Greg probably are more employable than Lakesha and Jamal.

Regardless of educational attainment by black workers, they typically have a higher rate of unemployment than their white counterparts. While college attainment helps all workers get more access to better-paying jobs with better benefits, the advantages still favor whites. Black workers, no matter their level of education, still face obstacles in the labor market such as unequal pay and systemic discrimination.

Criminal Justice

In her groundbreaking 2010 book—*The New Jim Crow: Mass Incarceration in the Age of Colorblindness*—Michelle Alexander provides indisputable evidence that Lady Justice is not colorblind. The author exposed racial discrimination in America's criminal justice system, which ranged from lawmaking, to policing, and to denying voting rights to ex-prisoners. Alexander's book helped to inspire tenets of the Black Lives Matter movement.

Throughout this book, we have discussed how the disparate treatment of blacks has created "gaps" in various areas of success (e.g., wealth and employment) between them and their white counterparts. Black people make up roughly 13 percent of the U.S. population and roughly 40 percent of the prison population. This yields a difference of 27 percentage points *above* what would be expected (13 percent) based on their population in the United States. Conversely, white people make up 64 percent of the U.S. population and roughly 39 percent of the prison population. This yields a difference of 25 percentage points *below* what would be expected based on their population. This is another significant race-based gap between blacks and whites.

Intuitively, we know that incarceration is seldom a pleasant experience, and it damages people in ways that often are irrevocable. For example, in the spring of 2010, Kalief Browder was 16 years old when he was arrested for an alleged robbery. This black teenager spent three years in Rikers Island (NY) jail—including two in solitary confinement—waiting for a trial that never happened. In other words, Browder was never convicted of a crime. Although his case was eventually dismissed, the trauma of those years alone behind bars lingered. At the age of 22, Kalief Browder committed suicide.

The collateral damage to the family members and loved-ones of inmates is often devastating, especially for African Africans. The wives, girlfriends, and children experience both emotional and economic distress. Studies show that the children of inmates often don't perform well in school and frequently exhibit behavior problems. Moreover, women partnered with inmates suffer from depression and monetary hardships.

Systemic racism has created a criminal justice system that is rooted in white privilege and oppressive to people of color. The prison system has a debilitating social and economic effect on black inmates and members of their families. The system fails to adequately "rehabilitate" black inmates, and they are frequently cycled back into the prison system. A study indicated that more than 58 percent of black men were reincarcerated in a North Carolina state prison within eight years following their release. By comparison, less than half of the white men and just over 41 percent of black women were reincarcerated during that same time period.

In America, there are two fundamental ways to strip a man of "life, liberty, and the pursuit of happiness." Those ways are through incarceration and denial of the right to vote. The United States remains one of the world's strictest nations when it comes to denying the right to vote to citizens convicted of crimes. An estimated 6.1 million Americans cannot vote because of "felony disenfranchisement" or laws that restrict voting rights to people convicted of felony-level crimes. Currently, more than 7.4 percent of the adult African American population in the U.S. is disenfranchised, compared to 1.8 percent of the non-African American population. Michelle Alexander's premise holds true, there is a neo-Jim Crow component in America's criminal justice system today.

Housing

A piece of forgotten, or hidden, history is how the government segregated America through housing. When the country was faced with a housing shortage at the conclusion of the Great Depression in 1933, the federal government began a program to increase (and segregate) America's housing stock. Under Franklin D. Roosevelt's New Deal, the government provided housing for middle-class and lower middle-class whites. African Americans and other people of color were excluded from the new suburban communities. Instead, they were pushed into urban housing projects.

When the Federal Housing Administration (FHA) was established in 1934, legalized or *de jure* segregation in housing continued in earnest. The FHA and private banks advanced the segregation efforts by refusing to insure mortgages in and near black neighborhoods. This policy was known as "redlining." All of this was occurring while the FHA was actually subsidizing builders who were mass-producing entire subdivisions for whites. And this was done with the mandate that none of the homes be sold to blacks.

Although redlining officially ended in 1968 with passage of the Fair Housing Act, the decades-old system of discrimination has had a lasting effect on people of color. Recent research shows that roughly 75 percent of the neighborhoods that were "redlined" on government maps 80 years ago continue to struggle economically today. Residents in these segregated, mostly metropolitan areas, face inequalities and limited opportunities to escape the grip of poverty.

Even when people of color have the financial means to purchase a home or rent a decent apartment, systemic racism creates barriers to discourage them. A new report from the U.S. Department of Housing and Urban Development found that when searching for homes or apartments, people of color are shown less units than their white counterparts. This type of discrimination raises the costs of the housing search for people of color and restricts their housing options.

As with other white-controlled institutions in America's system of racism, many banks and realtors have made it difficult for people of color to have access to decent, affordable housing. This system of racism has created yet another "equity gap" between blacks and whites in America. Black home-ownership, which has not changed much since 1968, continues to hover around 41 percent compared to 72 percent for whites.

Health Care

Racism has not spared America's health care system from inequalities that have a disproportionate impact on people of color and other marginalized groups. These inequalities contribute to uneven access to services, gaps in health insurance coverage, and poorer health outcomes among certain populations. African Americans comprise the group most adversely impacted by these health care challenges.

Black Americans are far more likely than whites to not have access to emergency medical care. The hospitals they go to tend to be less well-funded and staffed by practitioners with less experience. Even black doctors face discrimination. They are less likely than their similarly-credentialed white peers to receive government grants for research projects. Since African Americans have spent generations dealing with racism, it is highly possible that this has left many of them vulnerable to developing stress-related health issues that can lead to chronic issues later in life.

Blacks in particular have faced decades of discrimination in the area of health care. The Affordable Care Act (ACA) under President Obama helped to ensure health care coverage for millions of Americans. The uninsured rate among blacks declined after that law was implemented. Of the more than 20 million people who gained coverage under the ACA, 2.8 million were African American.

Yet, this population is still more likely to be uninsured than white Americans. As of 2018, the uninsured rate among blacks was 9.7 percent compared to 5.4 percent among whites. Coverage expansions under the ACA have accelerated the progress toward universal coverage in America. The continued high cost of many coverage options, however, means that access to affordable health care is still a challenge for many Americans, especially African Americans. It's even more challenging ever since the Trump administration has put forth an all-out effort to repeal the ACA; simply because it was a signature program of the Obama administration. This sort of smells like systemic racism.

Even with improved access to medical care under the ACA, the disparities in health outcomes between African Americans and whites are profound. Black women are three times more likely to die from pregnancy-related complications than white women. The African-American infant mortality rate is twice as high as the rate for white infants. African Americans are also more likely to die from cancer and heart disease than whites, and they are at a greater risk for the onset of diabetes.

African Americans have endured racism for hundreds of years. Despite the progress that has been made in recent decades, far too many African Americans still struggle to lead healthy and economically secure lives. This is due to the long-standing effects of systemic racism, which touches all African Americans, regardless of their gender or socioeconomic status. These effects can be reversed but it will take a real commitment and systemic change. Health care reform must be part of that effort.

Education

Throughout this book, we have focused on giving a detailed account of the evolution of K-12 public education in America. Through no fault of their own, black students have often struggled during that evolution. They are three times more likely to be suspended from school than white students, even when they commit the same infraction. Moreover, teachers are less likely to identify black children as gifted but more likely to identify them as needing special education services.

Like other white-controlled institutions in America, K-12 public education has been infected by systemic racism. Over 80 percent of the teachers in public education are white, predominantly middle-class females, and most of them are racially biased. Recently, a team of researchers from Princeton and Tufts universities analyzed data from Project Implicit, which collects hundreds of thousands of results from a series of self-administered tests that measure implicit and explicit biases. Responses from nearly 69,000 teachers are included in that database.

The results of the analysis indicate that teachers are just as racially biased as non-teachers in our society. The researchers found that 77 percent of teachers showed implicit bias as compared to 77.1 percent of non-teachers. Further, they found that 30.3 percent of teachers demonstrated explicit bias as compared to 30.4 percent of non-teachers.

This study should sound an alarm for educators. While the actions of most teachers are well-intentioned, their racial biases continue to adversely impact outcomes for students of color in their classrooms. White teachers tend to have significantly lower expectations for black students than they do for white students. This has caused an ongoing achievement gap between black and white students that has existed ever since public schools were desegregated.

Today, there is a clarion call across America to eradicate racism in all institutions that serve the people. The goal of that racism is to elevate white privilege through overt (explicit bias) and covert (implicit bias) discrimination against black and brown people. Public education is one of the institutions in that system of racism. We must reconcile the racist evils of the past because the future of our country is at stake. No evil institution in America can, and must not, prosper.

Public education is the institution that has the most direct impact on children. Invariably, many black children sit in classrooms across America and stare directly into the face of racism. It is incumbent upon educators and decision-makers to cease with their rhetoric and take action to rid our schools of any and all forms of bias.

Though our task is monumental, so is our determination. Let's begin this process now, even if we have to do it one school at a time. The future of our democracy is at stake. The next three sections of this chapter will provide a blueprint for change that can be used to transform schools into safe havens for racially unbiased teaching and learning.

STRATEGIC PLANNING TO MITIGATE RACISM IN SCHOOLS

School reform has been tried and hasn't really worked. For example, in the early 1970s, the reform movement of having "open classrooms" in schools was a novel idea but it faded away by the late 1970s. Fads and Band-Aids cannot mitigate systemic racism in our schools. What we need is systemic change to transform—not reform—our schools. Reform is akin to piecemeal change, which entails changing one or several parts of a system. Systemic change is more transformative; it involves changing all parts of a system.

While there are many definitions of systemic change, we believe this one hits the mark: *Systemic change is change that saturates all parts of a system and synchronizes those parts to create a mutually-desired outcome.* The two key components of this definition are *saturate* and *synchronize.* Saturate means the change must soak into all parts of the system. Synchronize means all parts must work together in harmony to achieve an outcome or change that all people agree is necessary. We will present a nine-step process that can be used to achieve the desired change.

Nine-Step Process for Change

The people—not the buildings—are the key "parts" of a school system, and they fall into one of six major groups: school boards, superintendents, principals, teachers, students, and stakeholders. For systemic change to occur, all of those parts must be saturated with a mindset that change is imperative, and the parts must work in harmony to achieve the desired change. The parts of a school system are randomly depicted in Diagram 3.

Diagram 3
Parts of a School System

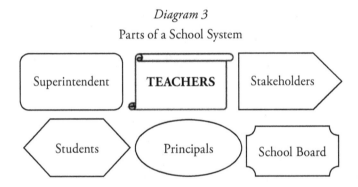

The entities in Diagram 3 represent a set of disjointed or separate parts of a school system. Each part has a different shape to indicate that they have different functions within the system. Typically, only a few parts are needed to make most changes in the system. For example, suppose there are 85 schools in a system and seven of them want to use SMART Boards instead of Promethean Boards in their classrooms. Would it be necessary for each of the six entities in Diagram 3 to be involved in that decision? Since this would involve piecemeal instead of systemic change, only two people are needed to make the change or reform. The principal would get input from teachers and then decide which interactive whiteboard to use.

Conversely, when systemic change is warranted, all parts of the system must come together and function as a unit. The only way to address systemic racism is through transformative or systemic change. School systems across America are infected with racism. If they want to fight that disease, they must saturate each part in Diagram 3 with a mindset that change is critical and necessary. Then these disjointed parts will become transformed into Diagram 4 and function as a synchronized unit to fight systemic racism.

Diagram 4
Parts of a School System Synchronized to Create Systemic Change

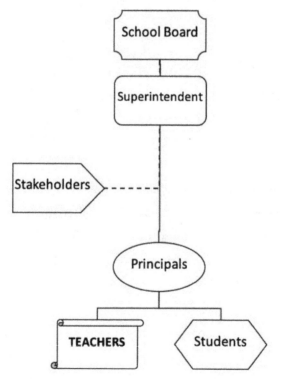

So, how does the change process begin? What is the triggering mechanism? And who is responsible for what? These are valid questions and, hopefully, all school systems across America are ready to pull the trigger and begin the process of eliminating systemic racism. The process for achieving systemic change involves developing and implementing a nine-step Strategic Plan (see Table 13).

Table 13

Nine Steps for a Strategic Plan

Step #	Description	Status
1	**Problem** must be acknowledged. *Throughout this book we have identified the problem as systemic racism, which is destroying and mutilating educational outcomes for black and brown students.*	Completed
2	**Causes** must be identified. *Systemic racism is caused by implicit and explicit biases that are held by educators. There is also a culture gap between teachers and their students.*	Completed
3	**Best Practices** must be explored. *A multicultural approach to pedagogy is essential.*	Completed
4	**Starting Point** must be determined. *In education, it is always prudent to address the instructional needs of your youngest and most vulnerable students first.*	Completed
5	**Emergency** must be declared.	Action Needed
6	**Strategic Plan** must be developed.	Action Needed
7	**Manage** the Plan.	Action Needed
8	**Implement** the Plan.	Action Needed
9	**Monitor** the Plan	Action Needed

It is vitally important to recognize that the nine steps for change in Table 13 involve a process, not an event. Meaningful change requires a change of heart, a change in beliefs or attitudes, and a change in practice. The effectiveness and sustainability of the nine steps in Table

13 will depend on the people who develop, manage, implement, and monitor the school system's strategic plan of action.

Step One in the nine-step process is to acknowledge that a *problem* exists. This book has chronicled the nature of the problem. Systemic racism in our nation's schools has perpetuated achievement gaps between students of color and their white counterparts.

Step Two requires school systems to identify the root *cause(s)* of the problem. Throughout this book, we have informed the reader of the debilitating effects that teacher-held biases and the culture gap have on student outcomes, especially for students of color. These are among the root causes of racism in our schools.

Step Three requires school systems to conduct research to identify evidence-based *best practices* that can be used to address the problem. We have conducted the research for you and identified a viable approach to address the race-based instructional challenges in our schools; namely—multicultural pedagogy.

Step Four provides the *starting point*. As always, it is sensible to address the instructional needs of your youngest and most vulnerable students first.

Thus, for each school system's convenience, this book has allowed us to complete the first four of the nine steps of a strategic plan to address systemic racism. The research has been reviewed and analyzed. You are aware of the nature of the problem (i.e., implicit and explicit racial bias) and the best practices (i.e., preschool education and multicultural pedagogy) that are needed to mitigate it. Steps Five through Nine require action. Each entity in the system plays a key role in completing those action steps, and their roles will be discussed in relation to the five remaining action steps.

Step Five: The school board must declare an *emergency.*

Communities typically elect a school board of five, seven, nine, or eleven trustees to oversee the local school district and make certain the desires of the community are met. As the governing body of the system, the school board has a responsibility to set a goal to protect all students and staff from anything that obstructs teaching and learning.

Systemic racism continues to cripple academic outcomes for a staggering number of children of color each year. A school board can (and must) sound the alarm and take decisive action in Step 5 to address the racial discrimination in schools that are under their jurisdiction. To that end, the school board must issue an official statement declaring that an emergency exists in their school system and give the superintendent a firm mandate to develop a Five-Year Strategic Plan. The plan will address racism with goals to have:

- ❖ The Teacher-Student gap closed
- ❖ High Expectations for all students
- ❖ Unbiased Student Discipline
- ❖ Multicultural Education
- ❖ Universal Pre-Kindergarten

Step Six: The superintendent must develop a five-year *strategic plan* of action. A school superintendent oversees the daily operations and long-range planning of a school district; supervises school principals and district staff; and works with the school board to manage fiscal operations. The superintendent is also responsible for preparing the agenda for school board meetings. The superintendent does sit in on all board meetings to make recommendations but is not allowed to vote on any of the issues. If the board votes to approve a mandate, then it is the superintendent's duty to carry out that mandate.

Once the school board issues its mandate, the superintendent must use all available resources to develop a comprehensive Five-Year Strategic Plan to combat systemic racism in the organization. The plan should be developed by a professional external vendor and updated every five years. The issues are far too sensitive and important to be placed into the hands of internal or inexperienced organizational planners. The superintendent should work collaboratively with the professional education firm or vendor throughout the process to ensure that all aspects of the school board's mandate are reflected in the plan. Accordingly, in Step Six:

- ❖ The Superintendent will hire a professional firm to develop a 5-year plan to address systemic racism in the school system.
- ❖ Areas of focus will include systemic racism in curriculum and instruction; hiring practices; student grading; and student discipline.
- ❖ The plan will include input from certified and classified employees, parents, teachers, students, and stakeholders.

Step Seven: Principals must *manage* the strategic plan. A principal is the instructional leader of a school. Principals who are effective leaders perform these duties and responsibilities well: Shape a vision of academic success for all students; facilitate a hospitable educational climate; improve classroom instruction; encourage others in leadership; and manage human and other resources and processes to foster continuous school improvement.

Once the Five-Year Strategic Plan is approved by the board, it is submitted to the superintendent for implementation. The superintendent should immediately meet with all principals in the system to make them aware of the importance of the plan and the expectations that are attached to it. As outlined in Step Seven, principals will bear the responsibility for managing the plans as follows:

- ❖ All principals will adopt a multicultural approach to pedagogy for teaching and learning in their schools.
- ❖ All teachers will receive ongoing, mandatory professional development in culturally responsive teaching strategies, which will facilitate student-teacher engagement and mitigate racial biases.
- ❖ All administrators will receive ongoing training in restorative justice and the principles of positive discipline to address disparities in student discipline.

Step Eight: Teachers must *implement* the strategic plan. The roles of teachers in today's multicultural society go beyond teaching. Some of those roles include being an external parent, counselor, mentor, and role model. Their primary role, however, is to engage students in classroom instruction to help them learn. The biggest impediment to classroom instruction is the culture gap between teachers and students, as well as their racial biases.

The successful mitigation of systemic racism in public education is largely contingent upon addressing those two factors—the culture gap and racial biases. The successful implementation of the strategic plan rests with the teachers because they have more direct contact with the largest and most important group in the school system, the s tudents. After receiving appropriate professional development to become certified as culturally competent teachers, they will begin to implement the key components of the plan in earnest as follows in Step Eight:

- ❖ Teachers will participate in ongoing professional development to become culturally competent instructors.
- ❖ They will use culturally responsive teaching strategies to better engage the culturally and racially diverse students in their classrooms.
- ❖ Teachers will make a commitment to have high expectations for all students, inclusive of every race, gender, religion, socioeconomic status, and culture.

The primary focus of the strategic plan is to mitigate the explicit and implicit racial biases that are directed at students of color. The evidence-based multicultural approach to pedagogy recognizes and embraces diversity by seeking ways to encourage student engagement. This is accomplished by creating a warm, positive, inclusive classroom where everyone feels like they belong. Ultimately, all students benefit from multicultural education, particularly in the areas of classroom engagement, cognitive development, and social and emotional learning.

Step Nine: Stakeholders must *monitor* the strategic plan. It is absolutely crucial to involve stakeholders in the planning and evaluation process. Once the school board sounds the alarm and declares the emergency, stakeholders or representatives in the community should be invited to contribute to the development of the 5-year plan. Community stakeholders include but are not limited to parents, members of faith-based groups, elected officials, small business owners, and former students.

While the superintendent and district-level staff will monitor the five-year plan internally to ensure continuous quality improvement, a process for external monitoring is equally as important to the overall success of the plan. Thus, Step Nine is outlined as follows:

❖ The school board will select an Oversight Committee consisting of at least five community stakeholders to monitor the progress of the plan on an ongoing basis.

❖ The committee will present progress reports to the board and community at least twice a year.

A SAMPLE PLAN WITH ONE GOAL

A strategic plan is a comprehensive document that tells people what the school system wants to achieve in the future and how it plans to get there. Developing that plan is an arduous process and should be conducted by a professional firm. A reputable firm such as the Cambridge Strategic Services or Taylor & Taylor Education Consultants should be hired to complete the planning process. Once the plan is written, the superintendent and staff should begin the process of implementing it.

A typical plan has three to five measurable systemwide goals that are targeted for completion within a five-year period. Those goals are determined by the school board with input from school staff and community stakeholders. For the purpose of illustration, we will develop a sample for one goal in a five-year plan to address the disproportionate suspension rates for black students. This is a national problem rooted in systemic racism.

The effects of school suspensions are well-documented. The

implicit bias of administrators often leads them to favor suspensions because they "push" black and brown students out of school. The students then lose valuable instruction and learning time. This time away from the classroom accumulates quickly and many black and brown students' grades drop as a result. Ultimately, repeated suspensions reduce the students' chances of graduating and impair their employment opportunities. Again, we will develop a sample for one possible measurable goal in a strategic plan, which is to reduce the disproportionate rate of suspensions for black students.

A. Description of the School District

Johnson County Public Schools (JCPS) is a hypothetical school system in the metropolitan area of Houston, Texas. It serves a highly diverse population of 155,000 students. Thirty-two percent of the students are black, 31% Hispanic, 22% white, 10% Asian, and 5% fall in the "other" category.

B. Statement of the Problem

In JCPS, black and Hispanic students are suspended at a disproportionate rate when compared to their white counterparts. Black students, in particular, are given out-of-school suspensions (OSS) at an alarmingly high rate. Although blacks represent only 32 percent of the student population in JCPS, they received 50 percent of the total number of OSS. This represents an 18-point "gap" or disparity. Hence, 50 minus 32 equals +18, which represents a high level of disproportionality or maltreatment. The hypothetical percent of OSS by race for the 2018-19 school year is presented in Table 14.

Table 14

Expected vs. Actual Percent of Out-of-School Suspensions for
Racial Subgroups based on Enrollment Percentages

Race	Expected Percent	Actual Percent	Disparity
Black	32	50	+18
Hispanic	31	35	+4
White	22	8	-14
Asian	10	2	-8
Other	5	5	0

Based on the data in Tables 14, this is the Statement of the Problem for JCPS:

Black students are given out-of-school suspensions at a significantly higher rate than their peers.

C. Measurable Goal

Goal #1: *Reduce the disparity (actual percent minus expected percent) for out-of-school suspensions for black students from +18 to zero over a five-year period.*

D. Action Steps to Achieve the Goal

To achieve the goal of reducing the 18-point disparity to zero in out-of-school suspensions for black students over a five-year period, JCPS must reduce the "gap" by an average of 3.6 points per year (5 x 3.6 = 18). These ongoing action steps (or strategies and activities) are designed to improve communication within the school system and community to reduce the disproportionate number of OSS for black students in JCPS:

1.1 Provide ongoing training in restorative justice for all administrators and staff members who issue suspensions to students.

1.2 Review the school district's discipline codes to ensure that they are appropriate and effective.

1.3 Monitor implementation of the discipline codes to ensure fair, unbiased and equitable administration.

1.4 Maintain a database on OSS disaggregated by student racial subgroups, school, grade levels, and type of infractions for each school in the district.

1.5 Generate and distribute individual monthly "discipline reports" to each school's principal.

1.6 Continually monitor the district's progress on reducing suspensions for black students.

1.7 Allocate resources to support and implement positive alternative-to-suspension programs.

1.8 Host ongoing discussions on school discipline to encourage community engagement, specifically the black community.

1.9 Provide ongoing professional development for teachers, administrators and other school staff that emphasizes the importance of evidenced-based positive school discipline, behavior management, cultural competence, and social justice and equity to meet the district's goals.

1.10 Prohibit school resource officers (SROs) from intervening in issues related to school discipline. This responsibility lies with school administrators, not SROs.

A district-level staff member should be assigned to monitor each step, and the Oversight Committee should receive quarterly written updates and briefings. The entire Five-Year Strategic Plan should be placed on the district's website for transparency and public viewing. The part of the plan that would address OSS is presented in Table 15. Anyone in the community should be able to look on the district's website to see the amount of progress that was being made toward reaching the goal of reducing the disproportionate out-of-school suspensions against black students from 50 percent to at least 32 percent, which is commensurate with their enrollment.

Table 15

JCPS Goal to Reduce the Disproportionate Percent of
Out-of-School Suspensions (OSS) for Black Students

School Level	Baseline	Year 1	Year 2	Year 3	Year 4	Year 5 (Goal)
Elementary (OSS)	50	37	36			*32*
Middle (OSS)	50	47	40			*32*
High (OSS)	50	45	41			*32*

NOTE: These are hypothetical data created by the co-authors for discussion purposes. Also, we are presenting the data in a format to indicate that there was no variation in OSS for black students across the three school levels. It was 50% (baseline) for all levels.

E. Financial Impact on the Budget

Strategic planning for every business requires weighing the pros and cons of any new intervention. In the corporate sector, this is usually done by conducting what is known as a cost-benefit analysis. In public education, which is funded primarily through tax revenue sources, the focus is primarily on the overall cost or *financial impact* the intervention would have on the school system's general fund.

The financial impact of mitigating disproportionate suspensions for black and brown students is minimal. Aside from the one-time fee the school system would pay a consulting firm to develop the 5-year strategic plan, there is virtually no cost involved. Schools simply need to change how they view, engage, instruct, and suspend students of color. And there are definite benefits because by eliminating frivolous and race-based suspensions—black and brown children will receive more classroom instruction, which would enhance their chances of graduating with their peers.

SUMMARY

Systemic racism is a loathsome disease that continues to divide our country. Social and economic institutions within our nation's infrastructure (e.g., health care, employment, housing, education, and criminal justice) continue to promote white privilege by discriminating against people of color. Racism in America's institution of K-12 public education is widespread and targets children of color. As lifelong educators, we can't think of anything more horrendous in public education than for a child to lose life or limb. Systemic racism does both. It either destroys or mutilates a child's educational dreams.

School systems across the nation are in a crisis because racism is gnawing away at our future. Racial inequity is baked into our education system, and black children face the most extreme hurdles to academic success. Within individual classrooms, teachers may mistake a black child's frown as an act of aggression instead of an expression of bewilderment. These scenarios often create tensions and, too often, result in a child receiving an unnecessary suspension from the classroom.

Inequities in our schools have compounded over the years. Some are deceptive and cloaked in implicit racial biases. These include persistent cultural messaging that black students are more physically aggressive and less academically capable than their white peers. Other inequities are overt and cloaked in explicit racial biases. These include school suspensions and arrests that are disproportionately imposed on black students.

This brings us back to the essential question that is posted at the beginning of this chapter: *How can schools mitigate the implicit racial biases that depress academic and behavioral outcomes for children of color?* School systems can accomplish this by declaring an emergency and developing a comprehensive Five-Year Strategic Plan to combat systemic racism in their schools. This chapter has outlined a nine-step process that can be used to create that outcome.

"Racism is a grown-up disease and we must stop
using our children to spread it."
— Ruby Bridges

CONCLUSION

THE PAST – THE PRESENT – THE FUTURE

In 1931, James Truslow Adams wrote an inspiring book titled *The Epic of America*. In that book, he stated that the American dream is: "That dream of a land in which life should be better and richer and fuller for everyone, with opportunity for each according to his ability or achievement...It's not a dream of motor cars and high wages merely, but a dream of social order in which each man and each woman shall be able to attain the fullest statue of which they are innately capable, and be recognized by others for what they are, regardless of the fortuitous circumstances of birth or position."

The last statement in the quote from Adams' book bears repeating: "regardless of the fortuitous circumstances of birth or position." This raises the question of race. Has race inhibited a person's ability to achieve the American dream of having a good job, a nice house and enough money to raise a family with access to reasonable comfort? Education was the pathway toward achieving the elusive American dream in the past; it remains the pathway in the present; and it will be the pathway in the future.

THE PAST

Throughout this country's history, the symbols of American democracy—opportunity, freedom, and prosperity—have been largely reserved for white people through the intentional exclusion and oppression of people of color. Harsh racial and ethnic inequalities were imposed during the Jim Crow era that were designed to create and maintain white supremacy. This system of explicit racism denied the overwhelming majority of black Americans access to the American dream.

A new American dream for black people emerged during the civil rights movement under the leadership of Dr. Martin Luther King, Jr. Under his leadership and prodding, some progress was made with dismantling some of the structural racism in America. The most sweeping changes in the 1960s and 1970s were wrapped in legislation that included voting rights, fair housing, equal employment opportunities, and the desegregation of schools.

The period between the 1980s and the first decade of the twenty-first century was somewhat of a golden age for blacks. While many of them were able to get a piece of the American dream, systemic racism continued to impose restrictions on their progress, especially in criminal justice and education. Blacks were incarcerated at a disproportionate rate, and the achievement gap between black and white students became a topic of discussion and negative messaging.

In the 1990s, the controversial book—*The Bell Curve*—claimed that the gaps in student achievement were the result of the so-called intellectual superiority of white students. This is a classic example of the use of systemic racism to denigrate and discriminate against blacks. Contrary to what proponents of white privilege would want to believe, the achievement gaps are primarily due to "opportunity gaps" in the resources available to students from disadvantaged versus advantaged households.

America's past was characterized by a society in which the doors to the American dream were not open to everyone. Despite their best efforts, many black people could never penetrate those doors. The face of systemic racism was bold and overt from the 1900s through the 1980s. Although it became more subtle and somewhat hidden during the period between the 1990s and 2019, systemic racism was just as prevalent and just as deadly.

Barack Obama's presence in the White House did not dismantle systemic racism; it only made most white-controlled institutions even more determined to promote white privilege. Essentially, many of the employment, housing, financial, and banking institutions remained "whites only" clubs. They controlled the resources blacks needed to pursue the American dream. While the American dream was alive and well for some people of color; for most of them—it remained just a dream.

THE PRESENT

The present began with the election of Donald Trump in 2016. Ever since his inauguration, the cultural climate in the United States has become increasingly more divisive and toxic. Hardly a day goes by without a tweet from his office about a fresh tale of political discord, "fake news" or social struggle. Opportunities for people of color to achieve economic success and social mobility through hard, honest work—the American dream—appeared to be dwindling.

While Trump touted the stock market as a measure of economic prosperity in the United States, which it isn't, systemic racism continued to promote white privilege and suppress the American dream for most people of color. Much of the racism was camouflaged and not visible to the naked eye. For example, on the surface, it seemed as if blacks were making gains in housing and wealth. In reality, whites were making economic gains at a much higher rate, and the "wealth gap" between blacks and whites was actually widening.

When the COVID-19 pandemic collided with the murder of George Floyd in 2020, it created an imperfect storm. Because of that storm, the rose-colored glasses were removed and the face of systemic racism was exposed. The world became equipped with 2020-vision and the imperfections in America's society were magnified. The world could see systemic racism more clearly; the picture was vivid. They could see how blacks were being marginalized through police brutality and racial discrimination. They could see how the ethos of white privilege was perpetuating "gaps" between black and white Americans in wealth, education, health care, housing, and criminal justice.

This clear vision of systemic racism sparked a global demand for social and economic justice for all. White privilege, which was viewed as exclusive and divisive, was upstaged by a more inclusive, uniting movement—Black Lives Matter. Billion-dollar institutions across the nation—such as Microsoft, Amazon, Google, and others—took homage and pledged their support for a more inclusive America where black lives did, indeed, matter. In perhaps one of the most surprising displays of solidarity, the state of Mississippi passed legislation in June 2020 to officially remove the Confederate symbol from its flag.

America's new 2020-vision also allowed people to see how both implicit and explicit racial biases were impacting many children of color in public education. This became even more noticeable because, in the year 2020, children of color became the majority in public schools across the entire United States. The year 2020 marked a pivotal time for school boards across America to develop strategic plans to mitigate systemic racism in public education. This book provides the steps needed to help develop those plans.

Presently, there are indications that some sustainable changes are occurring in America to mitigate systemic racism. It is our duty to maintain the momentum, sustain the current improvements, and seek more change. By working together—America can achieve even greater heights of excellence.

THE FUTURE

We should look into the future of America with guarded optimism. The awakening to systemic racism has created a sea change that, in all probability, the next generation will advance even further. An ongoing explosion in diversity will change the "color" of America. By 2045, the Census Bureau projects that the United States will become a "minority white" nation. Whites will make up 49.7 percent of the population as compared to 24.6 percent for Hispanics, 13.1 percent for blacks, 7.9 percent for Asians, and 3.8 percent for multiracial populations.

There is hope that the future leadership of America will be more diverse, more inclusive, and less tolerant of racism. Twelve-year-old Taylor McCray—a bright, well-rounded African American girl at North Gwinnett (GA) Middle School—provides a glimpse of what the future leadership in America would look like. When asked what she thought racism in America would look like in 20 years, Taylor replied:

> "I hope it's not [an issue] but with the changes that people are trying to make there's a chance it [racism] won't still be a problem. Especially, because the new generations—Gen Z—are more united than the previous generations. The next generations have the power to fix what the previous generations have done involving the Earth and racism."

Enough said. They "have the power to fix it."

> "As a nation and as a people, we're going to get there. We're going to make it. We're going to survive and there will be no turning back."
>
> – U.S. Congressman John R. Lewis
> February 21, 1940 – July 17, 2020

ACKNOWLEDGEMENTS

With so much inspiration coming from so many people, where do we begin with our acknowledgments and words of thanks? It's only fitting that we begin at the beginning and give special thanks to our parents. They provided real-time inspiration to us as we delved into America's ugly past in *The Imperfect Storm*. Our parents experienced the full gamut of Jim Crow laws. Their ability to rise above systemic racism and oppression has inspired many generations to remain steadfast and unmovable as they continue to pursue their dreams.

For much of her adult life, Jim's mother—the late Hattie Elizabeth Taylor—was a single parent who raised three children. Despite having to deal with economic hardships, she always stressed the importance of "getting a good education" and her children complied; we all have college degrees. We thank Mom for her tenacity, her wisdom, her inspiration and, above all—her love.

Wandy's mother—Grace Wallace—has provided immeasurable inspiration to us; simply through the life she has lived. She completed two years of college, raised ten children, earned a certificate as a technology specialist, and worked 30 years outside the home during that time. Mom's dedication to her family and the values she instilled in us have never changed. She has amazing strength and an uncompromising spirit that touches the lives of everyone she meets.

Wandy's father—Norris Wallace, Jr—is truly a living legend who embodies the essence of inspiration. He is a retired educator and judge who has lived a life that brings this book alive. He has seen it all. While raising a family of ten children in the Jim Crow South, Judge Wallace ensured that each of them understood their value, their worth, and their potential—regardless of the circumstances. Pride and dignity were fundamental in all that he taught and provided the foundation for Wandy to become the strong educational leader she has become today. Dad, we can't find the words to thank you enough for all you have done.

Lucille Swain, our godmother, celebrated her 100th birthday in 2020. What a blessing! She lives in Brooklyn, NY, and is a walking, talking history book. She continues to be an absolute marvel because of her sharp mind, elegant style, spirituality, and kind heart. Anyone who knows "Aunt Lue" comes away as a better person. She reminds us to be kind and to value each day as another gift of life.

When we look at our five adult children a broad smile creases our face, and we are overcome with pride and joy. They are our inspiration, and we never hesitated to get real-time input from them while writing this book. After all, three of them are educators! Eric is an administrator in Wake County (NC), and Nikki and Brittany are teachers in Georgia. Our oldest son, Terry, owns a business in real estate and Jay works as a medical technician. Our children always inspire us and they are living examples that the true measures of success are character and hard work—not the color of their skin!

We realize that some of the best gifts and sources of inspiration come in small packages. Our children have blessed us with ten wonderful grandchildren: Janai, Terrence Jr. (TJ), Jaylin, Erykah, Christian, Carter, Taryn, Savon, Taylor, and Kamryn. They inspire us every day, and we know they will learn valuable lessons about life from *The Imperfect Storm* and use them to help make America a better place for everyone.

Special thanks and acknowledgements are extended to Brianna McGagin (our niece), Tammy Wallace (our sister), Shaminy Manoranjithan (teacher), Tanisha Banks (teacher), Karen Watkins (school board member), Dr. Tarece Johnson (school board member), Rep. Donna McLeod (advocate for social justice), Dr. Noreen Freeman (assistant principal), Dr. Nikki Mouton (education administrator), and Dr. Sharon Smith (educator) for providing valuable insights that were used in our book.

And we thank our pastor—the Reverend Dr. Richard B. Haynes— for the inspiration he always provides through his thought-provoking sermons.

Last, but not least, our greatest source of inspiration continues to flow from our Lord and Savior—Jesus Christ. Through Him all things are possible and through His will we were able to write *The Imperfect Storm.*

NOTES

Introduction

xi **The term "perfect storm" was first used on May 30, 1850**. See blog in Grammarphobia by Patricia T. O'Conner and Stewart Kellerman (May 8, 2009) titled *The Imperfect Storm*. Retrieved from: https://www.grammarphobia.com/blog/2008/05/the-imperfect-storm.html

xii **teachers' biases lead to lower academic.** In his article, *Teacher racial bias matters more for students of color*, Hua-Yu Sebastian Cherng, assistant professor of international education at NYU, discusses the impact of implicit bias on outcomes for students of color. https://phys.org/news/2017-05-teacher-racial-bias-students.html

xii **schools are becoming increasingly more racially and culturally diverse.** Article by Grace Chen titled *White Students are Now the Minority in Public Schools*. Appeared in School Review on October 14, 2019. https://www.publicschoolreview.com/blog/white-students-are-now-the-minority-in-u-s-public-schools

xiii **"Racial Disparities in School Discipline are Growing, Federal Data Show"** See article by Moriah Balingit in the Washington Post on April 24, 2018.

xiii **Despite numerous efforts to contain and mitigate COVID-19.** The Centers for Diseases and Control provided ongoing updates and guidance on its website to keep people informed during the epidemic. https://www.cdc.gov/coronavirus/2019-ncov/cases-updates/cases-in-us.html

xiii **injecting disinfectants to kill the virus**. See article on the BBC titled *Coronavirus: Outcry after Trump suggests injecting disinfectant as treatment.* Retrieved from: https://www.bbc.com/news/world-us-canada-52407177

xiv **James Baldwin** 's quote https://www.kinfolk.com/confronting-history-james-baldwin/

Chapter 1

2 **"I did something good: I made Juneteenth very famous."** See article in Forbes by Tommy Beer on June 18, 2020. https://www.forbes.com/sites/tommybeer/2020/06/18/trump-claims-nobody-had-ever-heard-of-juneteenth-before-he-made-it-very-famous/#130be50b133e

2 **Story of Margaret Crittenden Douglass.** Portrayed online at Education @ Library of Virginia. https://edu.lva.virginia.gov/online_classroom/shaping_the_constitution/doc/margaret_douglass

3 **Ideology of Two Black Scholars**. The Debate between W.E.B. Dubois and Booker T. Washington. See on a site called Frontline. https://www.pbs.org/wgbh/frontline/article/debate-w-e-b-du-bois-and-booker-t-washington/

3 **Booker T. Washington encouraged blacks to distinguish themselves through hard work**. DuBois urged blacks to get an education in the liberal arts. See book - The African Americans: Many Rivers to Cross (1st ed.). USA: Smiley Books by Gates & Yacovone (2013) pages 173-182.

5 **Money Matters** See *How Money Matters for Schools*. School Finance series in Learning Policy Institute by B. Baker, July 17, 2018. https://learningpolicyinstitute.org/product/how-money-matters-brief

5 **Louisiana law** See brief written on 5-11-20 by Brian Duignan that provides an overview of the *Plessy v. Ferguson* Supreme Court decision of 1896. Retrieved from https://www.britannica.com/event/Plessy-v-Ferguson-1896

5 **"Social psychologist Kenneth Clark"** conducted a classic doll study in 1939. One of the authors, J.A. Taylor, replicated this study in 1975 for an unpublished master's thesis at the University of South Carolina titled – *Racial Preference and Social Comparison Processes – 36 Years Later.*

6 Ibid

7 **most black children today appear to have high levels of self-esteem and self-confidence.** See manuscript by Okeke-Adeyanju, Taylor et al. titled Celebrating the Strengths of Black Youth: Increasing Self-esteem and Implications for Prevention. 2014. Retrieved from: https://www.ncbi.nlm.nih.gov/pmc/articles/PMC4152398/

7 **"To separate [black children] from others of similar age…"** Chief Justice Earl Warren's written opinion on the U.S. Supreme Court's decision in Brown v. Board of Education http://landmarkcases.c-span.org/pdf/Brown_Warren_Opinion.pdf

7 **school buildings for blacks had leaking roofs** See Jim Crow's Schools by Peter Irons. Retrieved from: https://www.aft.org/periodical/american-educator/summer-2004/jim-crows-schools

8 **Julius Rosenwald** and "Rosenwald Schools" Much of Information for the section on school facilities for blacks during the Jim Crow era was taken from National Park Service's website, *The Rosenwald Schools: Progressive Era in Philanthropy in the Segregated South (Teaching with Historic Places)* https://www.nps.gov/articles/the-rosenwald-schools-progressive-era-philanthropy-in-the-segregated-south-teaching-with-historic-places.htm

9 Ibid

9 **the intent of equalization programs throughout the South.** See *Equalization Schools: A Lesson in Education and Civil Rights* by Sophia Dembling (September 3, 2015) Retrieved from: https://savingplaces.org/stories/equalization-schools-a-lesson-in-education-and-civil-rights#.XwfYBihKiUk

10 **Harvard Civil Rights Project, our nation's schools became increasingly more segregated.** See brief posted on the Harvard Graduate School of Education titled *School Segregation on the Rise Despite Growing Diversity among School-Aged Children.* Retrieved from https://www.gse.harvard.edu/news/school-segregation-rise-despite-growing-diversity-among-school-aged-children#:~:text=Almost%20a%20half%20century%20after,to%20intensify%20throughout%20the%201990s.

10 **School facilities can have a profound impact on outcomes** for both students and teachers. https://sites.psu.edu/ceepa/2015/06/07/the-importance-of-school-facilities-in-improving-student-outcomes/#:~:text=A%20growing%20body%

20of%20research,both%20teacher%20and%20student%20outcomes.&text=
With%20respect%20to%20students%2C%20school,learning%2C%20and%20
growth%20in%20achievement.

12 **Freedom Schools**. The article titled, *Exploring the History of Freedom Schools*, on the Civil Rights Teaching website provides an in-depth discussion of how the SNCC set up freedom schools in Mississippi during 1964. See https://www. civilrightsteaching.org/voting-rights/exploring-history-freedom-schools/

13 Ibid

13 **over 200 students in two all-black high schools…suspended**. See article by John Hale (1-8-18) titled Student Activism and the Mississippi Freedom Struggle. Retrieved from: https://www.aaihs.org/student-activism-and-the-mississippi-freedom-struggle/

14 **Marian Wright Edelman's** CDF Freedom Schools. https://www.childrensdefense. org/about/leadership-and-staff/leadership/

15 **Georgia spent $32 on each white child and just $7 on those that were black.** See comprehensive article by Peter Irons (2004) titled, *Jim Crow's Schools*. Retrieved from https://www.aft.org/periodical/american-educator/summer-2004/ jim-crows-schools

15 **Dine Hollow reflected the widespread findings across the 17 Jim Crow states**. See comprehensive article by Peter Irons (2004) titled, *Jim Crow's Schools*. Retrieved from https://www.aft.org/periodical/american-educator/summer-2004/ jim-crows-schools

16 Ibid

18 *"If we can organize the Southern States for massive resistance"* Retrieved from: https://www.lva.virginia.gov/exhibits/brown/resistance.htm#:~:text=%22If%20we%20 can%20organize%20the,campaign%20of%20delay%20and%20obfuscation

18 **"Massive Resistance"** to integration led by Senator Harry Byrd. Virginia Museum of History & Culture. https://www.virginiahistory.org/collections-and-resources/ virginia-history-explorer/civil-rights-movement-virginia/massive

18 **Little Rock Nine**. See History.com. https://www.history.com/topics/black-history/ central-high-school-integration

19 **Governor Faubus**. *Brown vs. Board of Education Documentary*. [You Tube}. This highly-informative 9-minute, 59-second video by Dapper Gaming (September 15, 2011) gives still photos and a narrative of the Little Rock Nine. The viewer becomes aware that Jim Crow was a cartoon-like character who mocked black people. https://www.youtube.com/watch?v=PLDlqiKXquo

20 Ibid

21 **Ruby Bridges**. *Biography*. June 22, 2020. https://www.biography.com/activist/ruby-bridges

23 **In 1996, Ruby and Mrs. Henry were reunited** on an episode of the *Oprah Winfrey Show*. See https://www.youtube.com/watch?v=qwb5xsRO1yc

23 **Kerner Commission** or National Advisory Commission on Civil Disorders. Summary Report. http://www.eisenhowerfoundation.org/docs/kerner.pdf

25 **"one black, one white; separate and unequal"** See Smithsonian Magazine, *The 1968 Kerner Commission Got it Right, But Nobody Listened.* https://www.smithsonianmag.com/smithsonian-institution/1968-kerner-commission-got-it-right-nobody-listened-180968318/

26 Ibid

27 **"Education has enhanced my senses…"** quote created by the co-author, Jim Taylor.

Chapter 2

28 **Shifting demographics**. See 2019 article by Grace Chen titled *White Students are Now the Minority in U.S. Public Schools* on https://www.publicschoolreview.com/blog/white-students-are-now-the-minority-in-u-s-public-schools

29 Ibid

30 **Seven major characteristics of culture**. See https://historyplex.com/characteristics-of-culture

31 Ibid

33 **"Aurat aiee, aurat aiee, tharki teri shaamath aiee!"** See article In NPR by Bina Shah (March 15, 2018) titled *Women in Pakistan Dared to March – And*

Didn't Care What Men Thought. Retrieved from: https://www.npr.org/sections/goatsandsoda/2018/03/15/593549219/women-in-pakistan-dared-to-march-and-didnt-care-what-men-thought

33 **Awá tribe in Brazil.** See article in USA Today (11-26-18) by Josh Hafner titled Many isolated tribes, like Sentinelese that killed American, still exist. Here's where. Retrieved from https://www.usatoday.com/story/news/nation/2018/11/26/beyond-north-sentinel-uncontacted-isolated-tribes/2117381002/

34 **the Kente cloth is a symbol of West African culture. See article by James Padilioni (May 22, 2017) in Black Perspectives titled *The History and Significance of Kente Cloth in the Black Diaspora*. Retrieved from:** https://www.aaihs.org/the-history-and-significance-of-kente-cloth-in-the-black-diaspora/

35 **Generation gaps**. Boomers, Gen X, Gen Y, and Gen Z Explained. See Kasasa. June 18, 2020. https://www.kasasa.com/articles/generations/gen-x-gen-y-gen-z

35 **Baby Boomers, Millennials, Generation Z.** See article by Ryback for characteristics of each generation. https://www.psychologytoday.com/us/blog/the-truisms-wellness/201602/baby-boomers-generation-z

36 **"a generation whose worldview is based on change"** See book edited by Christine Henseler titled Generation X Goes Global: Mapping a Youth Culture in Motion (1st ed). ISBN-13: 978-0415699440

37 **"Me-Me Generation"** See https://time.com/247/millennials-the-me-me-me-generation/

38 **more minority babies than white babies were born.** See article in Bloomberg by Frank Bass (5-17-12) titled *Nonwhite US Births Become the Majority for First Time*. Retrieved from: https://www.bloomberg.com/news/articles/2012-05-17/non-white-u-s-births-become-the-majority-for-first-time

40 **elements of a great workplace**. See article titled *Six Things to Build a Successful Workplace Culture and one to Tolerate*. https://www.forbes.com/sites/davidsturt/2018/11/05/6-things-to-build-a-successful-workplace-culture-and-1-to-tolerate/#2cf1c42f54fa

42 **"In fact, Mexico has the second largest professional diaspora in the United States."** Jonathan Karl of ABC News interviews Mexican Diplomat Claudia

Ruiz Massieu https://www.gob.mx/sre/en/articulos/crm-the-best-way-to-counter-misinformation-and-stereotypes-is-to-speak-with-facts-information-and-truth

43 **Cultural differences in the workplace**. See *Five Ways to Overcome Cultural Barriers at Work* by J. Whitmire. June 6, 2016. https://www.entrepreneur.com/article/276998

43 **the same explosion in diversity**. See Status and Trends in the Education of Racial and Ethnic Groups.

https://nces.ed.gov/pubs2019/2019038.pdf

44 **In California, for example, only 40 percent of the teachers are nonwhite**. See article (January 6, 2019) in Ed Source by Phillip Reese titled *With new hires, California's teaching corps become more diverse* Retrieved from: https://edsource.org/2019/with-new-hires-californias-teaching-corps-becomes-more-diverse/606370

44 **Community meeting held to offensive and inappropriate racist comments at Saline Area Schools**. See ABC News. https://abcnews.go.com/US/high-school-students-sue-michigan-administrators-suspensions-alleged/story?id=68936870

44 **Racial tension at Key Elementary School**. See article by Perry Stein, *A White Child Called Three Black Classmates a Racial Slur* in the Washington Post, March 12, 2019. https://www.washingtonpost.com/

45 **"It is important that we understand the role that implicit bias."** See *The Effects of Implicit Bias in Schools* by Gullo and Beachum (May 9, 2017). https://whyy.org/articles/essay-the-negative-effects-of-implicit-bias-in-schools/

47 **A study by Dr. Walter Gilliam of Yale**. See *The Role of Implicit Bias in Early Childhood Setting* by Marsha Basloe. https://www.childcareservices.org/2019/04/16/the-role-of-implicit-bias-in-early-childhood-settings/

47 **"the degree of attention, curiosity..."** See Glossary of Education Reform. Retrieved from: https://www.edglossary.org/student-engagement/

47 **Jenny Fulton** (2019). *Three Kinds of Engagement*. https://www.classcraft.com/blog/features/evidence-of-student-engagement/

50 **Audre Lorde** quote retrieved from: https://www.brainyquote.com/quotes/audre_lorde_390625

Chapter 3

51 **"This is the value of the teacher…"** See *What Makes an Extraordinary Teacher?* by P.B. Paresky, June 18, 2015. https://www.psychologytoday.com/us/blog/happiness-and-the-pursuit-leadership/201506/what-makes-extraordinary-teacher

53 **almost half of the teachers in the U.S. actively looking for another job** See article by Shane McFeely (March 27, 2018) titled *Why your Best Teachers are Leaving and 4 Ways to Keep Them.* Retrieved from: https://www.gallup.com/education/237275/why-best-teachers-leaving-ways-keep.aspx

53 **"When the elephants fight, it's the grass that suffers."** https://africageographic.com/stories/elephants-fight-grass-suffers/

53 **Sheldon Davis.** Interview on May 9, 2020.

54 **having just one – just one! – black teacher.** See article by Lauren Camera (Nov. 23, 2018) titled *Black Teachers Improve Outcomes from Black Students.* Retrieved from: https://www.usnews.com/news/education-news/articles/2018-11-23/black-teachers-improve-outcomes-for-black-students#:~:text=It%20found%20that%20having%20just,out%20by%20nearly%2040%20percent.

54 **Four of the most popular alternative programs.** See *The Fastest Way to Become a Teacher – Obtain a Certification in Record Time* by Lizzie Perrin, July 2, 2018. https://www.noodle.com/articles/fastest-way-to-become-a-teacher

56 **Gallup poll** shows teacher shortage in the U.S. *How to Fight the Growing Teacher Shortage* by Tim Hodges (March 15, 2019). https://www.gallup.com/education/247727/fight-growing-teacher-shortage.aspx?g_source=link_WWWV9&g_medium=TOPIC&g_campaign=item_&g_content=How%2520to%2520Fight%2520the%2520Growing%2520Teacher%2520Shortage

56 **"completely unprepared" or "mostly Unprepared."** See article, *Many White Teachers and Principals Feel Unprepared to Serve Diverse Students,* by Kim Doleatto in Herald-Tribune (September 2, 2019). https://www.heraldtribune.com/news/20190902/many-white-teachers-and-principals-feel-unprepared-to-serve-diverse-students

57 **teachers in New Jersey** See Op-ed by Darlyne DeHaan (January 24, 2020) titled *Teachers in NJ not Equipped to teach English Language Learners.* Retrieved

from: https://www.njspotlight.com/2020/01/op-ed-many-nj-teachers-are-not-equipped-to-educate-english-language-learners/

57 **"Diversity in the classroom was not a topic of discussion when I was in college in the 1980s."** Interview with Barbara Thompson on May 9, 2020.

58 **"I think the training I received at Teach for America prepared me well for the challenges I faced."** Interview with Brianna McGagin on June 2, 2020.

59 **"self-efficacy"** in preservice programs. See *How Do Sources of Self-Efficacy Predict Preservice Teachers' Beliefs Related to Constructivist and Traditional Approaches to Teaching and Learning?* *by* Cansiz & Cansiz (October 23, 2019). https://journals.sagepub.com/doi/full/10.1177/2158244019885125

60 **Enrollment in teacher preparation programs nationwide has declined.** *Sharp Nationwide Enrollment Drop in Teacher Prep Programs Cause for Alarm* by Lauren Camera, December 3, 2019. US News. https://www.usnews.com/news/education-news/articles/2019-12-03/sharp-nationwide-enrollment-drop-in-teacher-prep-programs-cause-for-alarm

62 **The Most Common Types of Teacher Professional Development.** *See* Schoology Exchange. (August 30, 2018). https://www.schoology.com/blog/three-most-common-types-teacher-professional-development-and-how-make-them-better

63 **after reading a news article in the** *Gwinnett Daily Post* **about her proposal to the school board.** (Note. Dr. Wandy Taylor is the co-author of this book, and the focus of her EdD dissertation was in the area of multicultural education). See article by Keith Famer (4-16-15) in the Gwinnett Daily Post titled *Gwinnett County Schools seeks to develop cultural competency, inclusiveness.* Retrieved from: https://www.gwinnettdailypost.com/archive/gwinnett-county-schools-seeks-to-develop-cultural-competency-inclusiveness/article_219b9478-262f-5620-b78a-f2aac73d0cf6.html

64 **Anderson & Ward Consulting Services** See https://www.andersonward education.com/

Chapter 4

67 **This gap, along with the implicit racial biases**. *See the Elephant in the Classroom.* The Grade Network. https://www.thegraidenetwork.com/blog-all/2018/8/1/teacher-bias-the-elephant-in-the-classroom

68 **Multicultural education**. See site at Univ. of Washington https://education.uw.edu/cme/view

70 **Cultural competence is a key factor**. See Diversity Toolkit: Cultural Competence for Educators. NEA. http://www.nea.org/tools/30402.htm

71 Ibid

73 **culturally responsive teaching (CRT) refers**. See unpublished dissertation (January 2015) by Wandy W. Taylor titled *Using Culturally Responsive Teaching Strategies to Impact Teachers' Perception of Classroom Engagement in a Culturally Diverse Title I Elementary School: An Action Research Study.* Published by Pro Quest. UMI Number: 37022771

73 **"a pedagogy that empowers students intellectually, socially, emotionally, and politically..."** The Dreamkeepers: Successful Teachers of African American Children by Gloria Ladson-Billings. (p. 13) ISBN-13: 978-0470408155

73 **"Culturally responsive pedagogy is a student-centered approach..."** See article by Matthew Lynch, *What is Culturally Responsive Pedagogy?,* The Edvocate website (April 21, 2016) https://www.theedadvocate.org/what-is-culturally-responsive-pedagogy/

73 Ibid

74 **So, what does CRT look like in the classroom?** See article titled *Culturally Responsive Teaching: What You Need to Know.* It also shows a You Tube video by educators with a group known as Understood. https://www.understood.org/en/school-learning/for-educators/universal-design-for-learning/what-is-culturally-responsive-teaching?utm_source=google&utm_medium=paid&utm_campaign=evrgrn-may20-edu&gclid=EAIaIQobChMIxMOXuO226gIVhJ6zCh38dAQLEAMYASAAEgIqffD_BwE

75 Ibid

76 **negative teacher expectations account for approximately five to 10 percent.** See article by L. Loewus in Education Week (1-16-13) titled *Research Review: Teacher Expectations Matter*. Retrieved from: https://blogs.edweek.org/teachers/teaching_now/2013/01/research_review_teacher_expectations_matter.html

78 **"being authentic with your students."** Conversation with Shaminy Manoranjithan on June 5, 2020.

79 **"Jighaboos."** See Travis Gettys' article, Texas nicknames her class 'Jighaboos' – then claims she didn't know the word is a racial slur: https://www.rawstory.com/2016/09/texas-teacher-nicknames-class-her-jighaboos-then-claims-she-didnt-know-word-is-a-racial-slur/

80 **Taylor Model** designed by the authors, co-owners of Taylor & Taylor Education Consultants, LLC.

82 **"Great teachers have…"** https://www.goodreads.com/quotes/1012798-great-teachers-have-high-expectations-for-their-students-but-even

Chapter 5

84 **Florida, Georgia, and Oklahoma are the only states that offer universal pre-K.** See brief by Amanda Rock, April 9, 2020. https://www.verywellfamily.com/universal-pre-k-2764970

84 **Soviet Union (USSR) launched Sputnik.** See Dissertation by H. Cha regarding its impact on education in America. https://tigerprints.clemson.edu/cgi/viewcontent.cgi?article=2551&context=all_dissertations

84 **many black children did not have access to the nation's initial STEM.** See Stephen DeAngelis' article titled *STEM Education: We Need another Sputnik Moment* (Marcch13, 2015). Retrieved from: https://www.enterrasolutions.com/blog/stem-education-need-another-sputnik/

85 **Project Head Start** https://www.acf.hhs.gov/ohs/about/history-of-head-start

86 **"If an unfriendly foreign power had attempted to impose on America…"** *A Nation at Risk Turns 30: Where Did it Take US?* by Edward Graham, NEA

Today (April 25, 2013) http://neatoday.org/2013/04/25/a- nation-at-risk-turns-30-where-did-it-take-us-2/

87 Ibid

87 **No Child Left Behind Act (NCLB).** George W. Bush. Executive Summary. US Department of Education. https://www2.ed.gov/nclb/overview/intro/execsumm.html

88 **Every Student Succeeds Act (ESSA).** Barack H. Obama. US Department of Education. https://www.ed.gov/essa?src=rn

88 **Twenty-three states were awarded three-year PDGB-5 grants for 2020.** Retrieved from: https://www.ffyf.org/preschool-development-grant-funding-awarded-to-26-states-for-2020/

90 **collapse of the Soviet Union on December 25, 1991.** https://www.ducksters.com/history/cold_war/collapse_soviet_union.php

91 **the "Coleman Report."** See article by Eric Hanushek titled, *What Matters for Student Achievement?* Education Next. https://www.educationnext.org/what-matters-for-student-achievement/

92 **"The Nation's Report Card"** All Data in the Tables and discussion for the NAEP Report's Reading & Math Assessments (Grades 4&8) were retrieved from: https://www.nationsreportcard.gov/mathematics/supportive_files/2019_infographic.pdf

96 **The Program for International Student Assessment (PISA).** All data that generated discussion were retrieved from the NCES website: https://nces.ed.gov/surveys/pisa/pisa2018/#/

98 **Both assessments (TIMSS & TIMSS-A).** All data for the discussion and the table were retrieved from https://nces.ed.gov/timss/timss2015/

100 **Nadia Comaneci began…at the age of six.** See article by Eli Laskey in Tie Breaker (December 12, 2010)

titled, Olympian Nadia Comaneci's Improbable Story of Success and Survival. https://www.tiebreaker.com/nadia-comaneci-improbable-story-success-survival/

101 **early brain development has a lasting impact...** See "Brain Development" on First Things First website: https://www.firstthingsfirst.org/early-childhood-matters/brain-development/

101 **there is a 30-million word-gap between children...**See article title *Let's Stop Talking about the 30 Million Word Gap* (June 1, 2018) by A. Kamenetz on NPR website: https://www.npr.org/sections/ed/2018/06/01/615188051/lets-stop-talking-about-the-30-million-word-gap

102 **conducted a study to evaluate the vocabulary gap.** Article by B. *Carey titled Language gap between rich and poor children begins in infancy, Sandford psychologists find.* Located in Stanford News (Sep. 2013). https://news.stanford.edu/news/2013/september/toddler-language-gap-091213.html#:~:text=Fernald%20suggests%20that%20slower%20processing,any%20new%20words%20that%20follow.

103 **"It is easier to build strong children than to repair broken men."** Quote by Frederick Douglass https://www.brainyquote.com/quotes/frederick_douglass_201574

103 **Perry Preschool Project.** See the Evidence Summary compiled by Social Programs that Work organization: https://evidencebasedprograms.org/document/perry-preschool-project-evidence-summary/

104 Ibid

114 **77 percent of the children in the program group graduated from high school.** See data dashboard https://highscope.org/perry-preschool-project/

115 Ibid

106 **latest results from this ongoing longitudinal study....of Perry participants at age 50-55.** Article compiled by L. Mongeau (May 14, 2019) for Hechinger Report. https://hechingerreport.org/sending-your-boy-to-preschool-is-great-for-your-grandson-new-research-shows/

106 **The Abecedarian Project.** See the summary compiled by Social Programs that Work organization. https://evidencebasedprograms.org/programs/abecedarian-project/

107 **Abecedarian group (1) had significantly higher scores on cognitive tests.** See *Groundbreaking Follow-up Studies* retrieved from: https://abc.fpg.unc.edu/groundbreaking-follow-studies

108 **In the mid-1960s, three major problems plagued Chicago's west side.** The history of the program is posted on Chicago Public Schools' website: https://cps. edu/Schools/EarlyChildhood/Pages/Childparentcenter.aspx

109 **Each site also had a Head Teacher.** This document provides a comprehensive history and overview of the Child-Parent Centers in the program. http://clstudy. org/Ch2/Index.html

109 **a federally-funded investigation of the CPCs was led by Arthur Reynolds of the University of Minnesota.** See University of Minnesota website with links to data for the Chicago Longitudinal Study: https://innovation.umn.edu/cls/

110 **"every dollar we invest in high-quality early education..."** See full transcript of Obama's 2013 State of the Union Address: https://obamawhitehouse. archives.gov/the-press-office/2013/02/12/remarks-president-state-union-address

111 **"Studies show students grow up more likely to read and do math at grade level..."** See full transcript of Obama's 2013 State of the Union Address: https:// obamawhitehouse.archives.gov/the-press-office/2013/02/12/remarks-president-state-union-address

112 Ibid

112 **After a thorough evaluation of 21 public preschool programs.** See article by Meloy, Gardner, and Darling-Hammond titled Untangling the Evidence on Preschool Effectiveness: Insights for Policy Makers (January 31, 2019): https:// learningpolicyinstitute.org/product/untangling-evidence-preschool-effectiveness-report

113 **Each state has its own formula.** See data for each state at: https:// worldpopulationreview.com/state-rankings/per-pupil-spending-by-state

114 *The State of Preschool 2019,* **the National Institute for Early Education Research (NIEER).** The NIEER's website provides tons of data at: http://nieer. org/state-preschool-yearbooks/2019-2

116 **In 2013, President Obama announced his bold** *Preschool for All* **proposal...** See article by Bornfreund and Loewenberg titled *The Obama Early Childhood Legacy* in New America Weekly (Dec. 15, 2016). https://www.newamerica.org/weekly/obama-early-childhood-legacy/

116 **following evidence-based building blocks … early childhood education programs**. See six-page brief by M. Wechsler et. al. on https://learningpolicyinstitute. org/sites/default/files/product-files/LPI_ECE-quality-brief_WEB-022916.pdf

117 Ibid

118 **Good to Great** by Jim Collins. Harper Business. 2001. ISBN 0-06-662099-6

120 Photo of Kamryn McCray 2 ½ years old and ready for school! She's also our granddaughter.

120 **"The goal of early childhood education…"** Quote by Dr. Maria Montessori https://www.applemontessorischools.com/montessori-quotes/

Chapter 6

122 Under President Lyndon B. Johnson…signed (ESEA) into law in1965. See ESEA Network at https://www.eseanetwork.org/about/esea

123 **Barack Hussein Obama II**. Biography: https://www.biography.com/ us-president/barack-obama

124 Ibid

125 **"I am the son of a black man from Kenya and a white woman from Kansas."** See the full transcript of Obama's March 18, 2008 speech: https://www.npr.org/templates/ story/story.php?storyId=88478467

126 **his first book, titled *Dreams from My Father*.** See three-part summary of the Obama's book: https://www.supersummary.com/dreams-from-my-father/summary/

127 Ibid

127 **"we're still locked in this notion that if you appeal to white folks…"** See article by William Douglas in The Mercury News (8-10-07) titled *Obama answers question: Is he 'black enough'?* Retrieved from: https://www.mercurynews. com/2007/08/10/obama-answers-question-is-he-black-enough/

128 **Arne Duncan was confirmed by the U.S. Senate on January 20, 2009**. See Duncan's bio and accomplishments: https://ballotpedia.org/Arne_Duncan

129 **Obama signed sweeping education reform.** The highlights of Obama's education plan were taken from this book: The Obama Education Plan: An Education Week Guide by Education Week Press and Jossey Bass 2009.

130 **Common Core.** See article by Robert Rothman titled Five Myths About the Common Core State Standards in the Harvard Education Letter. Volume 27, Number 5. September/October 2011.

131 **Obama even proposed a $75 billion plan to provide universal preschool.** See article by Dylan Scott in Governing (April 10, 2013) titled *Obama Proposes 4&5 Billion for Universal Preschool.* Retrieved from: https://www.governing.com/topics/education/gov-obama-proposes-66-billion-over-10-years-for-universal-preschool.html

132 **The Promise Neighborhoods was an initiative.** See Press Summary (December 19, 2011) from the U.S. Department of Education website titled *Obama Administration Announces 2011 Promise Neighborhoods Grant Winners.* Retrieved from: https://www.ed.gov/news/press-releases/obama-administration-announces-2011-promise-neighborhoods-grant-winners

132 **the high school graduation rate hit an all-time high of 83.2 percent.** See article by Kamenetz and Turner in NPR (10.17.16) titled *The High School Graduation Rate Reaches a Record High-Again.* Retrieved from: https://www.npr.org/sections/ed/2016/10/17/498246451/the-high-school-graduation-reaches-a-record-high-again#:~:text=The%20high%20school%20graduation%20rate%20in%20the%20U.S.%20reached%20an,fifth%20straight%20record%2Dsetting%20year.

133 **issue of "zero tolerance" in school discipline policies.** See article in The Atlantic (January 8, 2014) by Danielle Wiener-Bronner titled Obama Administration Asks Schools to Drop Zero-Tolerance Approach. Retrieved from: https://www.theatlantic.com/national/archive/2014/01/ending-zero-policy-discipline/356812/

133 **President Obama signed ESSA into law in December 2015**. See article by Andrew Lee, JD, in Understood titled *Every Student Succeeds Act (ESSA): What You Need to Know.* Retrieved from: https://www.understood.org/en/school-learning/your-childs-rights/basics-about-childs-rights/every-student-succeeds-act-essa-what-you-need-to-know

134 **opportunity to attend community college.** See White Press Release (January 9, 2015) titled *FACT SHEET: White House Unveils America's College Promise Proposal: Tuition-Fee Community College for Responsible Students*. Retrieved from: https://obamawhitehouse.archives.gov/the-press-office/2015/01/09/fact-sheet-white-house-unveils-america-s-college-promise-proposal-tuitio

135 **college costs and student debt were two major concerns for President Obama.** See official archived White House document (July 18, 2011). *Obama Administration Record on Education*. Retrieved from: https://obamawhitehouse.archives.gov/sites/default/files/docs/education_record.pdf

136 **"gainful employment."** See U.S. Department of Education archived document (July 1, 2015) titled Fact Sheet: Obama Administration Increases Accountability for Low-Performing or-Profit Institutions. Retrieved from: https://www.ed.gov/news/press-releases/fact-sheet-obama-administration-increases-accountability-low-performing-profit-institutions

137 **Donald John Trump.** Biography: See https://www.biography.com/us-president/donald-trump

138 Ibid

140 **"Donald worried that his grade point average,"** See article in The Guardian (July 7, 2020) by Martin Pengelly titled *Mary Trump's book: eight of its most shocking claims about the president*. Retrieved from: https://www.theguardian.com/us-news/2020/jul/07/donald-trump-mary-niece-book-eight-most-shocking-claims

141 **"legacy as an educator" by "imparting lots of knowledge."** See article by Boser, Schwaber, and Johnson, Trump University: A Look at Enduring Education Scandal, for detailed history of Trump University: https://www.americanprogress.org/issues/education-postsecondary/reports/2017/03/30/429573/trump-university-look-enduring-education-scandal/

142 **"There are people that borrowed $36,000 to go to Trump University."** See Stephanie Saul's article in the New York Times (Feb 26, 2016) titled *Trump University's Checkered Past Haunting Candidate*: https://www.nytimes.com/2016/02/27/us/donald-trump-marco-rubio-trump-university.html

142 **"the least racist person that you've ever encountered."** See article in the Telegraph (June 10, 2016) by D. Millward: https://www.telegraph.co.uk/news/2016/06/10/donald-trump-i-am-the-least-racist-person-that-youve-ever-encoun/

143 **Trump's company was accused of refusing to rent to or negotiate with black tenants**, See Mahler and Eder's article (April 27, 2016) in The New York Times titled *'No Vacancies' for Blacks: How Donald Trump Got his Start, and Was the First Accused of Bias*. Retrieved from https://www.nytimes.com/2016/08/28/us/politics/donald-trump-housing-race.html

143 **"When Donald and Ivana came to the casino, the bosses would order all black people off the floor,"** See article in Politi Fact by Clare O'Rourke (May 22, 2019). Retrieved from: https://www.politifact.com/factchecks/2019/may/22/viral-image/donald-trump-has-faced-allegations-racism-decades/

144 **"Central Park Five"** See Patrick Ryan's article in USA Today by Patrick Ryan. Retrieved from: https://www.usatoday.com/story/life/tv/2019/06/03/looking-back-trumps-involvement-1989-central-park-five-case/1212335001/

145 **"Black guys counting my money! I hate it."** The author of the book Trumped! In this Op-ed "Donald Trump *Says He's 'Never Used Racist Remarks.' I Know Better.* O'Donnell provides accounts of Trump using racist remarks. Retrieved from: https://www.politico.com/magazine/story/2018/11/07/donald-trump-says-hes-never-used-a-racist-remark-i-know-different-222314

145 **"they don't look like Indians to me."** See online video provided by the Washington Post. Retrieve at https://www.washingtonpost.com/video/politics/they-dont-look-like-indians-to-me-donald-trump-on-native-american-casinos-in-1993/2016/07/01/20736038-3fd4-11e6-9e16-4cf01a41decb_video.html

146 **"he was fired for being overeducated"** See article by Benjy Sarlin in TPM (May 9, 2011) titled *Former Apprentice Contestant: Trump 'Doesn't Like Educated African-Americana Very Much'* Retrieved by Former Apprentice Contestant: Trump 'Doesn't Like Educated African-Americans Very Much'

146 **referring to Muslims, "Well, somebody's blowing us up"** See transcript by America & Media Watchdog of dialogue between Trump and David Letterman. Retrieved from https://www.mrc.org/biasalerts/lettermans-irritation-trump-denounces-ground-zero-mosque-insensitive-somebody-knocked

146 **birtherism "is almost completely resistant to factual correction"** See pdf of a Klinkner's paper titled *The Causes and Consequences of 'Birtherism'* (p. 2) that was presented at the 2014 Annual Meeting of the Western Political Science Association. Retrieved from http://www.wpsanet.org/papers/docs/Birthers.pdf

147 **"from countries whose governments are a complete and total catastrophe"** See July 2019 article by M. Ygleslas titled *Trump's racist tirades against 'the Squad' explained*. Retrieved from: https://www.vox.com/2019/7/15/20694616/ donald-trump-racist-tweets-omar-aoc-tlaib-pressley

148 **"I'm a tremendous believer in education," Trump said**. See article in NPR Ed (9-25-16) by Turner and Westervelt titled Donald Trump's Plan for America's Schools. Retrieved from: https://www.npr.org/sections/ed/2016/09/25/494740056/ donald-trumps-plan-for-americas-schools

148 **DeVos has a history of not supporting K-12 public education.** See Education Votes website: https://educationvotes.nea.org/2019/03/22/devos/

149 **Devos used her family's wealth to privatize public schools.** Article by Corey Turner of NPR (September 25, 2016) titled Donald Trump's Plan for America's Schools provides an overview of Trumps' plan for education. Currently, he doesn't have a comprehensive written plan, just ideologies. Retrieved from: https://www.npr. org/sections/ed/2016/09/25/494740056/donald-trumps-plan-for-americas-schools

150 **There was a public outcry over from parents, students and educators.** See 2017 press release on the NEA's website: http://www.nea.org/home/69617.htm

150 **commencement address for historically-black Bethune-Cookman University**. See article by Brittany Fennell titled *Bethune-Cookman Graduates Turn Their Backs on Betsy DeVos* in Ebony Live (May 11, 2017): https://www.ebony. com/news/bethune-cookman-betsy-devos/

151 **In his proposed budget for fiscal year 2020**. See a summary of Trump's proposed budget retrieved from: https://www.budget.senate.gov/imo/media/doc/ SBC%20Trump%20Budget%20Reaction%203-20-19%20FINAL.pdf

151 **"I have been consistent in my opposition to Common Core"** See Trump's tweet retrieved from: https://twitter.com/realDonaldTrump/status/6976 13947655086080

152 **EFS proposal, taxpayers could make voluntary contributions to scholarship-granting organizations** See Derek Black's in USA Today (Feb 14, 2020) titled Trump's 'education freedom' plan is an attack on public schools. Retrieved from: https://www.usatoday.com/story/opinion/2020/02/14/donald-trump-education-freedom-school-choice-vouchers-column/4738012002/

153 **The Student Loans Proposal (SLP) is Trump's 10-point plan.** See article by Zack Friedman in Forbes (March 14, 2020) titled Trump: *My New Student Loan Plan Works Like This*. Retrieved from: https://www.forbes.com/sites/zackfriedman/2020/03/14/donald-trump-student-loans/#3509783946ff

155 **"American children have been trapped in failing government schools."** See transcript of Trump's State of the Union Address (February 4, 2020): https://www.whitehouse.gov/briefings-statements/remarks-president-trump-state-union-address-3/

156 **"Trump University was a fraudulent scheme…"** See article in NBC News (June 1, 2016) by Alexandra Jaffe titled *Trump University Staffers Describe 'Fraudulent Scheme'* in New Court Documents. Retrieved from: https://www.nbcnews.com/politics/2016-election/trump-university-staffers-describe-fraudulent-scheme-new-court-documents-n584071

157 **"You're living in poverty; your schools are no good…"** See article on The Guardian posted on August 19, 2016: https://www.theguardian.com/us-news/2016/aug/20/what-do-you-have-to-lose-donald-trump-appeals-for-black-vote

158 **"Leadership and learning are indispensable to each other"** Retrieved from: https://www.brainyquote.com/quotes/john_f_kennedy_130752

Chapter 7

159 **the WHO announced the official name of the disease – COVID 19.** See article by Erin Schumaker in ABC News (April 23, 2020) titled *Timeline: How coronavirus got started*. Retrieved from: https://abcnews.go.com/Health/timeline-coronavirus-started/story?id=69435165

160 **lynching of George Floyd.** See article by C. Lewis in Open Democracy (June 6, 2020). Retrieved from: https://www.opendemocracy.net/en/opendemocracyuk/george-floyd-was-lynched/

161 **"could have saved lives."** Dr. Fauci's comments to CNN's Jake Tapper. Video retrieved from: https://www.cnn.com/videos/politics/2020/04/12/sotu-fauci-full.cnn

161 **A retro-analysis conducted by scientists at the Columbia University.** Article dated May 21, 2020, and titled *COVID-19 Projections: Delayed Response to Rebound Would Cost Lives* retrieved CU's website: https://www.publichealth.columbia.edu/public-health-now/news/covid-19-projections-delayed-response-rebound-would-cost-lives

163 **More than 36 million of those American workers filed claims for unemployment insurance** See article by Sarah Hansen in Forbes (May 14, 2020) titled *Another 3 Million Filed for Unemployment Last Week – Two-Month Total Hits 38 Million.* Retrieved from https://www.forbes.com/sites/sarahhansen/2020/05/14/another-3-million-filed-for-unemployment-last-week-two-month-total-hits-36-million/#36313618c269

163 **Congress passed a $2 trillion stimulus bill.** See article by Leon LaBrecque in Forbes on March 29, 2020 titled *The CARES Act Has Passes: Here are the Highlights.* Retrieved from: https://www.forbes.com/sites/leonlabrecque/2020/03/29/the-cares-act-has-passed-here-are-the-highlights/#54eb187868cd

164 **retail sales in the U.S. fell 8.7 percent in March 2020** See press release from the Census Bureau: https://www.census.gov/newsroom/press-releases/2020/retail-trade-sector.html

165 Ibid

166 **seven of those deadly, biased diseases.** See article by D.J. DeNoon on Web MD's Website titled *Why 7 Deadly Diseases Strike Blacks Most.* Retrieved from: https://www.webmd.com/hypertension-high-blood-pressure/features/why-7-deadly-diseases-strike-blacks-most#1

167 Ibid

168 **New Orleans health officials realized**. See article (May 30, 2020) by Godoy and Wood titled *What Do Coronavirus Racial Disparities Look Like*

State by State? Retrieved from the NPR website: https://www.npr.org/sections/health-shots/2020/05/30/865413079/what-do-coronavirus-racial-disparities-look-like-state-by-state

169 **AMP researchers compiled these key findings.** Comprehensive data retrieved from the AMP website under the heading – *The Color of Coronavirus: COVID-19 Deaths by Race and Ethnicity in the US* (June 24, 2020): https://www.apmresearchlab.org/covid/deaths-by-race

170 Ibid

170 **median white wealth ($919,000) was over $700,000 greater.** See the third chart on this website: https://apps.urban.org/features/wealth-inequality-charts/

172 **America's ugly history of discrimination in health care.** See article (Feb 4, 2017) by E. Sanford III in Black Perspectives titled *Civil Rights and Healthcare: Remembering Simkins v. Cone (1963)* retrieved from: https://www.aaihs.org/civil-rights-and-healthcare-remembering-simkins-v-cone-1963/

173 **over 124,000 schools across America were closed.** See article (April 30, 2020) by C. DeAngelis titled *The Coronavirus Pandemic's Impact on Education and the Defenders of the Status Quo.* Retrieved from: https://reason.org/commentary/the-coronavirus-pandemics-impact-on-education-and-the-defenders-of-the-status-quo/

173 **about 17% of teens…often unable to complete homework assignments.** See article from the Pew Research Center (Oct. 26, 2018) by Anderson and Perrin titled *Nearly one-in-five teens can't always finish their homework because of the digital divide.* Retrieved from: https://www.pewresearch.org/fact-tank/2018/10/26/nearly-one-in-five-teens-cant-always-finish-their-homework-because-of-the-digital-divide/

174 **"This has been a real challenge…first-graders are active and need hands-on nurturing"** Interview with Brittany McCray on April 25, 2020.

175 **trying to provide "individualized" instruction over the telephone.** Interview with Annette Samuel on April 25, 2020.

176 **"summer learning loss"** See article in Brookings (September 14, 2017) by Quinn and Polikoff titled *Summer Learning Loss: What is it, and What*

can We Do About it? Retrieved from: https://www.brookings.edu/research/summer-learning-loss-what-is-it-and-what-can-we-do-about-it/

177 **NWEA projections, if students in primary grades return...will retain only about 70 percent.** See article in The Journal (March 21, 2020) by D. Schaffhauser titled *Research: Coronavirus Learning Loss Could Put Some Students Behind a Full Year.* Retrieved from https://thejournal.com/articles/2020/04/21/research-coronavirus-learning-loss-could-put-some-students-behind-a-full-year.aspx

178 **three million (12%) adolescents ages 12 to 17 had depression.** See report published April 21, 2020 titled *The Implications of COVID-19 for Mental Health and Substance Abuse.* Retrieved from KFF website: https://www.kff.org/coronavirus-covid-19/issue-brief/the-implications-of-covid-19-for-mental-health-and-substance-use/

179 **"I used to think school was so boring"** Interview with Taryn Greene on March 28, 2020.

180 **"summer nutrition gap"** See article in The Counter by Jessica Fu and Jimin Kang (July 3, 2018) titled *30 million children rely on free school lunch. Where do they eat when school's out?* Retrieved from: https://thecounter.org/summer-hunger-new-york-city/

182 **"I think we're about to see a school funding crisis"** See article (May 26, 2020) in NPR by Cory Turner titled *A Looming Financial Melton for America's Schools.* Retrieved from: https://www.npr.org/2020/05/26/858257200/the-pandemic-is-driving-americas-schools-toward-a-financial-meltdown

184 **many struggling historically black colleges and universities** See article (May 19, 2020) with a CNN video by Graver, Jarrett and Pomrenze titled *HBCUs doubly hurt by campus shutdowns in coronavirus pandemic.* Retrieved from: https://www.cnn.com/2020/05/18/us/coronavirus-education-hbcu-finances-hit-wellness/index.html

185 **"It is too early to predict implications for student loan debt"** See article (April 30, 2020) by A. DePietro titled *Here's a Look at the Impact of Coronavirus (COVID-19) on Colleges and Universities in the U.S.* Retrieved from: https://www.forbes.com/sites/andrewdepietro/2020/04/30/impact-coronavirus-covid-19-colleges-universities/#6667b0f061a6

186 **slave patrols – also known as "paddyrollers"** See article (Sep 17, 2018) by Ben Fountain titled "Slavery and the Origins of the American Police State" retrieved from: https://gen.medium.com/slavery-and-the-origins-of-the-american-police-state-ec318f5ff05b

186 **the Great Migration (1916-70) of African Americans from the rural South.** See the history *The Great Migration* retrieved from: https://www.history.com/topics/black-history/great-migration

186 **white police departments, were not accustomed to the presence of African Americans.** See article in Britannica (June 2020) by Leonard Moore titled *Police brutality in the United States.* Retrieved from: https://www.britannica.com/topic/Police-Brutality-in-the-United-States-2064580

187 **Watts Riots of 1965 and the Detroit Riot of 1967.** CNBC Slideshow (September 13, 2013) by Daniel Bukszpan titled *America's Most Destructive Riots of all Time.* Retrieved from: https://www.cnbc.com/2011/02/01/Americas-Most-Destructive-Riots-of-All-Time.html

189 **"I am not going to stand up to show pride in a flag"** See article (August 27, 2016) by Charles Curtis in USA Today titled *Colin Kaepernick 'I won't stand to show pride for a country that oppresses Black people'* retrieved from: https://ftw.usatoday.com/2016/08/colin-kaepernick-49ers-national-anthem-sit-explains

189 **"Get that son of a bitch off the field right now!"** See Trump's quote in NBC Bay Area article (9-22-17) https://www.nbcsports.com/bayarea/49ers/trump-anthem-protesters-get-son-b-field

190 **Ahmaud Arbery (age 25) – was shot to death after being pursued by two white men.** See Richard Fausset's excellent article (June 24, 2020) in The New York Times titled *What We Know About the Shoot Death of Ahmaud Arbery.* Retrieved from https://www.nytimes.com/article/ahmaud-arbery-shooting-georgia.html

191 **"The video was already out, we saw it..."** See article by Christian Boone in the AJC (May 8, 2020) titled *Glynn County commissioners say DA blocked arrests after fatal shooting.* Retrieved from https://www.ajc.com/news/local/watch-gbi-updates-following-arrests-ahmaud-arbery-shooting/1aJbZe2uL9HrndjyWYjB2L/

192 **John Perry said: "As I sit here and I look at you all"** See article (May 26, 2020) by Emma Hurt titled Arbery Shooting Sparks Racism, Corruption Questions About

Georgia County Retrieved from https://www.npr.org/2020/05/26/861992342/arbery-shooting-sparks-racism-corruption-questions-about-georgia-county

193 Ibid

193 **death of Breonna Taylor.** Bridgett Read's article in The Cut (June 2020) *Breonna Taylor was Shot and Killed by Police in her own Home*, provides a detailed account of this killing. Retrieved from: https://www.thecut.com/2020/07/breonna-taylor-louisville-shooting-police-what-we-know.html

194 Ibid

195 **"We strongly condemn the actions of the LMPD"** See statement in Paul Greely's article (May 30, 2020) titled *WAVE Condemns Police Shooting at its News Crew* retrieved from: https://marketshare.tvnewscheck.com/2020/05/30/wave-news-condemns-police-shooting-at-their-tv-news-crew/

195 **"They're killing our sisters just like they're killing our brothers…"** See article in The Cut (June 2020) by Bridget Read titled *Breonna Taylor Was Shot and Killed by Police in Her Own Home*. Retrieved from: https://www.thecut.com/2020/07/breonna-taylor-louisville-shooting-police-what-we-know.html

196 **John Legend penned an op-ed in *Entertainment Weekly*.** See article in Pop Sugar (June 5, 2020) by Monica Sisavat titled *John Legend Demands Justice for Breonna Taylor on What Would've been Her Birthday: 'Never Stop Fighting'* retrieved from: https://www.popsugar.com/celebrity/john-legend-tribute-for-breonna-taylor-on-her-27th-birthday-47531725

196 **The murder of George Perry Floyd, Jr.** This article (June 3, 2020), *This is how loved ones want us to remember George Floyd*, by Alisha Ebrahimii of CNN is comprehensive, informative and powerful. It is a quasi-autobiography with photos of George Floyd's life and death. Retrieved from: https://www.cnn.com/2020/05/27/us/george-floyd-trnd/index.html

197 Ibid

199 **"Men, women, people with different backgrounds …"** See article by D. Aldridge and video: https://www.11alive.com/article/news/local/protests/john-lewis-george-floyd-protests-today-show/85-75547b23-dbd4-4119-84e0-8801772e0ab4

199 **Commissioner Roger Goodell released this statement at the height of the Floyd-inspired protests:** See video from GMA and statement of NFL's apology. Retrieved from https://abcnews.go.com/US/nfl-apologizes-listening-players-racism-colin-kaepernick-remains/story?id=71122596

200 **Floyd-inspired protests were spurring meaningful changes in many major corporations.** See article by Gillian Friedman (June 22, 2020) titled *Here's What Companies Are Promising to Do to Fight Racism.* Retrieved from: https://www.nytimes.com/article/companies-racism-george-floyd-protests.html

201 **notable changes occurred in the area of police reform.** See article in the New York Times by P. Philbrick and S. Yar (August 3, 2020) titled *What has changed since George Floyd?* Retrieved from: https://www.nytimes.com/2020/08/03/briefing/coronavirus-vaccine-tropical-storm-isaias-tiktok-your-monday-briefing.html

201 **Floyd's death globalized the struggle against racism.** CNN provides a gallery of vivid slides of people across the globe in their homeland showing support for Black Lives Matter. Very Powerful! Retrieved from https://www.cnn.com/2020/06/06/world/gallery/intl-george-floyd-protests/index.html

202 **prompted systemic changes in international sports** See article in ESPN Sports (August 8, 2020) titled *New FA gridlines could see footballers face 12-match ban for racism.* Retrieved from: https://www.espn.com/soccer/english-premier-league/story/4155525/new-fa-guidelines-could-see-footballers-face-12-match-ban-for-racism

202 **Statements from the European Union offer a measure of the global reaction to Floyd's death.** See article by Eszter Zalan in the EU Observer (June 3, 2020) titled *EU calls George Floyd's death 'abuse of power.'* Retrieved from https://euobserver.com/foreign/148528

203 **American Public Health Association indicated**. See Press Release (May 29, 2020) from APHA titled *Racism is an ongoing public health crisis that needs our attention now.* Retrieved from: https://www.apha.org/news-and-media/news-releases/apha-news-releases/2020/racism-is-a-public-health-crisis

203 **"Racism is literally killing black and brown people."** See article in Yahoo News (7-30-20) by C. Wilson titled Austin, Texas, joins growing list of U.S. cities in declaring racism a 'public health crisis'. Retrieved from: https://news.yahoo.com/austin-texas-racism-public-health-crisis-louisville-minneapolis-191822382.html

204 **rename Robert E. Lee High after the late U.S. Rep. John R. Lewis.** See article (7-23-2020) by Michelle Basch of WTOP News titled Fairfax County high school to be renamed for Rep. John Lewis. Retrieved from: https://wtop.com/fairfax-county/2020/07/fairfax-county-high-school-to-be-renamed-for-rep-john-lewis/

206 **"If a man like Malcolm X could change, and repudiate racism"** Retrieved from https://www.brainyquote.com/quotes/eldridge_cleaver_156356

Chapter 8

207 **Joaquin Phoenix (who is Puerto Rican-American) called out systemic racism.** See article in BBC News (February 3, 2020) titled *Bafta Awards 2020: Joaquin Phoenix praised for calling out 'systemic racism.'* Retrieved from: https://www.bbc.com/news/entertainment-arts-51355206

208 Ibid

209 **Graph 4.** This model was designed by the authors, co-owners of Taylor& Taylor Education Consultants, to depict systemic racism.

213 **Systemic racism has created the unequal distribution of wealth in the United States.** See Nine Charts about Wealth Inequality in America (October 5, 2017) retrieved from Urban Policy's website: https://apps.urban.org/features/wealth-inequality-charts/

214 **was $727 from July 2019 to September 2019** See article in Center for American Progress (10-5-19) by J. Cusick *titled RELEASE: African Americans Face Systemic Obstacles to Getting Good Jobs.* Retrieved from: https://www.americanprogress.org/press/release/2019/12/05/478133/release-african-americans-face-systematic-obstacles-getting-good-jobs/

214 **white-sounding names get called back roughly 50 percent more often than applicants with black-sounding names** See article *by Marcel Schwantes titled Harvard Study Says Minority Job Candidates are "Whitening" their Resumes hen Looking or Jobs.* Retrieved from https://www.inc.com/marcel-schwantes/why-minority-job-applicants-mask-their-race-identities-when-applying-for-jobs-according-to-this-harvard-study.html

215 **Michelle Alexander.** It has been ten years since the publication of her book, and we continue to see the system racism Michelle Alexander describes in her book, <u>The New Jim Crow</u>, ISBN 978-1-59558-643-8

215 **Black people make up roughly 13% of the U.S. population and roughly 40% of the prison population.** Retrieved from: <u>https://www.benjerry.com/whats-new/2016/systemic-racism-is-real</u>

216 Ibid

216 **incarceration is seldom a pleasant experience.** See article in the New Republic (June 28, 2016) by Tony Brown and Evelyn Patterson titled *Wounds from Incarceration that Never Heal*. Retrieved from: <u>https://newrepublic.com/article/134712/wounds-incarceration-never-heal</u>

217 **how the government segregated America through housing**. Richard Rothstein's book, <u>The Color of Law</u> (published by Liveright in May 2017), documents how the government used discrimination in its policies to deny blacks the right to live where they wanted to and raise their children in good schools. The outcome was de facto segregation.

218 Ibid

219 **Blacks in particular have faced decades of discrimination in the area of healthcare.** See article by Jamila Taylor in The Century Foundation (December 12, 2019) titled *Racism, Inequality, and Health Care for African Americans*. Retrieved from: <u>https://tcf.org/content/report/racism-inequality-health-care-african-americans/?agreed=1</u>

221 **analyzed data from Project Implicit.** See article by the American Educational Research Association (April 15, 2020) titled *Research finds teachers just as likely to have racial bias as non-teachers*. Retrieved from: <u>https://phys.org/news/2020-04-teachers-racial-bias-non-teachers.html</u>

222 *"Systemic change is change that <u>saturates</u> all parts of a system"* This is a hybrid definition that was formulated by the co-authors.

223 **random parts of a school system.** The Flow chart was created by the co-authors

224 **must transform into Flow Chart.** The Flow chart was created by the co-authors

225 **process of change involves nine steps.** The nine-step model for change was developed by the co-authors.

226 Ibid

237 **"Racism is a grown-up disease"** Quote by Ruby Bridges retrieved from: https://www.brainyquote.com/quotes/ruby_bridges_991719

Conclusion

239 **"that dream of a land in which life should be better and richer and fuller for everyone"** From James Truslow Adams' book, <u>The Epic of America</u> (pp 214-215). ISBN-13: 978-1931541336; ISBN-10: 1931541337

244 **"I hope it's not [an issue]"** Quote from Taylor McCray, a future leader in America's quest to become a non-racial democracy. She's also our granddaughter.

INDEX